ALSO BY STEVE SHEINKIN

BORN TO FLY
The First Women's Air Race Across America

UNDEFEATED
Jim Thorpe and the Carlisle Indian School Football Team

MOST DANGEROUS
Daniel Ellsberg and the Secret History of the Vietnam War

BOMB
The Race to Build—and Steal—the World's Most Dangerous Weapon

THE PORT CHICAGO 50
Disaster, Mutiny, and the Fight for Civil Rights

THE NOTORIOUS BENEDICT ARNOLD
A True Story of Adventure, Heroism & Treachery

WHICH WAY TO THE WILD WEST?
Everything Your Schoolbooks Didn't Tell You About Westward Expansion

TWO MISERABLE PRESIDENTS
Everything Your Schoolbooks Didn't Tell You About the Civil War

KING GEORGE: WHAT WAS HIS PROBLEM?
*Everything Your Schoolbooks Didn't Tell You About
the American Revolution*

FALL

SPIES, SUPERBOMBS, AND THE

OUT

ULTIMATE COLD WAR SHOWDOWN

STEVE SHEINKIN

Roaring Brook Press
New York

Published by Roaring Brook Press
Roaring Brook Press is a division of Holtzbrinck Publishing Holdings Limited Partnership
120 Broadway, New York, NY 10271 • mackids.com

Library of Congress Cataloging-in-Publication Data
Names: Sheinkin, Steve, author.
Title: Fallout : spies, superbombs, and the ultimate Cold War showdown / Steve Sheinkin.
Other titles: Spies, superbombs, and the ultimate Cold War showdown
Description: First edition. | New York : Roaring Brook Press, 2021. |
Includes bibliographical references and index. | Audience: Ages 10–14 |
Audience: Grades 7–9 | Summary: "As World War II comes to a close, the United States and
the Soviet Union emerge as the two greatest world powers on extreme opposites of the political
spectrum. After the United States shows its hand with the atomic bomb in Hiroshima, the Soviets
refuse to be left behind. With communism sweeping the globe, the two nations begin a neck and
neck competition to build even more destructive bombs and win the space race. In their battle for
dominance, spy planes fly above, armed submarines swim below, and undercover agents meet in
the dead of night. The Cold War game grows more precarious as weapons are pointed toward each
other, with fingers literally on the trigger. The decades-long showdown culminates in the Cuban
Missile Crisis, the world's close call with the third—and final—world war"— Provided by publisher.
Identifiers: LCCN 2021019729 | ISBN 9781250149015 (hardcover)
Subjects: LCSH: Cold War—Juvenile literature. | United States—Foreign relations—Soviet
Union—Juvenile literature. | Soviet Union—Foreign relations—United States—Juvenile
literature. | Cuban Missile Crisis, 1962—Juvenile literature. | Espionage, American—Soviet
Union—History—20th century—Juvenile literature. | Espionage, Soviet—United States—
History—20th century—Juvenile literature.
Classification: LCC E841 .S54 2021 | DDC 972.9106/4—dc23
LC record available at https://lccn.loc.gov/2021019729

Our books may be purchased in bulk for promotional, educational, or business use.
Please contact your local bookseller or the Macmillan Corporate and
Premium Sales Department at (800) 221-7945 ext. 5442 or by email
at MacmillanSpecialMarkets@macmillan.com.

First edition, 2021 • Book design by Aurora Parlagreco
Printed in the United States of America by LSC Communications, Harrisonburg, Virginia

5   7   9   10   8   6   4

For my big sister, Rachel.
You showed me the path.

CONTENTS

You must take your opponent into a
deep dark forest, where two plus two
equals five, and the path leading out
is only wide enough for one.

—MIKHAIL TAL,
WORLD CHESS CHAMPION,
1960-1961

PROLOGUE
The Paperboy

THE KID HIKED UP THE dark stairwell to the sixth floor, hoping only for a decent tip, maybe fifteen cents. Busting up a Russian spy ring was an unexpected bonus.

It was a Friday afternoon in June 1953, collection day for Jimmy Bozart, a thirteen-year-old paperboy for the *Brooklyn Eagle*. The newspaper cost thirty-five cents a week, and most people threw in an extra nickel or dime. The two retired teachers on the top floor of this apartment building were a bit more generous. They usually gave him two quarters.

Jimmy knocked on the teachers' door. One of the women greeted him and dropped coins into his hand, more coins than usual. To be polite, he waited until the door was closed to look down at his palm.

It was good. One quarter and five nickels.

But as Jimmy started down the stairwell his heel caught on a step, and the money went flying—coins bounced down the stairs, clanking and spinning. He scrambled after them. He found the quarter first. Then four of the nickels. Where was the other one?

The bulb in the ceiling fixture was out. Searching step by step in faint light angling in from a high window, Jimmy spotted the familiar sight of Thomas Jefferson's Monticello home. The back of a nickel.

Only the back.

Jimmy picked up the sliver of silvery metal. The coin had no front.

He found the other side of the coin on the landing. It had the usual front and smooth sides of a Jefferson nickel, but it was hollow. Something was wedged in the space inside, something square and black. It looked like a tiny piece of film.

Jimmy pried the thing out and held it up to the window. He saw tiny numbers printed on the film, groups of five-digit numbers typed in neat columns. Some kind of secret code?

Jimmy raced home, wondering what he'd found. Everyone knew that Soviet spies had stolen American atomic bomb secrets during World War II. Now, with the United States and the Soviet Union locked in the Cold War, there must be new enemy spies out there. Could this coin have anything to do with that?

At the Bozart family apartment, Jimmy's dad studied the tiny piece of film through a magnifying glass. He had no idea what it was, or what the numbers meant. He told his son that he'd better show the strange find to the police.

Jimmy thought of Carolyn Lewind, a girl in his eighth-grade class whose dad was a detective. He ran to her apartment building and showed the coin and the film to Carolyn and her mother. But the detective was still at work. Jimmy dropped the coin into his pocket and left.

When Carolyn's father came home, his wife told him that a red-haired kid named Jimmy Bozart had come by with a hollow nickel and some kind of coded message he'd found inside. Detective Lewind growled at her for letting the kid leave with potentially explosive evidence of espionage. He hurried to the Bozarts' apartment.

Mr. Bozart didn't know where his son was. He mentioned that his wife was playing bingo at a nearby church. Maybe she'd seen the boy.

The detective charged into the church and interrupted the game. No Jimmy. Lewind seized the bingo prize money, just in case the nickel had somehow wound up there.

He stepped outside and saw a man pushing an ice cream cart down the sidewalk. He grabbed the ice cream man's change too, just in case.

Then he turned and saw a bunch of boys playing stickball in the street. He looked the kids over, one by one. His gaze froze on a kid with red hair and freckles. About his daughter's age.

Barging into the game, he said, "You're Bozart?"

Jimmy nodded.

"What did you do with the nickel?"

Jimmy reached into his pocket and held it out.

The man snatched the coin. He pulled a nickel from his own pocket and handed it over.

"So you're not out anything," the detective said.

Jimmy took the new coin and went back to playing stickball.

He would be a college student by the time he realized that he'd stumbled into a series of events that were moving the globe's two great powers to the brink of the third—and final—world war.

PART 1
Two Hollow
Coins

RUDOLF ABEL
top Soviet spy in America

JIMMY BOZART
paperboy hero

FRANCIS
GARY
POWERS
Force & U-2 pilot

ANDREI SAKHAROV
Soviet physicist &
H-bomb designer

JOSEPH STALIN
Soviet dictator,
ruled until death
in 1953

STANISLAW ULAM
(left) AND
EDWARD TELLER
designers of U.S.
H-bomb

DWIGHT EISENHOWER
U.S. president, 1953–1961

LAVRENTY BERIA
head of Soviet secret
police

LONA COHEN
American-born
Soviet spy

REINO HAYHANEN
Soviet spy,
Abel's assistant

LUCKY DRAGON
crew member

HARRY TRUMAN
U.S. President,
1945–1953

BARBARA POWERS
wife of Francis Gary Powe[r]

THE PLAYERS

COLD WARRIOR

THIS IS A STORY ABOUT spies and spy catchers. It's about superbombs, the space race, and the global clash between the United States and the Soviet Union. It's the story of the most intense years of the Cold War, building to the single most dangerous moment in human history. But even in such an epic struggle, small details and seemingly ordinary people play pivotal roles, shoving events in one direction or another.

What does a paperboy's tip have to do with the end of the world?

That took a while to figure out.

The New York police passed the hollow nickel on to the Federal Bureau of Investigation. Two FBI agents went to interview the teachers who'd given it to Jimmy Bozart—but who remembers where they got a particular coin? One of them must have picked it up as change at the grocery store, the women guessed. Or possibly when buying subway tokens. The women seemed credible. There was no point in questioning them any further.

Trying another angle, the agents visited magician supply shops around the city. They showed employees the hollow coin, hoping for clues to its origin.

"It's not suitable for a magic trick," one salesman told the agents. "The hollowed-out area is too small to hide anything aside from a tiny piece of paper." No good for a performer on stage, in other words.

Holding the separate sides of the coin in his hands, the salesman explained that he'd never seen anything like it. This was no cheap novelty, nothing mass produced in any factory. These were two sides of two different authentic nickels, expertly hollowed out, and—look at this—whoever made it had drilled an almost invisibly tiny hole in the R of the word *TRUST*. Someone who knew to look for the hole could stick in a needle to pop the coin open.

Who made stuff like this?

No one, as far as the salesman knew.

The agents thanked the man. They tried a few more shops and got the same dead-end answers. There wasn't much more to be done. The tiny piece of film was on its way to government code breakers in Washington, D.C. Maybe something would come of that. Maybe not.

In the meantime, the FBI moved on to other cases.

Jimmy Bozart finished eighth grade and continued delivering the *Brooklyn Eagle*.

And the man who'd hollowed out the nickel and hidden the coded message inside, the highest-ranking Soviet spy in America, went on living and working in Brooklyn, just a few miles from the Bozart family's apartment. He was Emil Goldfus.

And Andrew Kayotis.

Also Martin Collins.

His real name was William Fisher.

For the sake of clarity, let's use the name by which he would become infamous in America: Rudolf Abel. And let's follow him into the story by jumping back five years to 1948, to the Soviet capital of Moscow in the early days of the Cold War.

"I would rather perish than betray the secrets entrusted to me. . . . With every heartbeat, with every day that passes, I swear to serve the Party, the homeland, and the Soviet People."

Rudolf Abel swore this sacred oath in Moscow's Lubyanka building, headquarters of the Soviet Union's secret intelligence agency, the KGB. Later that evening he kissed his wife and daughter goodbye. For how long, he could not know. Years, certainly. Boarding a ship bound for Quebec, Canada, Abel set out on his new assignment: to expand the Soviet Union's spy network in America, to steal the technology behind new American bombs, and to help pave the way to a glorious Soviet victory in World War III.

That's all.

His entire life had built toward this mission. Abel was born in England to parents of German and Russian heritage. In 1921, when he was eighteen, the family emigrated to Russia. Communists had just taken over the country and would rename it the Union of Soviet Socialist Republics. Under communism, an all-powerful central government owns all the land and factories, controlling every aspect of the country's economy. In theory, the government uses its power to distribute a fair share of the country's income to every worker. Abel's parents believed in the promise of communism, and Abel came to agree. At a young age, he committed himself to the goal of helping the Soviet Union spread its form of government around the world.

Tall and thin, with a bony face and piercing eyes, Abel spoke fluent German and English, in addition to Russian. He had a gift for building gadgets and fixing machines. Useful qualities for a spy. Recruited into Soviet intelligence, he spent several years living undercover in Norway, posing as an electronics salesman while secretly setting up radio networks for fellow spies. When Germany attacked the Soviet Union during World War II, Abel took on the incredibly dangerous task of slipping behind enemy lines. He managed to convince German commanders he was on *their* side, then fed them damaging misinformation, diverting their attention from upcoming Soviet attacks.

Abel's reward was this new assignment. This time the enemy was the United States of America.

It was only three years since the end of World War II, but so much had already changed.

The Soviets and Americans had been allies in the war, united by their common enemy, Adolf Hitler's Germany. Together, they crushed Hitler. Together, they won the war in Europe. When the fighting ended in 1945, the United States and the Soviet Union were the biggest powers left standing.

The two powers immediately began to clash over postwar plans. What, for instance, would happen in the countries of Eastern Europe that had been conquered by Germany during the war? American leaders wanted to see the establishment of democratic governments—governments that would be friendly to the United States. Joseph Stalin, the Soviet dictator, had a very different vision. Stalin's army had driven Hitler from Eastern Europe at the cost of millions of Soviet soldiers. He now controlled that part of the globe and had no intention of letting it go. One by one, Stalin installed hand-picked puppets to lead new communist governments in Eastern Europe. He violently crushed any oppo-sition, any calls for freedom or democracy.

"An iron curtain has descended across the Continent," declared Winston Churchill, Britain's prime minister during World War II, while visiting America in 1946.

It was a vivid and frightening image—the drop of a barrier across Europe, a dividing line between free and communist worlds. What would stop Stalin from continuing to expand the borders of his empire? Who could prevent more people from falling under Soviet control?

The United States would take that job, declared U.S. President Harry Truman. In what became known as the Truman Doctrine, the president committed the United States to the goal of stopping the further spread of Soviet power.

And so by the fall of 1948, as Rudolf Abel sailed west across the Atlantic Ocean, the United States and the Soviet Union were locked in a struggle for power and influence all over the world: the Cold War.

It was understood, on both sides, that there could be only one winner.

Juggling a series of false names and forged passports, Rudolf Abel traveled by train from Quebec City to Montreal. He crossed the border by bus and headed south. In New York City, a Soviet diplomat slipped him $1,000 in cash. Abel rented a tiny apartment and began to explore his new home.

The next step was to meet the librarian.

Hollow nickel

Secret code

207

14546	36056	64211	08919	18710	71187	71?15	02906	66036	10922
11375	61238	65634	39175	37378	31013	22			23551
88527	10130	01767	12366	16669	97846	7			
19262	69849	90251	11576	46121	24666	0			
51911	78912	32939	31966	12096	12060	8			
76271	31154	26838	77221	58343	61164				
31734	27562	51236	12982	18089	66218	22577	09454	81210	
26986	89779	54197	11990	23881	48884	22165	62992	36449	41742
30267	77614	31565	30902	85812	16112	53312	71820	60369	12872
12458	19081	97117	70107	06391	71114	19459	59586	80317	07522
76509	11111	36990	32666	04411	51532	91184	23162	82011	19185
56110	28876	76718	03563	28222	31674	39023	07623	93513	97175
29816	95761	69483	32951	97686	34592	61109	95090	24092	71008
90061	14790	15154	14655	29011	57206	77195	01256	69250	62901
39179	71229	23299	84164	45900	42227	65853	17591	60182	06315
65812	01378	14566	87719	92507	79517	99851	82155	58118	67197
30015	70687	36201	56531	56721	26306	67135	91796	51341	07796
76655	62716	83588	21982	16224	87721	85519	23191	20665	45140
66098	60959	71521	02334	21212	51110	85227	98768	11125	05321
53152	14191	12166	12715	03116	43041	74822	72759	29130	21947
15764	96851	20818	22370	11391	83520	62297			

W 12740/622

HOLLOW COIN #1

HER NAME WAS LONA COHEN. The thirty-five-year-old New Yorker was a librarian by day—and a longtime secret agent for the Soviet Union. During the war she'd earned legendary status in the Soviet spy service by sneaking past FBI agents with atomic bomb plans hidden in a tissue box. With agents like that, Rudolf Abel hoped to build a new Soviet spy network in America.

They arranged to meet at the Bronx Zoo. Abel followed Cohen to the zoo, to make sure she wasn't being tailed. He saw right away he was dealing with someone trained in tradecraft— the tricks and techniques of espionage. Cohen dry-cleaned herself expertly, strolling in the front door of a crowded store and darting out a side exit. She got on a subway car and jumped off just as the doors were closing. A lesser spy than Abel would have lost her trail.

Abel and Cohen met outside the zoo's birdhouse, sat together on a bench, and began making plans.

The two spies met often over the following months, walking through parks and museums, looking like ordinary friends enjoying ordinary outings.

All the while, the Cold War was rapidly expanding.

The U.S. military built its arsenal of atomic bombs from 9 in 1946 to 170 in 1949.

The Soviets responded in August 1949 with a successful test of their first atomic bomb.

In October 1949, communists seized power in China, the world's most populous country.

President Harry Truman countered with the next major escalation. On January 31, 1950, Truman told the world that the United States was going to try to build a new kind of bomb. A superbomb, some called it. More accurately, a hydrogen bomb.

Rudolf Abel, a man who read physics textbooks for fun, understood the basic science. He could see why a hydrogen bomb's power would be virtually unlimited. Would it be possible to build such terrible weapons? Maybe — that was a question for the world's top physicists.

Would it be possible to steal some useful secrets from the Americans? Maybe — if Abel could build a good enough network of spies. But the ever-widening Cold War was making it harder than he had hoped.

On a hot day in June 1950, a young man in a suit walked a long, circuitous route through the streets of Manhattan's Upper East Side, glancing at reflections in shop windows to check behind him. Certain he was not being followed, the man entered an apartment building and knocked on the door marked 3B.

Lona Cohen came to the door in shorts. She was alarmed to see Yuri Sokolov, a Soviet official at the United Nations—and, secretly, an intelligence agent. It was a *major* violation of the rules of tradecraft for Sokolov to risk being seen at Cohen's home. She let him in, quickly closing the door behind him.

Lona's husband, Morris, a history teacher and fellow spy, came to greet the visitor. Sokolov made small talk, in case the room was bugged, while pulling out a pen and pad of paper.

The situation has changed, he wrote. *It's better for you both to leave the country.*

The Cohens understood. It was front-page news. British authorities had just arrested Klaus Fuchs, a physicist who had helped the Americans design the first atomic bomb. Fuchs had confessed to being a Soviet spy and was awaiting trial in London. In Philadelphia, the FBI had picked up Harry Gold, who'd worked as Fuchs's courier, delivering stolen bomb plans to the Soviets. Now the whole world knew that the Soviet Union had built its atomic bomb with plans stolen from an American lab. Lona Cohen had been part of the theft—and could not know how long that would remain a secret.

Probably the FBI will know about yourselves, Sokolov wrote. *So it is better not to wait.*

Morris grabbed the pen. *Is it an order? Or advice?*

An order.

Lona Cohen gathered the notes and burned them in the bathroom sink.

Just like that, Rudolf Abel was all alone.

There was no panic. Trained to play the long game, Abel went about establishing what looked like a normal life in New York. He opened a bank account and chatted with the owners of neighborhood shops. He rode subways and buses, learning the routes and stops. He went to the movies and strolled through parks, casually making note of potential dead-drop locations. In his apartment, he made clever spy gadgets, crafting pencils with hidden chambers under removable erasers, cutting hidden compartments into cuff links and batteries.

His masterpiece was a hollow nickel. He carved it by hand from two real nickels. On the front, where it said *IN GOD WE TRUST*, he drilled a tiny hole into the letter *R*.

THE SUPER

"HAVE YOU GOT A PROBLEM for me to solve?"

A young physicist named Edward Teller sat on a train with a fellow scientist, Otto Frisch. This was back in the early 1930s, years before World War II. Teller and his friend were taking a break from the German university where they worked—but Teller's brain did not do well with breaks. He needed a problem, a puzzle, *anything*.

Frisch couldn't think of one. Teller would not relent.

Finally, Frisch came up with something: place eight queens on a chessboard so that no one queen can capture another. It's a tricky puzzle. The most powerful piece on a chessboard, the queen can move horizontally, vertically, or diagonally.

Also, they had no chessboard.

Teller was quiet for twenty minutes. Then he called out the solution, naming each square on which a queen could safely be placed.

Then he said, "Do you have another problem for me?"

* * *

Another problem. A harder problem. Like food and water, scientists need a steady supply.

Along with many other Jewish scientists in Europe, Edward Teller fled from Germany as Adolf Hitler began stripping Jews of their rights. Teller found a new home in the United States. During World War II, he was among the elite scientists recruited to a secret lab called Los Alamos, in the mountains of New Mexico. Their job was to beat Hitler in the race to make the world's first atomic bomb.

When the work at Los Alamos began in 1943, scientists understood the basic structure of atoms, the tiny particles that make up the matter all around us. They knew that atoms, in turn, are made up of even smaller particles. In the nucleus, the center of the atom, protons and neutrons are packed tightly. Electrons spin in orbits around the nucleus.

Scientists realized that if they could break apart an atom's nucleus, it would release energy as it split, a process they named fission. If they could cause enough atoms to split rapidly enough, they'd have a new kind of bomb, one *far* more powerful than conventional explosives such as TNT. Led by a physicist named Robert Oppenheimer, the team succeeded, testing the world's first atomic bomb in the New Mexico desert in July 1945. The bomb exploded with the awesome force of twenty thousand tons of TNT. Three weeks later, the United States dropped two of these bombs on Japan.

Those bombs—just two bombs, each small enough to fit in a plane—destroyed the cities of Hiroshima and Nagasaki, killing more than 200,000 people.

World War II was over. But the story does not end there.

Because when a bunch of geniuses are stuck together on a remote mountaintop for a few years, they're going to toss around ideas. At Los Alamos, even as they figured out how to make bombs by splitting atoms, scientists began to wonder if they could make *bigger* bombs by fusing atoms together.

Another problem. A harder problem.

Again, the basic science was well understood. In the process of nuclear fusion, the nuclei of small atoms combine to form larger ones. This happens in the center of the sun and other stars.

Let's start with this fact: the sun is big. It's not just the largest object in our solar system—it contains 99.8 percent of *all* the matter in the solar system. More massive objects have more gravity. The sun's gravity compresses its core into an area of enormous pressure and temperature. In these extreme conditions, atoms of hydrogen, the lightest element, smash together and combine, forming a new element, helium. The process releases vast amounts of energy—it's the energy from fusion that gives the sun its light and heat.

Edward Teller knew all this. So the question was unavoidable: If the goal is to make a powerful bomb, why not try to harness the power of fusion? The main obstacle was that the overwhelming pressure and heat needed to cause atoms to fuse simply did not exist on earth.

Until, for a fraction of a second, they *did* exist—inside an exploding atomic bomb.

When the scientists tested their fission bomb in the New Mexico desert, a key part of the problem was solved. A fission bomb could create the heat and pressure needed to fuse hydrogen atoms. In theory, a fission bomb could ignite a fusion bomb.

Even before the weapon existed, people started naming it. The hydrogen bomb. The H-bomb. The superbomb. The Super.

* * *

The Super made for fascinating theoretical discussions. But when World War II ended, most of the scientists at Los Alamos wanted to go back to what they loved—research and teaching, not making bombs. Many wrestled with regret over having used the laws of physics, which they revered, to devise a weapon of mass destruction. Robert Oppenheimer argued against pursuing the Super. He wasn't sure hydrogen bombs could be made, but if they could, they'd simply be too destructive, too much of a threat to the entire human species.

Edward Teller disagreed. There was genuine evil in the world, he argued. Look at Hitler, who had murdered six million European Jews during the war, including hundreds of thousands from Teller's native country, Hungary. Look at Stalin, who used his secret police to imprison and murder millions in the Soviet Union—and was expanding his power into Eastern Europe.

Evil like that must be confronted, Teller insisted. Ideally, with superior firepower.

Teller stayed at Los Alamos and aimed his relentless brain at the challenge of the Super. There was one part of the riddle he couldn't crack. To create the type of thermonuclear burning that occurs inside stars would require tremendous heat and pressure. A fission bomb could provide this—but too slowly. The massive power of the fission bomb would blow everything apart before the fusion could begin. Teller's team tried different designs, using some of the world's first computers to churn through calculations of what would happen in each millionth of a second inside a hydrogen bomb. The results were discouraging, infuriating. Fighting back tears of frustration, Teller hit one dead end after another.

Many scientists breathed a quiet sigh of relief.

*   *   *

She would never forget the look on her husband's face that day.

One afternoon in late January 1951, nearly a year after President Truman announced that the United States was going to develop a hydrogen bomb, Françoise Ulam walked into the living room of the Los Alamos home she shared with her husband, Stanislaw. She found him gazing out the window to the garden, but not at the plants, not at the sky. Stan was a brilliant mathematician. Françoise was used to seeing him lost in thought, his mind wandering through some abstract idea maybe ten people on earth might understand.

This was different. There was something oddly unsettled about the look on his face.

"I found a way to make it work," he said.

"What work?" she asked.

He was still staring out the window.

"The Super," he said. "It is a totally different scheme, and it will change the course of history."

Ulam told Teller his idea. They batted it back and forth, debating, refining, and quickly working out what would come to be known as the Teller-Ulam configuration.

The physics gets complicated, and some of it's still classified, but the key point is that they figured out a way to ignite a fusion bomb using the X-rays produced by a fission blast. Both bombs would be housed inside the casing of a single warhead. The fission bomb would spark thermonuclear burning in the fusion bomb, and you would get the combined power of both explosions.

The design was still only sketches and numbers and symbols. Lots of difficult engineering work remained, but the fundamental problem had been solved. From this point on, the scientists at Los Alamos *knew* the Super was going to work.

Meanwhile, the Cold War was turning violent. Backed by Joseph Stalin and the communist government of China, the forces of communist North Korea poured across the border into South Korea. The United States sent troops to help South Koreans fight back the invasion, and opposing armies battled to a bloody stalemate. Nearly forty thousand Americans died preventing the communists from taking over South Korea. In November 1952, Dwight Eisenhower won the U.S. presidential election, promising to bring the Korean War to an end.

Just two weeks after the election, news of the Super hit American newspapers.

Only rumors at first. There had been some sort of colossal explosion on a coral island in the South Pacific. The U.S. government was evasive about exactly what had happened, saying only that "the test program included experiments contributing to thermonuclear weapons research."

Vivid details trickled in as letters from American sailors who'd witnessed the test began arriving back in the States. Even facing away from the blast, on ships thirty miles from the test site, the men had seen a flash of light much brighter than the sun. Then came the heat of the explosion, like an open oven on their backs.

"You would swear," wrote one sailor, "that the whole world was on fire."

A New York *Daily News* editorial guessed that this was a hydrogen bomb, perhaps five to ten times as powerful as the fission bomb that destroyed the Japanese city of Hiroshima.

The newspaper was right about the bomb, but wrong about its power.

The world's first hydrogen bomb was five hundred times more powerful than the Hiroshima bomb. It exploded with a force of 10.4 megatons—the equivalent of 10.4 *million* tons of TNT. It was more powerful than all the explosives used in World War II put together.

This was a major turning point in human history. For the first time, human beings held in their hands the power to wipe all life from the face of the earth. Of course, a species that is smart enough to pack the power of the stars inside a bomb is also smart enough to avoid fighting a war with such weapons.

Right?

Nuclear
test in
U.S. desert

THE LONG GAME

THE MONSTER WAS IN THE mood for a dance.

It was many hours into a boozy New Year's Eve party, just two months after the American hydrogen bomb test. All the top Soviet officials were gathered at Joseph Stalin's sprawling dacha, a country home, in the woods near Moscow.

Stalin stumbled to the record player and put on a Russian folk song. The leader wanted people to dance, so they danced. But not Svetlana, Stalin's daughter. She was leaning against a wall, ready for sleep.

Stalin shuffled to her. "Well, go," he said, slurring his words, "dance!"

"I've already danced, Papa," she said. "I'm tired."

Stalin grabbed his daughter by the hair and yanked her onto the dance floor. Then the dictator himself, a man who had spent the past two decades terrorizing his own people, spread out his arms and began lurching to the music.

A fifty-eight-year-old Soviet official named Nikita Khrushchev watched the whole scene. He saw Svetlana's face flush, her eyes fill with tears. He felt sorry for her.

But he'd come too far to turn back now.

Khrushchev moved his short, round body onto the dance floor. With the grace of a cow on a frozen pond, he swayed back and forth alongside his leader.

This was Nikita Khrushchev's life. He and the other members of Stalin's inner circle would be summoned to Stalin's home. They'd sit through endless dinners, laugh at Stalin's stupid jokes, listen to his drunken rants until five in the morning. If he said dance, they danced.

It was the price they paid to be near the center of power.

After one typically torturous evening in early 1953, Khrushchev spent a quiet Sunday with his family at his own dacha, pleasantly surprised not to have heard from Stalin all day. He was in pajamas, getting ready for bed, when the telephone rang.

"They think something has happened to him," Georgy Malenkov, another top Soviet official, told Khrushchev. "We'd better get over there."

Khrushchev pulled on a suit and rushed to Stalin's dacha. The guards standing outside Stalin's bedroom door explained that the leader had been in his room all day. They'd wondered why he hadn't come out, but were too terrified of his wrath to open the door and check on him. Finally, they'd convinced a maid to go in. She found Stalin lying on the floor in a pool of cold urine.

He had suffered a massive stroke. As he lingered near death, unable to speak, the inevitable power struggle began. No one thought Nikita Khrushchev would come out on top.

Lavrenty Beria, the ruthless head of Stalin's secret police and the dictator's most fawning sidekick, fully expected to take the reins. He stood hour after hour at Stalin's bedside. Anytime Stalin showed the slightest sign of life, Beria would fall to his knees and kiss his dear leader's hand. Then, when Stalin drifted back into sleep, Beria would drop the limp hand and spit on the floor.

Khrushchev was in the room when Stalin finally died. He was watching Beria's face. There was no mistaking the glowing smile of triumph.

Observers of Soviet politics figured Khrushchev was about the fifth most powerful figure in Stalin's inner circle. Standing five foot two, with his baggy suits and gap-toothed smile, he was used to being underestimated. Overlooked. That was fine with him. It was just where he wanted to be.

Born in a tiny village in southern Russia in 1894, Nikita Khrushchev grew up with his parents and sister in a wooden hut. From the age of six, in shoes made from tree bark, he gathered wood and water for the family and herded cows and sheep for nearby landowners. At fourteen, his red hair cut short, Nikita began working twelve-hour days as an equipment repairman in a coal mine.

Even by the standards he'd grown up with, Nikita was shocked by the extreme poverty of the miners, the criminally low pay, the miserably hot mines, the constant threat of deadly fires and cave-ins, the filthy, disease-ridden barracks. All of this was surrounded by a bleak, treeless landscape of mud—while clearly visible in the distance, like a taunt, wealthy mine owners lived in grand houses on leafy lanes.

There *had* to be a better system than this, a fairer way to distribute a country's wealth. Khrushchev became interested in communism, which he believed would improve life for workers and their families. He met Nina Petrovna Kukharchuk, a devoted communist who lectured miners on the basics of communist philosophy. They were married, and with Nina's help and advice, Nikita began working his way up in the Soviet Union's all-powerful Communist Party.

Khrushchev quickly realized that the Soviet Union was not the workers' paradise he'd heard described in lectures. The Soviet government truly controlled *everything*. There were no elections, no free press, no freedom of speech or religion. When Joseph Stalin seized control in the mid-1920s, he stamped out every hint of opposition, jailing, starving, outright murdering millions of citizens to tighten his grip on power.

Khrushchev marched with Stalin every step of the way. The workers' paradise—that would come someday, he convinced himself. In the meantime, he focused on surviving Stalin's rages, moving up step by step. Even as his own friends were dragged off in the night by the secret police, declared "enemies of the people," and shipped to slave labor camps, Khrushchev continued to praise his boss.

"Our hand must not tremble," he said in defense of Stalin's brutal crimes. "We must march across the corpses of the enemy toward the good of the people."

Now, in the months after Stalin's death, Khrushchev set out to seize the opportunity of a lifetime. He could not stand to see Stalin be replaced by Lavrenty Beria, another mass murderer. And he knew that if Beria took over, no one—including himself—would be safe. One by one, Beria would eliminate all potential rivals. Khrushchev used this fear to his advantage.

"Listen, Comrade Malenkov, don't you see where this is leading?" Khrushchev said in a private meeting with his colleague. "We're heading for disaster. Beria is sharpening his knives."

"You want me to oppose him all by myself?" Malenkov asked.

"There's you and me," Khrushchev suggested. "That's already two of us."

Behind the scenes, one conversation at a time, Khrushchev lined up alliances against Beria within the Presidium—the council of top Soviet officials. By June, he was ready. The night before the trap was to be sprung, Beria and Khrushchev drove home from work together. As they shook hands before parting, Khrushchev could barely hold back a laugh of satisfaction.

You scoundrel, he thought, smiling at his rival. *This is our last handshake.*

The next day, Presidium members met in a conference room in the Kremlin, a complex of government buildings in Moscow. Khrushchev proposed that the group discuss the matter of Comrade Beria.

Beria's rat instincts tingled. He grabbed Khrushchev's hand.

"What's going on, Nikita?"

"Just pay attention. You'll find out soon enough."

Khrushchev and his allies took turns attacking Beria, accusing him of betraying the ideals of communism. Beria squirmed, realizing he'd been outmaneuvered. Right on cue, military officers loyal to Khrushchev charged in, shouting, "Hands up!"

They dragged Beria downstairs, shoved him into a car, and dumped him in prison.

Khrushchev drove out to his dacha that evening, drained and satisfied. He loved to get away from the noise and smog of the city and was happiest at his country home, a two-story cottage with a greenhouse, acres of rose bushes and fruit trees, and a wooded path down to the Moscow River.

There was much work ahead. Nikita Khrushchev still believed

in the goal that had driven him since youth, the dream of improving life for the Soviet people. He believed the Soviet Union deserved to be respected as a world power equal to the United States. Eventually, he expected to win the Cold War. Those were problems for another day.

Nina and their teenage son, Sergei, greeted Nikita as he drove up to the dacha.

"Today Beria has been arrested," the new Soviet leader told his family. "It seems that he is an enemy of the people."

THE WORST SPY

AND NOW WE'RE NEARLY BACK to where we began, with a paperboy's tip cracking open in a Brooklyn stairwell.

While Nikita Khrushchev consolidated power in Moscow, Rudolf Abel continued to prepare for a more active phase of his mission in America. The Soviet spy walked the streets of New York, neighborhood by neighborhood, picking out ideal dead-drop locations. He found a hollow space in the base of a lamppost in Fort Tryon Park. He noticed a bit of loose carpet beneath a seat in the balcony of the Symphony Theater.

Perfect spots to hide a coin with a coded message inside.

He worked out a signaling system. After loading a dead-drop, he'd put a chalk mark on the wall of a certain subway station, indicating the particular drop that held a message. It would be a great system—if he had anyone to share secret letters with.

Abel moved to Brooklyn and rented an art studio on the fifth floor of a downtown building, a little room with soot-stained walls and large windows looking out at a federal courthouse. He was retired, he told people in the building. He'd saved some money and wanted to take up painting.

It was a fine cover story, and Abel really *was* interested in painting. He bought paints and brushes and threw himself into the work. Striking up friendships with other artists in the building, Abel became known as an amusing eccentric. He did crossword puzzles in a flash and was a wonderful classical guitarist. He could fix any kind of electronic equipment—must be the field he'd retired from, people figured.

He stayed late in his studio many nights, which was not unusual for painters. But Abel's nighttime work was art of a different kind. He'd hang a copper wire out the window facing the courthouse, connect the homemade antenna to his shortwave radio, and exchange coded messages with Moscow. There was good news—Abel's bosses had finally decided to send him a new agent, someone who could help rebuild the Soviet spy network in America.

Rudolf Abel had no way of knowing his new partner was going to be just about the worst spy of the entire Cold War.

A stocky man in his early thirties crossed Central Park West and entered Manhattan's famous Central Park. He looked for the Tavern on the Green restaurant, and it was there, just like on the map he'd studied. Behind the restaurant he found the dirt bridle path. The white sign was there, right where it should be:

BE CAREFUL, HORSE RIDING

The man glanced left. He looked right. The coast was clear.

He pulled a white thumbtack from his pocket and stuck it in the white paint of the sign.

Mission accomplished, he turned and ambled farther into the park.

This was Reino Hayhanen, New York's newest Soviet spy. The thumbtack was a signal to his new boss, Rudolf Abel: he'd arrived safely and was ready to work.

Back in his studio, Abel prepared a coded message for the new agent. He hid it inside the hollow nickel he'd made, put the coin in one of his dead-drop locations, and marked the subway station wall with chalk.

Reino Hayhanen saw the signal. He found the coin.

Somewhere in Brooklyn, he spent it.

The coin made its way to two retired teachers and then to the paperboy, Jimmy Bozart. Bozart gave it to the New York City police, who passed it on to the FBI.

A blowup of the film found inside the coin arrived at the desk of Robert Lamphere, an FBI counterintelligence agent in Washington, D.C. Lamphere was a spy catcher. He'd helped track down the spies who'd stolen American atomic bomb secrets during World War II. This new piece of film reminded him of that operation. The message had a three-digit number at the top: 207. Beneath that were twenty-one lines of five-digit numbers. The first line read:

14546 36056 64211 08919 18710 71187 71215 02906
66036 10922

Lamphere recognized the hallmarks of a message coded by Soviet spies using what's called a one-time pad.

The system was simple but highly secure. Soviet agents used a well-guarded codebook, a kind of secret dictionary, with thousands of words. Each word was assigned a five-digit number. To encode a message, you first convert the message from words to the corresponding five-digit numbers from the codebook. Next, you take a sheet from a one-time pad. The sheet has rows and rows of random five-digit numbers. Add the first five-digit number from the sheet to the first five digits of the message, the second five-digit number from the sheet to the second five digits of the message, and so on. Note that this is a modified form of addition, with no carryover. You don't want to add extra digits, so four plus six equals zero, not ten. Eight plus seven equals five.

You also need to indicate which one-time pad sheet you used—that's why Abel added 207 to the top of his message. The message can then be sent by radio, telegraph, messenger—or hidden inside a hollow nickel.

To decode the message, the receiver finds the correct one-time sheet. The five-digit numbers from the sheet are subtracted from the five-digit numbers of the coded message. What remains is the original group of numbers. The receiver looks these numbers up in the codebook, and the message is turned back into plain language.

Sender and receiver both destroy the one-time sheet so it can never be used again.

This is time-consuming, but if done correctly, it is absolutely unbreakable. Even a modern computer cannot crack a message sent by the one-time pad system.

For a spy catcher like Lamphere, it was maddening. In his hand was *proof* that the Soviet Union had active spies here in the United States.

But until they made a mistake, they'd be impossible to find.

Rudolf Abel had no idea the nickel was missing.

Using another dead-drop message, Abel directed his agent

to meet him in person in the men's room of a movie theater in Queens. Hayhanen put on a blue tie with red stripes, stuck a pipe in his mouth, and headed for the theater.

Abel had been told by Moscow to watch for the tie and pipe as recognition signals. He got to the theater first and hung back, observing. And there was his new man in an ill-fitting suit and gaudy tie, puffing on a pipe like a kid with a theater prop.

Hayhanen ducked into the men's room. Abel waited for a group of teenagers to leave, then slipped in. The two agents looked each other over. Hayhanen was trained not to speak to anyone until the pre-arranged password was given. Abel knew this, but was suddenly in no mood for spy games.

"Never mind about the passwords," he said. "I know you are the right man."

This was poor tradecraft. Rude, too. Right away, Hayhanen knew his new boss did not respect him.

"Let's go outside," Abel said.

They walked out of the theater and down the street. As they began to talk, Abel was horrified by Hayhanen's poor English. Everything about the man stood out. Rudolf Abel had a bad feeling about his new partner.

THE TURTLE AND THE DRAGON

IT WAS MAYBE THE WORLD'S first reality television show.

And quite possibly the creepiest.

Picture this: You turn on the TV and see families in average suburban homes. Parents and children sit at a kitchen table. Kids have a game set up in a living room. An older couple relaxes in comfortable chairs, holding magazines.

But something's off. The lighting's too bright. Everything's too posed. No one's moving.

And you realize—these are mannequins.

We cut to an exterior shot. Quiet little houses in the desert, just before sunrise.

And then everything blows up.

With cameras rolling, a "small" atomic bomb—fifteen kilotons—detonates in the distance. There's a blinding flash of light, and almost instantly the sides of the buildings facing the blast char and smoke. Then comes the blast wave—a wall of compressed air expanding out from the explosion faster than the speed of sound—and the houses shatter.

The sun comes up and cameras show the carnage. A house 3,500 feet from the bomb is gone. Pieces of mannequin lay scattered in the rubble.

A house 7,500 feet from the bomb is scorched and slanting. Mannequins are tilted over on couches and chairs, grinning open-eyed at the ruins of their home.

In case you haven't learned your lesson, a deep-voiced narrator delivers the message the U.S. government wants you to hear. In this new age of Cold War and massive bombs, Americans had better start building shelters in their basements and backyards.

"Prepare now against the threat of atomic warfare," a government spokesman tells viewers. "Or will you, like a mannequin, just sit and wait?"

Kids had their own special Cold War programs, including the government-made instructional film *Duck and Cover*.

We open with an animated turtle in a bow tie ambling upright along a pleasant country lane. A catchy little song begins:

> *There was a turtle by the name of Bert.*
> *And Bert the Turtle was very alert.*

As Bert walks up, a monkey in a tree lowers a stick of dynamite on a string. The fuse is burning.

> *When danger threatened him, he never got hurt.*
> *He knew just what to do.*

39

Bert hits the ground and pulls his legs and head into his shell just before the dynamite explodes, making a smoking ruin of the tree. No sign of the monkey.

> He'd duck and cover, duck and cover.
> He did what we all must learn to do,
> you and you and you and you.
> Duck and cover!

That's how American kids learned what to do in case the Soviets attacked. At "duck and cover" drills in school, students crouched under their desks with their hands over their heads. What if you didn't happen to be in class when the bombs fell? The film covered that in a series of short scenes, each a little black-and-white nightmare.

A boy rides his bike through a park.

"Here's Tony going to his Cub Scouts meeting," says the friendly narrator. "Tony knows the bomb can explode at any time of the year, day or night. He's ready for it."

There's a bright flash.

"Duck and cover!"

The boy jumps off his bike, dives to the curb, and lies facedown.

"Attaboy, Tony! That flash means act fast!"

Another scene shows a family picnic: two teenage kids, a mother laying out plates on a blanket, a father fanning campfire flames with a newspaper.

"Sundays, holidays, vacation time," says the narrator, "we must be ready every day, all the time, to do the right thing if the atomic bomb explodes."

Bright flash.

"Duck and cover!"

The kids and mom get under the picnic blanket.

The dad shields his head with his newspaper.

There was no hiding from the real thing.

Before dawn on March 1, 1954, a Japanese fishing boat named *Lucky Dragon* drifted in calm South Pacific waters. There were twenty-three crew members aboard, a few on deck but most still asleep in their bunks.

In an instant, the sky far to the west switched from black to yellowish white, as if someone had flipped on a light in a dark room. The men on deck watched, mouths hanging open.

Others scrambled up to the deck. A fiery orange glow spread above the horizon.

Someone shouted, "The sun rises in the west!"

The light faded as silently as it had come. The sky was black again. The boat swayed gently on calm water.

Seven minutes later the men heard a sound like a rumble of thunder, and the boat rocked. Clouds drifted in from the west. Pale gray flakes started falling from the sky. The sticky clumps coated the ship and the men. It stung their eyes and felt gritty in their mouths.

Aikichi Kuboyama, the boat's radioman, did some rough calculations. Whatever had happened, the light would have reached them almost instantly, but sound travels much slower. Seven minutes from flash to boom. Four hundred and twenty seconds. Sound takes about five seconds to travel a mile, so whatever happened was a bit over eighty miles away.

Kuboyama found a chart of nearby islands. To the west, about eighty miles, was Bikini Atoll, a group of small coral islands. The Americans had tested bombs there before.

By that evening, many of the crewmen had begun to suffer

from classic symptoms of radiation poisoning: weakness, head-aches, fevers, and nausea. As they headed home, sores blistered the men's skin. Their hair fell out in clumps. The *Lucky Dragon* reached Japan two weeks later.

"I don't know exactly what happened," Aikichi Kuboyama told his wife, "but on our way home we encountered something—an atom bomb, I think."

A hydrogen bomb, to be precise. The Super. A fifteen-megaton beast, 750 times the explosive force of the bomb that had destroyed Hiroshima.

The explosion obliterated a coral island in Bikini Atoll, sucking millions of tons of coral dust into the sky. The blast also created radioactive atoms—atoms with unstable nuclei that break apart, ejecting particles and rays as they decay. Radioactive atoms stuck to the coral dust, drifted in the wind, and dropped from the sky as deadly fallout on the *Lucky Dragon*. Radiation penetrated the men's bodies, damaging cells and weakening their immune systems.

From his hospital bed, Aikichi Kuboyama offered a plea to the world: "Please make sure that I am the last victim of the bomb."

Kuboyama died of liver failure at the age of forty, six months after coming home. The other crew members survived but would suffer lifelong health problems.

Moved by the terrifying reality that humans must now live along-side the Super, a Japanese filmmaker named Ishiro Honda reworked his script for a new monster movie. In this revised ver-sion, a hydrogen bomb test awakens a giant fire-breathing mutant, which then rises out of the sea and marches into Tokyo.

Godzilla was a whole new kind of story—for a whole new kind of world.

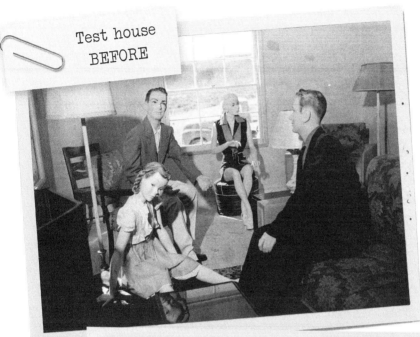

Test house
BEFORE

Test house
BEFORE

AFTER

EARLY WARNING

"ATTENTION! THE PLANE IS OVER the target. Five minutes to the drop!"

November 22, 1955—a cold, clear day in the dry grasslands two thousand miles southeast of Moscow. A thirty-four-year-old physicist named Andrei Sakharov stood with scientists and Soviet officials on an outdoor platform about forty miles from ground zero.

"The bomb has dropped!" roared a voice over the loudspeaker. "The parachute has opened! One minute!"

The Soviets had stolen the secret of the fission bomb from the Americans. This time, for the Super, Sakharov and his team figured it out on their own. This test would be the proof.

The observers turned their backs to the falling bomb.

"Five, four, three, two, one, zero!"

A silent flash filled the sky.

After the flash, it was safe to turn and look. Sakharov felt heat on his face. He watched a huge yellow fireball rise and grow, turning orange, then red, kicking up towering swirls of dust, boiling itself into the shape of a giant mushroom.

The bomb's blast wave cut a visible path in the steppe, flattening the tall grass as it sped toward the platform.

"Jump!" Sakharov shouted.

Everyone leaped off the platform—except for one bodyguard, who was knocked over as the wave barreled past.

"It worked!" cried Yakov Zeldovich, Sakharov's colleague. "It worked! Everything worked!"

Sakharov's own reaction was remarkably similar to what Robert Oppenheimer had experienced when he watched the world's first atomic bomb test in the New Mexico desert ten years before. A mix of pride, patriotism, relief, and horror.

The Soviet Union's first hydrogen bomb was even more powerful than expected. A young soldier watching from a trench was killed. A two-year-old girl died in a collapsed bomb shelter that should have been well out of the danger zone.

At the government's celebratory banquet that night Sakharov was the man of the hour, the young genius who'd matched the arrogant Americans. When a top military official gave him the honor of making the first toast, Sakharov stood and raised his glass of brandy.

"May all our devices explode as successfully as today's," he said, "but always over test sites and never over cities."

The room went silent. The generals scowled.

Sakharov understood. He had stepped out of line.

"We, the inventors, scientists, engineers, and craftsmen, had created a terrible weapon, the most terrible weapon in human history," he would recall realizing at this moment. "But its use would lie entirely outside our control."

*   *   *

The U.S. government continued pouring money into both fission bombs and hydrogen bombs, expanding its nuclear arsenal from 2,400 weapons in 1955 to 3,700 in 1956. And from this point on, Americans were on the lookout for Soviet bombs. Every second, day and night.

If Soviet bombers ever headed for America, they wouldn't fly west over the Atlantic or east over the Pacific. They'd come from the north, cutting over the Arctic, taking the shortest route to American cities. With this in mind, the U.S. military built early-warning radar stations in Alaska and Canada. At a command center in Colorado Springs, Colorado, radar technicians constantly monitored screens for any signs of enemy invaders.

Late in 1955, just after the Soviet hydrogen bomb test, the phone in the command center began to ring.

Colonel Harry Shoup picked up. "Colonel Shoup."

A young boy, hesitation in his voice, asked, "Is this . . . Santa Claus?"

"Is this a joke?" Shoup snapped. "Just what do you think you're doing?"

Silence on the line. Then quiet sniffling.

It turned out the boy had seen a Sears newspaper ad with a picture of Santa Claus saying, "Hey, kiddies! Call me direct on my telephone!" He'd misdialed. The poor kid had just wanted to talk to Santa. Instead, he got an alarming lesson in current events.

"There may be a guy called Santa Claus at the North Pole," Shoup told the boy, "but he's not the one I worry about coming from that direction."

In case of war, Francis Gary Powers would be crossing the Arctic in the opposite direction.

A twenty-six-year-old pilot stationed at Turner Air Force Base in Georgia, Powers was trained to deliver atomic bombs behind the iron curtain. A job he hoped he'd never be called on to do.

One afternoon in January 1956, after an uneventful practice flight in his F-84F Thunderstreak, Powers was surprised to see his name on a list stuck to the squadron bulletin board. What had he done wrong? What sort of extra duty was he about to be assigned?

The paper didn't say. Just told him to report to wing command headquarters at 8:00 the next morning.

Powers did as told. At least he wasn't alone; a few other young pilots showed up too, equally perplexed. A major called them into his office.

He told the men: You've been selected for your outstanding pilot ratings, your experience in single-pilot jets, and your top-secret clearances. Some men would like to meet you, talk to you about an opportunity. Interested? Go, one at a time, to the Radium Springs Inn. Knock on the door of cottage 1. Ask for Mr. William Collins.

Powers left the meeting with more questions than answers.

Intrigued, he drove to the motel that evening. He walked to the end of a row of tiny buildings, feeling like a character in one of those new James Bond spy novels everyone was reading. Only he wasn't a spy, and he didn't know how this story was supposed to go.

He knocked. The door opened. A man in a business suit stood there, waiting for the visitor to speak.

Powers said, "I was told to ask for a Mr. William Collins."

"I'm Bill Collins. You must be . . . ?"

"Lieutenant Powers."

The man gestured for Powers to come inside. Two more civilians in suits stood in the main room. Everyone shook hands. They sat down.

Collins said, "I suppose you're wondering what this is all about?"

47

SECRET WORLD

FRANCIS GARY POWERS—FRANK TO his friends—drove home to talk with his wife.

They'd met at the air base three years earlier. He was at a cafeteria counter late one night, sipping coffee and glancing over at a young woman sitting at a table with a book. He couldn't know that she'd driven farm trucks since the age of twelve, that she'd skipped two grades and graduated high school at fifteen. But he sort of could. She had that kind of energy.

"Golly, I'd sure like to meet that girl over there," Powers confided to the cashier.

The cashier smiled. "That shouldn't be very difficult. That's my oldest daughter."

Powers felt his face burn a deep shade of red.

The cashier introduced her daughter, Barbara Moore. Frank and Barbara soon began dating, bonding over a shared love of adventure and action.

Now, at home, Powers told his wife about the mysterious meeting in cottage 1. Mr. Collins had informed Powers he'd been chosen for a "special mission." He'd said the job would include a certain level of risk and would be "important for your country." The only thing he'd been clear about was that the work would require a long overseas deployment. No family allowed.

Frank and Barbara had been married just nine months. Frank's first thought was that the no-family rule was a deal-breaker, but Barbara encouraged him to grab the opportunity. She could live with her mother and keep her job as a secretary at the nearby Marine base. They could save up a lot of money. Besides, she could see that he really wanted to do it.

Powers called a phone number Mr. Collins had given him. He was told to return to the motel the next evening.

When they met again, Collins explained to Powers that he worked for the Central Intelligence Agency, a government agency tasked with gathering and interpreting secret information from around the world and running covert operations against enemies of the United States. Should Powers accept this new assignment, he'd leave the Air Force and work directly for the CIA. He'd be trained to fly a new kind of airplane, a top-secret design. The pay would be high, about what a commercial airline pilot would earn.

If it sounded dangerous, that's because it was. His mission would be to fly over the Soviet Union.

"How do you feel about it now?" Collins asked.

Flying had always been Frank Powers's dream—yet he still felt restless, unsatisfied. He'd been too young to serve in World War II. He'd been hit with appendicitis just as he was about to ship out to the Korean War. Here was a chance to do his part in the Cold War.

"I'm in," he told Collins.

"Take another night to think it over."

"That's not necessary," Powers said. "I've decided."

Frank Powers slipped into a secret world, a hidden layer beneath the surface of everyday life.

Like anyone new to tradecraft, he learned by trial and error. Here's a tip: while checking into a hotel under a fake identity, be sure to memorize your false address ahead of time, so you're not in the ridiculous position of standing at the registration desk with a pen in your hand, trying to remember where you live.

And when you're meeting with an agent, if the agent turns a radio up loud while you talk, leave the dial alone. Soon after signing up, Powers and a small group of other pilots met with Mr. Collins in a Washington, D.C., hotel room. Music blared on the radio as Collins showed the pilots a photo of the new plane they'd been recruited to fly.

"What do you call it?" asked one of the fliers.

"No one calls it anything publicly yet," Collins said. "But for your information, it's been dubbed the Utility-2."

It was the most boring name they could think of and would hopefully deflect unwanted attention.

Powers could barely hear over the music. He turned it off.

Collins stopped talking and glared.

Powers suddenly got it. The music was meant to cover their conversation, in case the room was bugged by Soviet spies. He flicked the radio back on, and the briefing continued.

The pilots were flown to a remote base in the Nevada desert. It wasn't much—a control tower and a six-thousand-foot runway, mobile homes, and a mess hall. The base was so secret that it didn't have an official name. On confidential government maps, it was labeled only as "Area 51."

There, finally, Powers got a close-up look at the Utility-2—or, as they'd started calling it, the U-2.

The thing looked like a glider with a jet engine, its wings twice as long as its body, so long they drooped when the plane was at rest. To achieve minimum weight, the designers had built the plane's sleek frame of aluminum just 0.02 inches thick. The tail was held on with three small bolts. It carried no weapons, no defense. The U-2's superpower was altitude. It would fly so high, it simply could not be hit.

That was the theory, anyway.

Nothing about flying this plane was easy. Before every takeoff, pilots did two hours of "pre-breathing"—breathing in pure oxygen to eliminate nitrogen from the blood. At high altitude, if there was a sudden loss of air pressure in the cockpit, nitrogen in the pilot's blood would expand into bubbles, causing the excruciating and often deadly condition known to scuba divers as the bends. As an extra layer of protection, pilots wore tight helmets and full-body pressure suits so stiff they left bruises.

There was no way to eat during flight. No way to drink or use the bathroom. There was never a moment to relax, because the maximum and minimum speeds at which the U-2 could stay aloft were nearly the same. Fly any faster, and the flimsy craft would literally break apart under the strain. Fly any slower, and the airflow over the wings would be insufficient to keep the plane in the sky. The plane would drop into a dive, gain speed—and break apart under the strain.

All that said, Powers loved the U-2, the thrill and the challenge of it. Alone at 70,000 feet, above the clouds and weather, he felt no sense of speed. The earth below curved away like the surface of a globe, and the sky above shaded to a spacy blue-black.

As the pilots trained at Area 51, people all over the American West started seeing oddly shaped ships soaring far higher than any plane they knew of. There was a sharp rise in reported UFO sightings.

Even Barbara Powers was kept guessing. Frank knew he was going to be sent to an American air base in Turkey but could not tell his wife where he was going or what he was doing. He handed her a CIA-prepared sheet of paper with a California address to which she could write. From there her letters would be forwarded to her husband. There was a phone number with a Virginia area code that she could call—but only in the case of dire emergency.

Before leaving the country, Frank Powers visited his parents in the small town of Pound, in southwestern Virginia. He told them he was heading overseas to do weather research for the government.

His sister Jan didn't buy it. "Why do you have to go all the way over there to study the weather? We have weather here."

In the summer of 1956, American pilots began flying U-2s over the Soviet Union. Using cutting-edge cameras in the bellies of the planes, the pilots photographed Soviet factories, military bases, rocket launch sites. The film was rushed back to the United States and analyzed by expert photo interpreters in Washington. Magnified prints were sent to President Dwight Eisenhower at the White House.

Eisenhower was impressed. A career military man, commander of Allied forces in Europe during World War II, he'd seen plenty of aerial reconnaissance photos. But never anything like these U-2 images. The views were so sharp you could identify Soviet planes on the ground, count the tanks and missiles.

The president worried, though. Imagine if the Soviets sent similar planes into American airspace. Eisenhower would consider that nothing less than an act of war.

On this point, he and Nikita Khrushchev were in complete agreement.

Soviet radar picked up the American planes the moment they neared the border. After the first U-2 flights over Soviet territory, Khrushchev had delivered a formal protest to the U.S. government.

The White House denied sending Air Force planes over the Soviet Union. This was technically true. The planes belonged to the CIA.

The overflights continued, with no further protest from Moscow.

Khrushchev's son Sergei, who was training to be a rocket scientist, asked his father why he didn't roar to the world about the offensive and illegal American flights.

Nikita told his son: "The weak complain against the strong."

The Soviet premier had quotes and proverbs for every occasion:

"They do not see with their eyes but with their asses—all they can see is what's behind them."

"Any fool can start a war."

"Fear has big eyes."

Another favorite, one he very much hoped to apply by shooting down an American U-2:

"The way to teach a smart aleck a lesson is with a fist."

Francis Gary
Powers next to
U-2 plane

WE WILL BURY YOU

"MOST OF THESE ARE STILL in progress, but this one is finished."

Rudolf Abel gestured to his newest painting. A young painter from a studio down the hall, Burt Silverman, studied the canvas, an image of homeless men on the street in New York.

"It has some strong qualities," Silverman said.

Except the drawing was quite poor, he pointed out. The composition was awkward. The color choices were dull.

"Well," Abel said, "this is one of the first things I did."

The spy took the criticism to heart. When he wasn't busy trying to recruit new agents or receiving coded radio messages from Moscow, Abel worked on improving as a painter. Other artists gathered in his space, drinking coffee, talking art and love and current events. His new friends often criticized the American government, especially the country's economic inequality and its shameful record of racism.

Abel just listened, as if he didn't care much about politics. It was a smart move.

The decade of the 1950s was the time of the Red Scare. American leaders whipped up fear of communists, warning there were enemy agents lurking everywhere—in schools, government offices, movie studios—secretly paving the way to Soviet world domination. Anyone who showed any interest in communism, or even in its goal of a fair distribution of wealth, risked being branded as disloyal, an enemy to America.

In a way, it made no sense. There's nothing in the U.S. Constitution that limits what sorts of political beliefs a citizen can have. Americans were so proud of their freedom—yet here they were, turning on each other for having different ideas. But in another way, it was perfectly understandable. Communism may have been inspired by noble goals, but Americans could see what real-world communist countries looked like. What if that kind of government grabbed control in America?

Rudolf Abel knew this was pretty unlikely. Sure, there *were* a few Soviet agents at work in the United States. But, sadly for Abel, not nearly as many as frightened Americans seemed to think. That's how it is when you're scared—you start to see your enemy everywhere.

As they say, fear has big eyes.

The level of fear rose higher when Americans saw how Nikita Khrushchev responded to a freedom movement in Hungary, one of the Eastern European countries controlled by the Soviet Union.

Hungarians marched in the streets in the fall of 1956, calling for free elections. Khrushchev sent Soviet troops and tanks into Budapest, the Hungarian capital, killing at least twenty-five hundred civilians. Khrushchev was no Stalin—he did not murder millions of his own citizens—but this action showed how ruthless he could be when faced with a threat to Soviet power.

In the face of protest from around the world, Khrushchev was defiant.

"Whether you like it or not, history is on our side," he lectured Western diplomats in Moscow. "We will bury you."

This would become Nikita Khrushchev's most famous line. Almost his slogan.

"We will bury you."

He claimed over and over that he did not mean it *literally*. He meant the communist system would, over time, prove itself superior to American-style capitalism and democracy.

Either way, Rudolf Abel would have liked to help with the burial.

But how was he supposed to get anything done with an assistant like Reino Hayhanen?

Hayhanen had been a brave and skillful agent during World War II but had gone soft in the years since. When Abel ordered him to open a photography shop in New Jersey as cover for planned operations, he never got around to it. When Abel provided Hayhanen with living expenses, Hayhanen blew it all on booze. When the two spies buried $5,000 in Bear Mountain State Park, north of the city, stashing it away for the wife of a Soviet spy who was doing time in Alcatraz, Hayhanen returned to the park, dug up the cash, and spent it.

Abel was out of patience. He informed his KGB bosses in Moscow. In early 1957, the Soviet intelligence agency ordered Hayhanen to return home for a vacation.

Hayhanen had been in the KGB long enough to know that such "vacations" usually included long stays in Siberian prison camps. He got as far as France before deciding to travel no farther east. After downing a few drinks, he stumbled into the American embassy in Paris.

"I'm an officer in the Soviet intelligence service," he blurted. "For the past five years, I have been operating in the United States. Now I need your help!"

It was hard for the American officials to know whether they should take this guy seriously. He was rambling. He stank of alcohol. But then he pulled out a coin, a Finnish five-mark coin, popped it open with a pin, and dumped out a tiny piece of microfilm.

The Americans flew Hayhanen back to the States, where FBI agents locked him in a hotel room and grilled him for seven days straight.

When Hayhanen disappeared, Abel sensed trouble. He checked into a seedy Manhattan hotel under yet another false name. The FBI tracked him down, knocking on the door early on the morning of June 21, 1957.

The door opened an inch. The FBI men shoved their way in. The top Soviet spy in America returned to the bed and sat naked on the edge of the sagging mattress.

"Colonel," began one of the agents, "we have received information concerning your involvement in espionage."

Abel's face flashed a hint of dread. The use of "colonel" was bad. That meant they'd gotten to Hayhanen. No one else in America could have told them his rank in the KGB.

Regaining his composure, Abel assured his visitors he knew nothing about spying.

The agents told him to put on some underwear.

They'd barely begun to search when they spotted a shortwave radio, with a wire snaking into the bathroom and dangling out the window.

"Colonel, you have lots of trouble."

"I can see that," he said.

When the FBI raided Abel's Brooklyn studio, the haul of evidence included stacks of American cash, spy gadgets Abel had crafted over the years, and Abel's KGB codebook and one-time pads. Now, *finally*, the FBI was able to decipher the hollow nickel message that had baffled them for four years.

```
WE CONGRATULATE YOU ON A SAFE ARRIVAL....
THE PACKAGES WERE DELIVERED TO YOUR WIFE
PERSONALLY. EVERYTHING IS ALL RIGHT WITH
THE FAMILY. WE WISH YOU SUCCESS. GREETINGS
            FROM THE COMRADES.
```

After all that drama and mystery, it was just a routine welcome message.

BROOKLYN ARTIST ARRESTED AS RED SPY
TOP RUSSIAN SPY CAUGHT
U.S. UNMASKS MASTER SPY

The headlines varied from town to town, but the facts were the same—a top Soviet agent had been at work right here, under Americans' noses, for nine years. That menacing message was soon followed by an even more frightening development.

"Ladies and gentlemen, we are bringing to you the most important story of this century."

With those words, on the evening of October 4, 1957, NBC radio announced the start of the Space Age. Soviet rocket scientists had just launched the world's first satellite, Sputnik, a 184-pound aluminum sphere that was orbiting Earth every ninety-six minutes at 18,000 miles per hour.

Americans dashed onto streets and lawns and farm fields and gazed up. And those who looked in just the right spot at just the right time saw it, a tiny dot reflecting the sun's light back to Earth as it sped across the night sky. Curiosity. Wonder. Shock. Fear. Here was another turning point in human history—and an undeniable triumph for the Soviet Union.

"America sleeps under a Soviet moon," crowed Nikita Khrushchev.

It was a brag. It was a threat.

Because rockets powerful enough to launch satellites into space could also be used to deliver hydrogen bombs to American cities.

If there was ever a good time to be on trial as a Soviet spy in America, this was not it.

In a packed Brooklyn courtroom, prosecutors displayed Abel's spy gadgets to the jury. Jimmy Bozart, now a college student, told his story of finding the hollow nickel. Reino Hayhanen, who'd cut a deal to disappear into the government's witness protection program, made a dramatic entrance in dark sunglasses, his hair, eyebrows, and new mustache dyed deep black, and gave devastating testimony about secret codes and dead-drops.

"This is an offense directed at our very existence," the prosecutor said of Abel's mission in America, "and through us at the free world and civilization itself."

Abel sat through it all, doodling in a notebook as if enduring a boring meeting.

The jury convicted him, leaving the judge with two sentencing options: a long prison sentence or the electric chair. Abel's lawyer, James Donovan, argued successfully against the death penalty by pointing out that one day the U.S. government might want to send Abel back to the Soviet Union as part of a trade.

True, Donovan conceded, the Russians did not have an important American spy in custody at the moment. But that could always change.

Barbara Powers was lonely, bored, and tired of waiting for answers.

Frank had been gone for more than a year, and she still didn't know where he was or when he might return. She understood, of course, that military personnel had to leave home sometimes. But her husband had resigned from the Air Force. Why? His Air Force career meant everything to him. Who was he working for? Why were they paying him so much?

One of Frank's letters had mentioned something about Athens, Greece. It was a place to start.

Barbara found the sheet of paper with the emergency contact information and dialed the Virginia phone number.

A man's voice: "Yes?"

"This is Barbara Gay Powers, the wife of Francis Gary Powers. And I just wanted to inform you that I am flying to Athens, Greece, tomorrow morning to be with my husband."

Brief silence on the line.

"Mrs. Powers, do you, er, think this is wise?"

Her mind was made up. "You bet your boots, mister. I'm on my way!"

MAN OR MONSTER?

LESS THAN A WEEK LATER Barbara and Frank Powers sat at a table in an Athens nightclub, toasting her arrival with champagne. He was thrilled to see her, she could see that in his eyes. But there was something else, something bothering him.

He put his glass down and fidgeted with its long stem.

"I might as well tell you this right off the bat," he began. "Sugar, this wild trip of yours over here isn't gonna exactly solve our problem."

"What do you mean? We're here now, together!"

"But not for long." He had to force out the next sentence. "Barbara, I am not stationed in Greece."

"Well, where *are* you stationed?"

"I still can't tell you that."

He'd heard that she was on her way to Athens and had come to meet her, he explained. If she decided to stay, he could fly in once or twice a month.

Barbara made the best of it. She worked at an air base in Athens, then another in Tripoli, Libya. Finally, in early 1958, the CIA agreed to let the U-2 pilots' wives join them at their base—Incirlik Air Base in Adana, Turkey.

"There she is," Frank Powers announced, "the U-2!"

Barbara Powers and a few other spouses were touring the base with their husbands. Barbara stood in front of the spy plane. Like a black crow, she thought, enormous and hungry.

"So," one of the women said, "this is John's other wife."

It was a joke, and not a joke. Life in Turkey was, in Barbara's words, a "marriage of three"—husband, wife, and the strange plane in which Frank conducted what he described as "weather reconnaissance flights." She still didn't know who he was really working for.

Approval for all overflights came directly from the White House. The pilots were then assigned specific routes and targets to photograph. Pilots call routine flights "milk runs." There were no milk runs over Soviet territory.

Keeping the U-2 in the air was hard enough. On top of that, the pilots knew they were being tracked by Soviet radar. The Soviets fired missiles at the American planes and gave chase in their own MiG fighters. The U-2, as its designers had promised, flew too high to be hit.

Yet Frank Powers couldn't help but wonder—what if he *was* hit? What if he was taken prisoner? What was he supposed to do?

His CIA bosses never discussed the topic. The most they did was offer pilots the option of carrying an "L pill"—L for lethal. The label of the bottle instructed users to crush a capsule between the teeth and inhale the toxic cyanide through the mouth. "It is expected that there will be no pain, but there may be a feeling of constriction about the chest," read the directions. "Death will follow."

Best not to think about it.

Between flights, it was easy not to. Frank and Barbara got their own three-bedroom trailer on base and were assigned two maids and a gardener. Barbara arranged parties, and Frank bought a slick Mercedes convertible. They adopted a massive German shepherd named Eck von Heinerberg, and the three of them crowded into the front seat of the sports car for epic drives through the Turkish countryside.

On the overcast afternoon of September 15, 1959, about 200,000 Americans lined the streets of Washington, D.C. Not cheering. Not booing. Just watching the surreal sight in silence.

There, in a car rolling slowly down the street, smiling and waving, was Nikita Khrushchev.

There was Mr. "We will bury you" taking in the sights like a tourist.

President Eisenhower had invited the Soviet leader to America. The rival powers were speeding toward a war that no one could win. Khrushchev had agreed it was time to talk. But Americans had no way of knowing what was really on his mind.

One newspaper captured the mood in a headline: "Khrushchev: Man or Monster?"

From Washington, Nikita, his wife, Nina, and Khrushchev's four grown children set off on a trip across America. The strange scenes played out on the TV news each night—Khrushchev cracking jokes with farmers, chowing down in corporate cafeterias, watching a movie being filmed in a Hollywood studio. His one disappointment was that the family visit to Disneyland was canceled at the last moment.

"Just now, I was told that I could not go," Khrushchev announced at a banquet full of movie stars. "I asked, 'Why not? What is it? Do you have rocket-launching pads there?'"

The audience roared with laughter as the words were translated into English.

Were the Los Angeles police worried about his safety, Khrushchev continued? Or was there another reason? "Have gangsters taken hold of the place? Your policemen are so tough they can lift a bull by the horns. Surely they can restore order if there are any gangsters around."

People chuckled. He was doing a comedy bit—right?

So why was his face turning so red?

"That's the situation I find myself in," Khrushchev ranted, punching the air. "For me, such a situation is inconceivable!"

Silence. Confusion. Was this guy joking or making threats? Was the man with his finger on the trigger of rockets and bombs pointed at the United States really getting this upset over not meeting Mickey Mouse? Was it because he felt disrespected? Was he just trying to keep his enemies guessing?

Man or monster?

"Please forgive me if I was somewhat hot-headed," Khrushchev said, ending his speech with a smile. "But the temperature here contributes to this."

Everyone clapped. Then the Soviet leader was led to one of the tables to meet Marilyn Monroe.

The important part of Khrushchev's visit came last: a meeting with President Eisenhower at Camp David, the presidential retreat in Maryland.

At sixty-nine, nearing the end of his second term as president, Eisenhower—Ike, as Americans called him—was just about worn out. Only one major goal remained. A huge one. Before stepping away from public life, he was determined to get the United States and the Soviet Union off the road to World War III.

Ike had seen the horrors of World War II up close. The next war, if it happened, would be far worse. The U.S. stockpile of nuclear weapons was up to twelve thousand and rising. The Soviets had far fewer, but enough to kill millions of Americans in a matter of minutes. Both powers were racing to build more bombs, faster planes, more powerful rockets. Eisenhower's goal was to make it less likely that future confrontations would lead to all-out war. This would be his crowning achievement—a thawing of Cold War tensions. The dawn of a new, less dangerous era. Not a bad way to finish his life's work.

Walking together on wooded paths at Camp David, Eisenhower and Khrushchev made a small step toward finding common ground. The United States and Soviet Union would always be rivals, that was a given. What they needed to do, both leaders agreed, was find a way to compete without letting events slip out of control. Without destroying each other's cities. They agreed to hold formal talks on these issues at a summit meeting in Paris in May 1960. Eisenhower would then travel to the Soviet Union, making the first ever visit by a U.S. president.

Both leaders saw Khrushchev's visit as a success. Both saw it as in their interests to slow down the march toward a war no one could win. Both wanted to continue battling for advantage around the world, without resorting to hydrogen bombs.

Both truly believed their side would win the Cold War.

Khrushchev returned home and began preparing to host the American president. Teams of workers scrubbed streets and buildings, and broke ground on the nation's first and only golf course. President Eisenhower, it was understood, greatly enjoyed golf.

In Washington, Eisenhower turned to a vital question: Should he continue to approve U-2 flights over Soviet territory in the early months of 1960?

On the one hand, the flights were risky. They could wreck the fragile goodwill Ike had built with the Soviet leader. On the other hand, the spy planes brought back priceless intelligence on Soviet military strength. And Khrushchev had stopped complaining about the overflights years ago. Maybe he'd learned to accept them.

It was a tough call. The Paris summit was set to start on May 16, 1960.

Eisenhower decided the U-2 flights could continue until the first of May.

The last overflight before the Paris summit was assigned to Francis Gary Powers.

HOLLOW COIN #2

FRANK POWERS LOOKED OVER THE new piece of equipment a CIA officer had just handed him. A shiny silver dollar. But not an ordinary one.

The coin had a tiny metal loop attached to the top, like some sort of good-luck charm you'd hang on a keychain. Turn the loop and the coin opened. It was hollow. Inside was a pin, its tip covered with something sticky and brown. Curare, the officer explained, a highly lethal toxin. A quicker version of the L pill. One prick would be deadly. There'd be no danger of being tortured by the Russians.

The coin was optional. Pilots were not ordered to take it along. Or to use it.

Powers decided to take it, just in case. Then he brought up the topic they'd all been avoiding.

"What if something happens and one of us goes down over Russia?" he asked. Suppose they don't use the coin? What then?

"Is there anyone there we can contact? Can you give us any names and addresses?"

"No, we can't."

"All right, say the worst happens," Powers said. "A plane goes down, and the pilot is captured. What story does he use? Exactly how much should he tell?"

"You may as well tell them everything," said the CIA man. "Because they're going to get it out of you anyway."

Barbara Powers packed her husband a bag with thermoses of coffee and soup, six sandwiches, pickles, and cookies. Frank couldn't tell her where he was going, of course, but she knew he often flew to other bases for these secret missions. She did not expect to see him again for a few days.

Frank Powers flew to an American air base at Peshawar, Pakistan, the jumping-off point for his twenty-eighth overflight. It would be his longest, the longest for *any* pilot—from Pakistan all the way over Russia to an air base in northern Norway. Nine hours of flight time, most of that in Soviet airspace.

After tossing and turning on a cot in a hangar, Powers rolled out of bed at 2:00 a.m. on May 1, 1960. He ate a big breakfast, did his pre-breathing, pulled on his pressure suit, climbed into his plane, and took off, soaring high above the peaks of the Hindu Kush mountain range. Crammed into the cockpit of his U-2, Powers felt the usual tension as he neared the enemy frontier. Reaching for his radio, he sent the pre-arranged code to the base in Pakistan: two quick clicks. A response of three clicks would mean return to base. One click would mean proceed.

The signal came back: *CLICK*, and silence.

*   *   *

It was the special phone that woke him that morning.

Nikita Khrushchev opened his eyes in his dark bedroom and reached for the red phone on his bedside table. The minister of defense, Rodion Malinovsky, was on the line. Khrushchev listened, then hung up, his Sunday already ruined. He dressed in a suit and tie and trudged downstairs for breakfast.

His son Sergei, now twenty-four, wondered what was wrong. May 1 — May Day — was a Soviet workers' holiday, a day of celebrations and parades that Khrushchev always enjoyed. But the way his father was clinking his spoon on the side of his glass of tea — that was a "do not disturb" sign.

It was a silent meal. Khrushchev got up and walked out.

Sergei was too curious to resist. He ran outside. His father was about to get into a black government car but stopped when he saw Sergei. Nikita Khrushchev often confided in his son when they were alone. He did so now.

"They've flown over us, again."

"How many?" Sergei asked.

"Like before — one," Khrushchev said. "It's flying at a great height."

"Will we shoot it down?"

"That's a stupid question." Softening his tone, he added, "It all depends on what happens."

Soviet air defense had improved its weapons, but the American pilot would have to fly near enough to a missile base to give them a decent shot. They would need a bit of luck.

Two hours into the flight, Frank Powers switched on his plane's cameras and photographed Baikonur Cosmodrome, the site from which Soviet scientists had shocked the world with their Sputnik launch.

Powers continued northwest for another two hours. The rounded tops of the Ural Mountains came into view. He was on course. The skies ahead were clear. It was a beautiful spring day. He was making a note in his flight log when he felt a thump.

His seat jerked forward and the sky flashed orange.

"My God," he shouted, "I've had it now!"

The nose of the plane dipped. Powers pulled back on the wheel to bring it up. No response. Either the control cable to the tail had snapped, or the tail itself had been shot off. The plane tipped into a nosedive. Its long wings sheared off. The fuselage swung nose-up and dropped like a spent rocket. All Powers could see was spinning blue sky.

He reached for the self-destruct switch. Once he flipped it, he'd have seventy seconds before an explosive charge blew the cockpit apart, destroying the plane's secret technology. The procedure was to start the self-destruct countdown, then blast himself free in his ejection seat. But Powers's knees were jammed under the instrument panel. If he tried ejecting now, he'd leave his legs behind.

The accelerating free fall created tremendous g-force, which Powers felt as crushing weight on his body, making every movement a battle.

The altimeter was spinning crazily—but accurately—past 35,000, under 34,000 . . .

Powers had the presence of mind to know he was beginning to panic.

"Stop," he told himself. "Stop and *think*."

He reached up and unlatched the clear canopy over the cockpit, and the whole thing cracked off and spun into the sky. Blinding frost instantly covered the faceplate of his helmet. Managing to yank his legs loose with his hands, he unfastened his seat belt and felt his body being ripped from the plane, then jerked to a stop, held back by the oxygen hoses attached to his flight suit. He kicked and twisted, and the hoses snapped, and he was free, tumbling toward the earth.

His parachute opened at 15,000 feet. Everything slowed down. There was no sound. The air was frigid, but breathable.

Powers lifted his faceplate just in time to see pieces of his plane rain past. He looked down at a landscape of hills and forests, farmland, and a small town. It looked pleasant and peaceful. Almost like his home state of Virginia.

It was definitely not Virginia.

Now Powers had a few minutes to take stock, to prepare for the worst. He reached into a pocket of his flight suit, pulled out a map of his flight plan, ripped it to small pieces, and let them fall. What other evidence did he have of his spying mission?

The coin. The hollow coin.

Powers took the silver dollar from his pocket. He unscrewed the loop and the hollow coin split open.

There was the needle. One prick would be plenty.

The Soviet military paraded past massive crowds in Moscow's Red Square, displaying some of its latest weapons and missiles. Then came more peaceful marchers—ballerinas dancing, singers and musicians, farmers holding government-approved banners with stirring slogans such as MORE FERTILIZER FOR AGRICULTURE!

Nikita Khrushchev and other top officials watched from atop the red granite mausoleum holding the bodies of the former Soviet leaders Vladimir Lenin and Joseph Stalin. The sun was shining. The views of the grand buildings around the square, including the colorful onion-shaped domes of Saint Basil's Cathedral, were impressive. But what caught Khrushchev's eye was the sight of

Marshal Sergei Biryuzov, commander of Soviet air defense, pushing his way through the VIP seats on the mausoleum.

Everyone in the grandstand noticed. They watched Biryuzov work his way to Khrushchev's seat, lean down, and whisper in his ear.

The wreckage
of Powers's
U-2

ZUGZWANG

ALL THE MAN WANTED TO do was play golf and save humanity from nuclear annihilation. Now it looked like he wouldn't get to do either.

On the morning of May 1, at Camp David, President Dwight Eisenhower stood on a porch looking out at a cold, steady drizzle. There'd be no round of golf today. He took Mary Jean, his four-year-old granddaughter, to Camp David's two-lane bowling alley. He ate lunch with his wife, Mamie. Between downpours, he did a little skeet shooting at the rifle range.

Then the phone call came. It was General Andrew Goodpaster, one of the president's top military advisers, calling from Washington.

"One of our reconnaissance planes on a scheduled flight is overdue," Goodpaster said, "and possibly lost."

Climbing into a helicopter for the short flight back to Washington, Eisenhower braced himself for what could be a difficult few days. What if the Soviets had managed to shoot down the U-2? That would be bad. But the president had one valuable asset: deniability. Khrushchev could never *prove* to the world that the United States had sent a spy plane over Soviet territory. The Central Intelligence Agency had assured Eisenhower of this again and again. The U-2 was simply too fragile. If it were ever hit in the sky it would be blown to bits. And there would be absolutely no chance to question the pilot.

"It would be impossible, if things should go wrong, for the Soviets to come in possession of the equipment intact," CIA Director Allen Dulles had promised the president. "Or, unfortunately, a live pilot."

Back home that evening, Nikita Khrushchev lowered himself into his favorite chair, a wooden rocker in the living room. Books, mostly about Lenin and Stalin and communist political philosophy, lined the walls of the cozy room. There was a large photo of Grand Kremlin Palace. It was a nice place to sit after work. A nice place to think.

Nina padded up in her slippers, bringing rolls and glasses of tea with lemon. She sat with her husband. It had been a good day. Soviet pride had been avenged.

The Cold War was like a chess match played on a global board. Chess was practically the Russian national sport, and Khrushchev relished the chess-like aspects of his job, the cunning calculation of moves and countermoves. The United States was richer. They had more bombs. So he would have to be the smarter player.

Nikita sipped his tea and considered his next move.

At the White House the next morning, General Goodpaster walked into the Oval Office. Bad news. President Eisenhower could see it on his aide's face.

"Mr. President, I have received word from the CIA that the U-2 reconnaissance plane I mentioned yesterday is still missing," Goodpaster said. "With the amount of fuel he had on board, there is not a chance of his being aloft."

Goodpaster showed Eisenhower the cover story the CIA had prepared in partnership with NASA, the U.S. space agency. Eisenhower read it over. He nodded his agreement. The story was a lie, of course, but it should do the job. The important thing, with the big Paris summit coming up, was to prevent a crisis with the Soviet Union.

The Soviet chess champion David Bronstein once said, "The most powerful weapon in chess is to have the next move."

It's true—except when it isn't.

The game is so complex, with more possible combinations of moves than there are atoms in the known universe, there's an exception to every rule. Sometimes, in rare cases, it's a disadvantage to have the next move. There's even a term for it, a German word, *zugzwang*, meaning "compulsion to move." A player in zugzwang has no good moves. You *have* to move—but any move will weaken your position.

Eisenhower was about to be in zugzwang, and he didn't even know it.

Khrushchev saw this. All he had to do was make what chess players call a waiting move, an insignificant move that changes nothing important on the board and gives your opponent the next turn.

May 3 was a rainy day in Moscow. Khrushchev stopped by a trade fair in a city park. He chatted with reporters and admired displays of goods manufactured in communist countries. No mention of Cold War tensions or the upcoming summit in Paris. Not a word about spy planes or missing pilots. A waiting move.

There was a shooting gallery at the fair, and Khrushchev took the opportunity to show off his marksmanship. As a crowd gathered to watch, he lifted his rifle and fired a bull's-eye, setting off a loud clanging of bells.

That same day, at 2:15 p.m., sirens wailed on the streets of New York City.

The signal for an incoming Soviet attack.

Cabs and buses pulled to the side of the street. People raced into buildings or down the steps of the nearest subway station. Children in schools ducked under desks and covered their heads. A zookeeper at the Bronx Zoo shoved an elephant, trying to move the animal inside. At Yankee Stadium, where the Yankees were hosting the Detroit Tigers, the players ran off the field.

This was Operation Alert, an annual drill held by the government since 1954. The goal was to prepare Americans for the outbreak of World War III. Planners wrote out realistic scenarios for the alerts—in this case, one twenty-megaton bomb detonated above LaGuardia Airport. Another hit the Naval Yard in Brooklyn, and a third was aimed at the Queensboro Bridge.

That level of firepower—the destructive energy of three thousand Hiroshima bombs exploding all at once—would flatten every building in the city. Of New York City's eight million residents, the government estimated, four million would be killed instantly. Most of the rest would die of injuries and radiation poisoning.

This time it was only a drill. At 2:30 p.m., right on schedule, the city came back to life.

President Eisenhower's phony cover story hit newspapers the next morning, May 4.

"AF Searching for Lost Plane," read one typical headline.

"U.S. Air Force planes circled over the mountainous wilds of southeastern Turkey today searching for an experimental jet plane that vanished with its pilot three days ago," the article began. "The plane belonged to the National Aeronautics and Space Administration. Name of the pilot was withheld."

Eisenhower had made his move. Now it was Khrushchev's turn.

ALIVE AND KICKING

THE NEXT MORNING, IN MOSCOW, U.S. Ambassador Llewellyn Thompson walked into the grand auditorium of Kremlin Palace. The place was packed with thirteen hundred Soviet officials, gathered to hear an address from their leader. Thompson figured he'd sit with the other diplomats, as always, but was ushered instead to the front row.

Why? He'd have to wait and see.

The Soviet premier strode onto the stage. He spoke of economic plans and labor policy, then moved on to international affairs.

"Comrade Deputies," he said, his voice rising in volume. "I must report to you on aggressive actions against the Soviet Union in the past few weeks by the United States of America. The United States has been sending aircraft that have been crossing our state frontiers."

He described the most recent overflight and his orders to destroy the invader.

"This assignment was fulfilled. The plane was shot down."

"Correct! Correct!" someone shouted.

"Shame to the aggressor!"

"Outright banditry!"

"Just imagine," Khrushchev continued, savoring the moment, "what would have happened had a *Soviet* aircraft appeared over New York, Chicago or Detroit! How would the *United States* have reacted?"

He glared directly at the American ambassador in the front row. "What was that? A *May Day* greeting?"

Soviet officials roared and stamped their feet.

Someone was pounding on the door of the trailer. Eck von Heinerberg, the giant German shepherd, was snarling and barking, eager to attack.

Barbara Powers opened the trailer door. Two stern-faced men identified themselves as agents of the Central Intelligence Agency. They told her to pack a few things. Her other belongings would be shipped home. She was leaving Turkey. Right now.

"Where's my husband?" she demanded, fighting back panic.

"Everything is going to be all right, Mrs. Powers," said one of the men. "Now please, just do as we say."

"What about my dog? I can't just leave him here."

"You can bring him right along with us on the plane, Mrs. Powers."

Thirty minutes later she was in the air, flying back to the United States. She kept asking for information about Frank. And whatever was going on, what did it have to do with the CIA?

The men would tell her nothing. They just kept pouring her drinks.

Eisenhower stood on the White House lawn smiling for the cameras, but without joy, like a kid forced to pose for a family photo. He climbed aboard a helicopter and headed west out of the city, toward the Blue Ridge Mountains.

This was the government's version of Operation Alert, a day for top officials to rehearse evacuating Washington. In his eighth year as president, Ike had long since lost any enthusiasm for these drills.

"I am not sure whether I would really want to be living," he said privately, "if this country of ours should ever be subjected to a nuclear bath."

With the rise of the Super, the U.S. government had begun spending billions of dollars trying to figure out how the country could emerge from the ashes of World War III. The best solution, leaders decided: move underground. At Mount Weather in Virginia, the government expanded an abandoned mine, constructing a small city inside the mountain: reservoir, power plants, sewage plants, cafeterias, a hospital, a crematorium. There was enough food and space for three thousand people to live for a month. Only the president, cabinet members, and the justices of the Supreme Court got private rooms.

No one could bring their families.

In the bunker war room, red bulbs dotted an enormous map of the United States—one bulb would glow to mark each nuclear blast. In a TV studio with a large photo of the Capitol building as a backdrop, the president could broadcast messages to whatever was left of the American population.

Officially, Mount Weather did not exist. Though local

residents did notice that the road up the hill was always plowed quickly after snowstorms.

It took the helicopter just twenty minutes to reach the bunker. Eisenhower walked through the five-foot-thick steel blast gate, past the decontamination chamber, and met in the war room with cabinet officials who were also participating in the drill. They'd heard nothing from Moscow about the missing U-2. It looked like the cover story was holding.

Until CIA Director Allen Dulles was handed a note just in from Moscow. Khrushchev had given a speech. He'd said something about shooting down an American plane. Nothing about a pilot. More details to follow.

Eisenhower decided to stick with his "weather research gone wrong" story. Without the pilot, the Soviets couldn't prove otherwise.

At a press conference that afternoon, U.S. State Department spokesman Lincoln White repeated the fiction. "It is entirely possible," he told the press, "that having a failure in the oxygen equipment, which could result in the pilot losing consciousness, the plane continued on automatic pilot a considerable distance and accidentally violated Soviet airspace."

No one had told White the cover story was a lie.

"Comrades, I must let you in on a secret."

Nikita Khrushchev was back on stage at the Kremlin, again playing to a crowded house, loving every minute of the building tension.

"When I made my report two days ago, I deliberately refrained from mentioning that we have the remnants of the plane."

Dramatic pause . . .

"And," he continued with obvious delight, "we also have the pilot, who is quite alive and kicking!"

The hall erupted in thunderous applause.

"Now, when they learn that the pilot is alive, they will have to think up something else," Khrushchev said. "And they will!"

Khrushchev insisted that he still wanted peace—but how could one deal with a government that told such stupid lies? The plane was studying weather! The oxygen equipment failed! The poor pilot got dizzy!

"Such a pirate, prone to dizziness, may in fact drop a hydrogen bomb on foreign soil. And this means that the peoples of the land where this pirate was born will unavoidably and immediately get a more destructive hydrogen bomb in return!"

Thirteen hundred Soviet officials jumped to their feet and pounded the backs of benches with their fists.

CENTER STAGE

"UNBELIEVABLE," EISENHOWER GROANED on hearing of Khrushchev's latest performance.

The Soviet premier had worked him like a puppet, leaving him with two awful options. He could deny knowledge of the U-2 flights—but that would make it look like he didn't know what his own government was doing. He could take responsibility—but no American president had ever admitted to spying on other nations.

Until now. Ike directed the White House to release a statement acknowledging that an American pilot, Francis Gary Powers, had been shot down on a reconnaissance flight over Russia and that President Eisenhower had personally approved the flight.

It was humiliating to have fallen so deeply into Khrushchev's trap. But Eisenhower was willing to take the heat, as long as there was still a chance for his meeting with the Soviet leader to succeed.

*   *   *

"Why should I bother answering your questions?" Frank Powers asked his interrogators. "As soon as you have everything you want, you're going to take me out and shoot me."

A group of military officers and men in business suits sat with the American prisoner at a long table in the KGB's Lubyanka prison. An interpreter translated. A stenographer took notes.

"There may be a way," a Soviet officer suggested.

Powers said he couldn't see it.

"There may be a way."

"Then tell me what it is."

"Think about it," the officer said. "You go back to your cell and think about it."

It didn't take much thinking. They wanted Powers to flip. Switch sides and return to America as a Russian asset, a double agent. That wasn't going to happen. But the alternatives were not particularly attractive.

Powers had tossed aside the hollow silver dollar while drifting down to Soviet soil—he was going to survive this ordeal, if possible. He'd been immediately captured, flown to Moscow, and locked in prison. Between interrogation sessions, he lay in a tiny cell. A bright bulb above the door never went out. When he put his eye to a peephole in the cell door, the eye of a guard stared back at him.

Over and over, the examiners made Powers repeat his story. He told *some* of the truth about his mission, as much as he figured they already knew. They demanded technical information about the U-2. He denied having any, portraying himself as a glorified bus driver. They didn't buy it. And around and around they went.

At the start of each day, Powers was ordered to initial a transcript of the previous day's interrogation.

"But they're in Russian," he said. "I can't read Russian."

"That doesn't matter. It is required."

Nikita Khrushchev spent the morning of May 16 strolling the streets of Paris. He joked around with people on their way to work. When a young student walked by, he asked if she'd passed her latest school exams.

"I did," she said.

Khrushchev patted her on the head. "Good girl!"

That afternoon the leaders of the United States, Great Britain, France, and the Soviet Union walked into a large room in Élysée Palace. Light poured in from the garden, but the air inside was cold with tension.

"We are gathered here for the Summit Conference," began French President Charles de Gaulle. "Does anyone wish to say anything?"

Khrushchev stood. Had he come to Paris to speak of serious issues, or to score more points against the Americans? That was not clear—until he opened his mouth.

"President de Gaulle," he began. "Prime Minister Macmillan. President Eisenhower. Permit me to address you with the following statement: A provocative act is known to have been committed recently with regard to the Soviet Union by the American Air Force."

This was nothing less than an invasion, Khrushchev charged, an act of war. The American president had confessed to the crime—but offered no apology, no promise to punish those behind the U-2 program. Under such conditions, it was impossible to hold useful talks. The Paris summit, in spite of the world's hopes for peace, must fail.

"Let the disgrace and responsibility for this," he said, "rest with those who have proclaimed a bandit policy toward the Soviet Union."

Also, Eisenhower was no longer invited to Russia.

"I'm just fed up!" Eisenhower ranted, back at the U.S. ambassador's residence that evening. "I'm just fed up!"

As if the Soviets were angels! As if they didn't believe in spying! The president had hoped there would at least be a chance to talk things through with Khrushchev, but the man insisted on playing the victim, putting on a show. Ike flew home in a foul mood. His dream of ending his presidency with a step toward peace was shattered.

Khrushchev stuck around Paris to give one more performance.

At a press conference packed with reporters and spectators, the Soviet leader strutted onto the stage, clapping his hands as some in the audience hooted and booed.

"If you boo us and attack us again, *look out!*" he threatened. "We will hit you so hard that there won't be a squeal out of you!"

Khrushchev was well aware he was pushing the world closer to war. It was all part of the game. The more frightened people were of the Soviet Union, the more power he held in his hands.

Members of the press shouted questions over the bedlam. Khrushchev, as always, had a story at the ready, telling the crowd that Eisenhower and his U-2 pilot reminded him of a trespassing cat. "If at the mine where I was raised, a cat was caught climbing into the pigeon coop, it would be grabbed by the tail and thrown to the ground. After that, the cat understood better the lesson he'd been taught."

*   *   *

A week later, a somber President Eisenhower sat at his desk in the Oval Office, addressing the nation on live TV.

"Tonight I want to talk with you about the remarkable events last week in Paris and their meaning to our future."

Ike defended the U-2 flights as necessary when dealing with a secretive and unpredictable adversary. He blamed Khrushchev for the failure of the summit. The United States would remain strong, he vowed—but Americans should not view the Cold War as business as usual. Throughout human history, rival powers had built weapons and moved inevitably toward the next war. This must not be allowed to happen again.

"Whether started deliberately or accidentally, global war would leave civilization in a shambles," Eisenhower warned the nation. "In a nuclear war, there can be no victors—only losers."

Three months later, on his thirty-first birthday, Francis Gary Powers was led by guards onto—appropriately enough—the stage of a massive theater.

High-profile trials in the Soviet Union were nothing more than scripted theatrics. Playing the role of Powers's defense lawyer was Mikhail Grinev, a wispy-goateed attorney whose job was to lose important cases to the government. Grinev had represented Khrushchev's rival for power, Lavrenty Beria. Right before they shot him in the head.

Barbara Powers sat in a private box, silently praying. She and Frank's parents had gotten permission to come to Moscow to attend the trial. She watched as guards guided Frank to the witness stand. He looked healthy but thin, swimming in the boxy suit they'd given him. He was squinting through the bright TV lights, trying to find his family in the crowd.

Three judges in dress uniforms sat at a table center stage. One of the judges, speaking Russian, read the official charge of spying. Powers and his family listened over headsets to an English translation.

"Do you understand the charge brought against you?"

"Yes," Powers said.

"Do you plead guilty of the charge?"

"Yes, I plead guilty."

He said he was sorry—because he genuinely was. And because it was his only chance to avoid the firing squad. "There was, I suppose, a great increase in tension in the world," he explained to the court, "and I am sincerely sorry I had anything to do with this."

As the trial moved to the question of sentencing, the prosecutor attacked Powers as a dangerous criminal, the foolish tool of a reckless government bent on starting a new world war.

"I have all grounds," the prosecutor concluded, "to ask the court to pass an exceptional sentence on the defendant."

I was right, Powers thought. *They're making an example of me.*

"But, taking into account Defendant Powers's sincere repentance before the Soviet court of the crime which he committed, I do not insist on the death sentence being passed on him, and ask the court to sentence the defendant to fifteen years' imprisonment."

Flash bulbs popped in Powers's eyes. He was in shock, unable to react.

Barbara's first thought was *Thank God he will not be executed.*

Frank's father, Oliver, leapt to his feet, bellowing, "Give me fifteen years here! I'd rather get death!"

LITTLE BOY BLUE

"DROP DEAD, YOU SCUM!"

This was how New Yorkers greeted Nikita Khrushchev as his ship docked at a Manhattan pier a month after Frank Powers's trial in Moscow. Longshoremen were supposed to help moor incoming ships—instead, they shouted curses. A banner draped over a boat floating nearby offered the Soviet leader a poem of welcome:

> *Roses are red,*
> *Violets are blue,*
> *Stalin dropped dead.*
> *How about you?*

Well, Khrushchev was used to such rudeness. The way American newspapers caricatured his portly build and bald head, portraying him like some stubby supervillain sprung from the pages of one of their ludicrous comic books.

That was fine. Let them laugh. Just so long as they respected the might of the Soviet Union.

Khrushchev was in New York for a meeting of the United Nations, and it was here that he joined forces with the controversial new ruler of Cuba, Fidel Castro.

Just thirty-four, Castro had overthrown a corrupt tyrant and seized control of Cuba less than two years before. Ever since, he'd been inching closer to communism. Closer to the Soviet Union. Now, outside a hotel in Harlem, in front of crowds and reporters, Castro and Khrushchev met for the first time. The bearded six-foot-two Cuban embraced the five-foot-two Russian, and Khrushchev would later describe the pleasant sensation of nestling in the arms of a bear.

There was opportunity in that hug.

The United States had dominated and exploited Cuba for decades. Now Castro was rejecting American influence, kicking out American businesses, setting a defiant example that other countries might choose to follow. Cuba was an island just ninety miles from the coast of Florida. A square on the American side of the Cold War chessboard. Khrushchev particularly admired Castro's combative style. He was an attacker—big, loud, radiating intensity and confidence.

At the United Nations, before an audience of world leaders in dark suits, Fidel Castro strode to the front of the room in green army fatigues. Launching into the longest speech in U.N. history, he chided the United States for supporting dictators around the world, just because they sided with America in the Cold War. He mocked Senator John Kennedy, a candidate for U.S. president, calling him a "millionaire, illiterate and ignorant."

Khrushchev laughed and cheered and pounded his desk, loving every minute—all 269 minutes—of the speech.

President Eisenhower saw Fidel Castro as a growing threat. A communist country right off the shores of America was bad enough. But the real danger, from the U.S. government's point of view, was that Castro would spread his revolution through Latin America and beyond.

With the full knowledge and support of the president, CIA planners and gadget-makers began devising plots to humiliate the Cuban leader. One idea was to poison Castro's cigars with drugs that would make him hallucinate and act crazy. Another was to sprinkle a special chemical into his shoes that, once absorbed into the bloodstream, would cause his famous beard to fall out.

And then there was the more direct approach.

Just a short cab ride from the U.N. building, a silver-haired man in diamond cuff links checked into New York's Plaza Hotel. This was Johnny Rosselli, Handsome Johnny to his friends. To the government, he was a high-ranking organized crime figure suspected of several murders. But the government was not looking to arrest Rosselli. It was looking to hire him.

American mobsters hated Castro for shutting down the casinos they'd been running in Cuba. For the right price, the CIA figured, maybe the mob would do the government's dirty work. Rather than deal with the mobsters directly, the agency sent what's known in the language of spies as a cut-out. A middleman, in other words. Plausible deniability. The cut-out, a private detective named Robert Maheu, made his way up to Rosselli's suite at the Plaza and got right to the point. Maheu was authorized, at the highest levels, to offer Johnny Rosselli $150,000 to murder Fidel Castro.

This story is well documented in the CIA's own files.

Rosselli said he'd do it. Not for money, forget the one-fifty. He'd do it, he said, as a patriotic American.

"The Soviets have made a spectacle before the world of the U-2 flight and the trial of our pilot," U.S. Senator John Kennedy told American voters, "and have treated this nation with hostility and contempt."

With the election just weeks away, Senator Kennedy, the Democratic nominee for president, warned that America was losing the Cold War. Losing in Cuba, in space, everywhere. He vowed to do better, to protect Americans from the Soviet advance.

Vice President Richard Nixon, the Republican candidate, fired back that Kennedy lacked experience and toughness. Kennedy was the "kind of man Mr. Khrushchev will make mincemeat of," Nixon charged.

Nikita Khrushchev followed the election with great interest. For the first time, American presidential candidates debated on live television, and Khrushchev was fascinated by the back-and-forth combat. Kennedy seemed to handle the pressure better. He was quick-witted and well-informed. He sweated less, for what that was worth.

When reporters asked Khrushchev which candidate the Soviets favored, he shrugged. "As we Russians say, they are two boots of the same pair."

That was the public line. In private, he wanted Kennedy. He'd spent time with Nixon and found him abrasive and inflexible. The young Kennedy might be easier to deal with. Easier to intimidate.

Was there some way Khrushchev could influence the election? Perhaps. He had Francis Gary Powers in prison. The Americans wanted to get Powers back. Khrushchev was willing to let the man go if there was something in it for the Soviets. But if he sent the pilot home now, it would be a win for Eisenhower and his vice president, Richard Nixon.

So why not wait a bit?

John Kennedy won a very close election. For the rest of his life, Nikita Khrushchev would claim that he had cast what he called "the deciding ballot."

January 19, 1961, was a cold, gray morning in Washington, D.C. Outside the Capitol building, crews of workers set up platforms and chairs for the inauguration ceremony the next day.

A black car stopped in front of the White House and John Kennedy jumped out. This would be his home in twenty-four hours. For now, he was here to meet the outgoing president.

At forty-three, Kennedy was the youngest person ever elected president. Eisenhower was the first president to serve into his seventies. Privately, Kennedy had mocked Ike for being old and out of touch. Eisenhower had dismissed Kennedy as "that young whippersnapper." Also "Little Boy Blue." But the transition from one president to the next was too important for politics or personal feelings. They were on the same side, after all. And there was business to discuss.

Across the president's desk in the Oval Office, Eisenhower warned Kennedy of the many Cold War challenges ahead.

"It's a high-stakes poker game," Ike said. "There's no easy solution."

Of course the most pressing issue was nuclear war. How to avoid it. If necessary, how to fight it.

Eisenhower described the procedure a president would use to launch an attack. There was no big red button. There was the "football"—a black briefcase carried by military officers, handed off from one to the other, kept close to the president at all times. Inside the football were folders with the secret commands needed to launch a nuclear strike.

The president would give his orders to the Pentagon by phone. From there, the orders would be relayed to bombers, submarines, and missile bases. The crews were trained, drilled, ready to go at a moment's notice. To achieve a maximum state of readiness, the Air Force kept some of its bombers airborne at all times. Fully loaded with hydrogen bombs, the bombers could be refueled in the air, giving them the range to reach Soviet targets. Even if Khrushchev launched a surprise attack, even if American cities and military bases lay in smoking ruins, the president could still order those bombers to deliver a devastating counterpunch.

"Watch this," Eisenhower said, lifting a phone on his desk. "Opal Drill Three!"

He set down the receiver. He told Kennedy to check his watch. Then he stood and turned to the French doors leading out to the White House lawn.

In exactly three minutes a Marine helicopter set down on the grass.

Kennedy was in awe.

Three minutes. A football, a phone call, a few commands.

Three minutes, and he could be on his way to a bunker carved into a mountain.

Three minutes, and he could be leading his country into World War III.

Francis Gary Powers shivered through a long winter in a tiny cell in Vladimir Prison, 150 miles east of Moscow. He shared the twelve-by-eight-foot space with Zigurd Kruminsh, a political prisoner from Latvia who'd been convicted of treason for trying to free his country from Soviet rule. They had two beds, a table, and a bucket for use between trips to the bathroom. A window high in the wall showed a tiny square of the sky.

Barbara Powers moved in with her mother in Milledgeville, Georgia. Reporters followed her around at first, snapping photos of the wife of the famous spy pilot, before gradually losing interest. Still, she didn't exactly blend in—driving around town in the Mercedes convertible she and Frank had bought in Turkey, with Eck von Heinerberg in the passenger seat.

One hundred miles northwest, in Atlanta's federal penitentiary, the FBI finally gave up on trying to flip Rudolf Abel. The man simply would not crack. Three years into a thirty-year sentence, the Soviet spy battled boredom and loneliness with letters to his wife and daughter, crossword puzzles, and chess in the prison yard. He got a set of paints and worked on a portrait of John Kennedy.

Somewhere in New England, Reino Hayhanen was living under a new name, drinking too much, terrified of being hunted down by Soviet agents.

Jimmy Bozart, the hero paperboy, was back in college in upstate New York, driving a new Oldsmobile given to him as a reward by a wealthy citizen.

In Miami, Handsome Johnny Rosselli began putting together a team of mobsters for his special assignment in Cuba.

At a secret training base in a forest near Moscow, twenty young pilots competed for the honor of being strapped to the top of a rocket. American pilots, in their own secret spots, were doing the same. Both sides were racing to launch the first man into space.

In Washington, a day before becoming president of the United States, John Kennedy stepped out of the White House into a cold morning. "No easy matters will ever come to you as president," Eisenhower had told him. "If they are easy, they'll be settled at a lower level."

Up on Capitol Hill, crews continued assembling the stands for the inauguration. A light snow began to fall.

FIDEL CASTRO
Cuban dictator

JOHN KENNEDY (*right*) with his
brother BOBBY KENNEDY

IVAN IVANOVICH
Soviet astronaut
mannequin

OLEG
PENKOVSKY
Soviet intelligence
agent and spy

WALTER ULBRICHT, East German ruler,
with NIKITA KHRUSHCHEV

HARRY SEIDEL
cyclist and escape
tunneler

ROTRAUT SEIDEL
with her son, ANDRE

GREVILLE WYNNE
salesman and MI6 agent

JANET CHISHOLM
Penkovsky's British
contact in Moscow

ALAN SHEPARD
U.S. astronaut; first
American in space

SERGEI KOROLEV
Soviet rocket scientist

ERNEIDO OLIVA (left) and
PEPE SAN ROMÁN
anti-Castro rebel leaders

THE PLAYERS

ORIGIN STORY

"THIS IS HOW IT FEELS to be killed."

That thought flashed through U.S. Navy Lieutenant John Kennedy's mind as a Japanese destroyer sliced his boat in half on the moonless night of August 2, 1943. Kennedy's back slammed into the boat's steel hull, a gas tank exploded, and by the light of the flames he watched the enemy ship disappear into the dark.

He shouted, "Everybody into the water!"

Most of the thirteen-man crew were already overboard, paddling between floating puddles of burning fuel. As the fires burned down, the men's eyes, which had adjusted to the bright flames, could see nothing. Following each other's voices, they gathered at a floating chunk of what had been the bow of their small patrol-torpedo boat, PT-109.

Kennedy and his crew had been patrolling passages in the Solomon Islands of the South Pacific, one of many World War II battlegrounds between the United States and Japan. The situation was dire. The bow of PT-109 was sinking. Two of the sailors were dead, and several wounded. Patrick McMahon was hurt the worst, with severe burns on his face, arms, and feet.

Sunrise made the situation even more desperate. The closest bases were all Japanese. If anyone was likely to see them, it was the enemy. Kennedy had to get his men out of the water—the shark-infested water—but how?

"We'll swim to that small island," he told the crew, pointing to Kasolo Island, a dark shape about four miles in the distance. He hoped it was uninhabited. "I'll take McMahon with me. The rest of you can swim together on this plank."

Someone said, "Will we ever get out of this?"

"It can be done," Kennedy said. "We'll do it."

Kennedy used his knife to cut a strip of material from McMahon's life vest, leaving one end attached to the vest and locking the other end between his teeth. He began to swim, pulling the wounded man along with him. They stopped to rest every fifteen minutes.

It took five hours to reach the island.

Gasping for air and vomiting salt water, their legs sliced open by sharp coral, Kennedy dragged McMahon onto the beach. Both men collapsed with their feet still in the sea. The other men crawled onto the sand. Just minutes later, they heard the hum of an engine. Everyone dove under bushes and watched a Japanese naval boat cruise past the island on its way to a nearby base.

Kennedy's injured back was beginning to throb. He and his men were stuck on a tropical island about the size of a football field. There were a few trees but no edible plants. No fresh water. They were surrounded by Japanese bases. The nearest Allied-held island was Rendova—they could see Rendova Peak in the distance to the southeast. It was forty miles away.

The lives of eleven young Americans, including twenty-six-year-old John Kennedy, could easily have ended right there, on a spit of land in the Solomon Islands in the middle of World War II.

Three days later, two young men were paddling their canoe near tiny Naru Island, about two miles southeast of Kasolo Island, when they spotted something interesting.

Biuku Gasa and Eroni Kumana were both in their late teens, both fishermen and canoe makers born on nearby islands. Both had volunteered for the perilous job of scouting for the Allies, observing and reporting on the movement of Japanese forces.

Cautiously, they paddled closer to Naru. Stuck on the reef near shore was the wreckage of a small Japanese boat. Gasa and Kumana decided to take a look at the wreck, see if there was anything worth salvaging. And it was a good find: maps, cooking pots, a sword, a gun. They started gathering the stuff—then froze when they noticed they were being watched.

Two men stood on the beach of Naru Island, staring at them.

Gasa and Kumana couldn't make out details from this distance but figured the men must be Japanese sailors from the wreck. They jumped into their canoe and sped off.

At the same time, the men on the beach dove under a bush. They, too, thought they'd just been spotted by the enemy.

They were John Kennedy and fellow sailor Barney Ross.

Kennedy had spent the last three days trying to keep his crew alive. He'd spent an entire night treading water between islands, fighting currents, terrified of sharks, beyond exhausted, hoping an American ship would pass. No luck. He and his crew had swum another mile to Olasana Island in search of food and water. Nothing. That morning, with his men dying of thirst, Kennedy had swum to Naru with Ross. They saw some sort of wreckage on the reef—but were spotted by men in a canoe and dove for cover.

Gasa and Kumana raced to what they hoped was a safe distance from Naru. It was thirsty work. Gasa suggested they stop for coconuts at Olasana Island. They were near the shore when a white man in rags staggered out of the bushes, waving his arms and shouting:

"Navy! Navy! Americans! Americans!"

Those were two of the few English words the scouts knew. They paddled to the beach. More Americans emerged, some injured, all starving. Gasa and Kumana made a fire and shared the food they had in the canoe. When John Kennedy returned to the island that evening, he tripped up to Gasa and Kumana—and fell into their arms.

In the morning, the group gazed at Rendova Peak, forty miles in the distance. The Americans could never get there. The scouts could, maybe.

Gasa husked a coconut and used hand gestures to convey his idea. Kennedy understood. He took out his knife and carved an SOS message in English into the shell of the coconut.

The scouts set out to deliver the message, paddling fifteen hours through choppy waters patrolled by the Japanese military, knowing they'd be killed if caught helping Americans. They showed the coconut to an amazed American officer. The crew of PT-109 had been given up for dead.

A PT boat picked the men up just after midnight on August 8, six days after PT-109 was destroyed. Kennedy was guided below deck, where he broke down in tears, his body drained and aching, his six-foot-one frame wasted to a skeletal 110 pounds.

"And so, my fellow Americans . . ."

Eighteen years later, still thin but no longer cadaverous, John

Kennedy sat in the bathtub in his Washington home, soaking a back that had never fully healed, practicing the inaugural address he'd give in a few hours. He'd worked through many drafts and revisions to get it just right—short and decisive, focused on the dangerous road ahead.

He recited the lines aloud again over bacon and eggs at the breakfast table.

"And so, my fellow Americans . . ."

Kennedy's rise had been quick. A year after World War II ended, he ran for Congress. At a campaign event in Boston, a high school student asked the young candidate what he'd done to become a war hero.

Kennedy smiled and said, "It was easy—they sank my boat."

That was Kennedy's style, to crack a self-deprecating joke. But he needed the PT-109 story, and he knew it. It was his origin story, proof he wasn't just a pampered kid who'd had everything handed to him by a rich father. He was elected to the House of Representatives in 1946, the Senate in 1952, and the White House just eight years later.

With his thick dark hair, quick smile, and custom suits, John Kennedy was something new—a stylish young president. A cool president. Voters had no idea that behind the slick image was a man who battled several chronic illnesses, who required a mix of shots and pills, plus three hot baths for his back, just to get through each day.

Inauguration morning was sunny and cold in Washington, about 20 degrees. A fresh layer of snow covered the city. Kennedy stood at the podium outside the Capitol, no hat or coat, puffs of frost coming from his mouth along with his carefully crafted words.

"Let every nation know, whether it wishes us well or ill, that we shall pay any price, bear any burden, meet any hardship, support any friend, oppose any foe to assure the survival and the success of liberty."

The human species had reached a turning point, he argued, a testing point. The Cold War was going to go one way or the other—sooner rather than later. "In the long history of the world, only a few generations have been granted the role of defending freedom in its hour of maximum danger. I do not shrink from this responsibility—I welcome it."

With one of the most quoted lines of the century, Kennedy challenged all Americans to face the coming test together. "And so, my fellow Americans: ask not what your country can do for you—ask what you can do for your country."

John Kennedy
in PT-109, 1943

FIRST PITCH

EARLY THE NEXT MORNING, A middle-aged woman named Evelyn Lincoln sat in the passenger seat as her husband, Abe, drove the family car along Washington streets. Abe pulled up to the gate at the White House. The security guard didn't know Mrs. Lincoln. He took her word that she worked for the new president.

"I'll call you later," Abe said.

Lincoln carried her briefcase to the West Wing, a separate building begun by Teddy Roosevelt in 1902 when the White House ran out of room for staff. She introduced herself as President Kennedy's personal secretary. A guard led her down a hallway to a small room.

"I guess this will be your office," he said.

She liked it. A window with a view of the Rose Garden. One door opening to the Cabinet Room, with its long table, bronze bust of Abraham Lincoln, and portrait of George Washington on the wall. A second door opened right into the Oval Office.

She walked into the president's office. It really was oval. The walls were bare, freshly painted a drab green she knew her boss would hate. The glass in the windows was two inches thick. Bulletproof. Tiny holes dotted the carpet, making a path from the desk to the doors leading out to the lawn. Golf shoes, she realized. Eisenhower used to put on golf cleats at his desk and walk outside to hit a few balls.

"Good morning, Mrs. Lincoln, is there any mail?"

A familiar voice. She'd worked for John Kennedy since he was first elected to the Senate eight years before. The president came in and sat at the desk, getting the feel of the spot at the center of power.

"This desk is too big," he said.

And he wanted his favorite rocking chair, the one that eased his stiff back, brought in and put by the fireplace. Plus they'd need a nicer sofa. Also, something would have to be done about the paint color.

First Lady Jacqueline Kennedy managed the remodeling, replacing the furniture, repainting the walls a warm off-white, hanging family photos, and bringing in the kind of stuff her husband liked—naval paintings, ship models, and his favorite artifact, the coconut shell with his SOS message from World War II.

Everything was ready just in time for a relentless string of disasters.

Four days after John Kennedy took office, the U.S. Air Force dropped two hydrogen bombs on North Carolina.

Not on purpose.

Shortly after midnight on January 24, 1961, ten hours into a routine flight along the East Coast of the United States, a B-52 bomber suffered a fuel leak, went into a spin, and broke apart as it fell. Five members of the eight-man crew managed to eject safely and open their parachutes.

The plane's two four-megaton bombs also fell free. One slammed into a wetland and buried itself deep in the mud without exploding. The other worked exactly as designed in case of war. As it fell, a series of automatic triggers inside the bomb engaged. Just one single safety switch prevented detonation.

The bombs each carried two hundred times the power of the bomb that destroyed Hiroshima. Radioactive fallout could have poisoned communities all the way to Washington, D.C., and beyond.

Secretary of Defense Robert McNamara had been in the job three days. A month before, he'd been head of Ford Motor Company. McNamara knew very little about hydrogen bombs. Just enough to be horrified.

"By the slightest margin of chance," he'd later admit, "literally the failure of two wires to cross, a nuclear explosion was averted."

A few weeks later, in Miami, Robert Maheu entered Handsome Johnny Rosselli's hotel room with a briefcase in his hand. The CIA cut-out sat on the edge of the bed and dumped out a pile of cash.

About $10,000, Rosselli judged with an expert eye. Just enough.

He hadn't changed his mind—he wasn't asking to be paid for the Castro job. But there were expenses to be covered.

Rosselli had consulted with a few mobster friends, and they'd decided a guns-blazing gangland-style shooting would be too messy. Who'd be crazy enough to take that job? Instead, Rosselli had asked whether the CIA could maybe get him some kind of poison. Government chemists produced a batch of six pills with what the lab described as "high lethal content." Botulinum toxin, to be specific. The victim would be sick for several days before dying, making it hard to trace the source of the poison.

After Rosselli gathered up the money, Maheu handed over the six capsules. They wouldn't dissolve well in hot drinks or soup, Maheu explained. Cold drinks should be fine.

The next step was to get the pills to the Cuban capital of Havana, where Rosselli had a contact who knew a waiter at a restaurant where Castro often dined.

How much did John Kennedy know about this assassination plot? That's still not clear, even now. Most historians think he must have been informed.

In any case, that was just one of several plans. Under President Eisenhower, the military and CIA had begun planning a far more ambitious operation to get rid of Fidel Castro—a full-blown invasion of Cuba. On March 11, standing before a map of Cuba on a podium in the Cabinet Room, the CIA's Richard Bissell updated Kennedy on the plan.

Fourteen hundred anti-Castro Cubans were training at a secret base in the mountains of Guatemala. Morale was high. They were ready to go. But the Soviets were starting to send military supplies to Cuba. Castro was getting stronger. And rumors of the invasion force were starting to spread. Time was running out.

The plan, explained Bissell, was to land the invasion force near the Cuban city of Trinidad. U.S. Air Force planes would fly overhead during the landing, bombing Castro's forces, while U.S. ships brought in supplies.

Kennedy didn't like it.

"It sounds like D-Day," he objected. "You have to reduce the noise level of this thing."

Make it look less like an American operation, Kennedy ordered, more like Cubans liberating their own country. He worried that a failed invasion would be a huge humiliation to the United States. And to him, personally. Kennedy wanted the option, if things went wrong, to deny this was an American-led attack.

The plan had been a year in the making. Now the CIA and military had a few days to rework it. The revised plan called for a quieter landing, at night without air cover, at a rural spot on the southern coast called Bahía de Cochinos. In English, the Bay of Pigs.

Between briefings on Cuba, Kennedy slipped out to the lawn to toss a baseball. Opening day for the Washington Senators was coming up, and it was traditional for the president to throw a ceremonial first pitch. Kennedy agreed to do it, but his bad back made throwing painful. He wanted to get in some practice before the big day.

There was news from Havana that week.

"Did you see the paper?" a giddy Robert Maheu asked one of his partners. "Castro's ill. He's going to be sick two or three days. Wow, we got him."

But Castro got better.

The CIA never did figure out what went wrong. It's possible the waiter got scared and never used the pills, or maybe he got fired before he had the chance. Or maybe Castro just stopped going to that restaurant.

Well, there was always the invasion, set to begin in a few weeks. That should finish off Castro once and for all.

On the chilly afternoon of April 10, the stands of Griffith Stadium were packed for the Washington Senators' opening-day game against the Chicago White Sox.

In his seat by the first-base dugout, President Kennedy took off his overcoat, stood, and loosened up his arm. Players from both teams moved in close. They knew the drill—important officials tossing out ceremonial pitches could never really throw.

But *everything* was a competition to Kennedy. He wound up and whipped the ball over the heads of the nearby players. It bounced off the gloves of two unsuspecting players, finally landing in the bare hand of White Sox outfielder Jim Rivera.

The crowd roared. Kennedy smiled and waved, and settled in to enjoy the game.

That same day, in the mountains of Guatemala, José Peréz San Román—Pepe to his men—spoke to the fourteen hundred men he was about to lead into battle. Training was over. It was time, he told them, to liberate their homeland.

Cheering, singing patriotic songs, the men climbed into trucks and rolled down dirt roads out of the mountains to an air base. They got on transport planes for a night flight to Puerto Cabezas, on the eastern coast of Nicaragua, the jumping-off point for the Bay of Pigs invasion.

THE COUNTDOWN

EARLY THE NEXT MORNING, AT the Baikonur Cosmodrome in the Soviet Union, Sergei Korolev stood outside a massive hangar as the doors slid open. Korolev, the Soviet Union's top rocket scientist, watched his creation roll out—a 112-foot-long rocket on its side, strapped to the platform of a flat train car.

As the Bay of Pigs invasion force gathered on the beach in Nicaragua, the Soviets were set to launch a surprise mission of their own. Two of the biggest events of the entire Cold War were playing out at the exact same time.

Korolev walked alongside the train tracks as the flatcar moved slowly, gently, from the hangar to the launch pad. This rocket, the R-7, was his masterpiece, a leap forward in rocket design. With this technology, Korolev had put the first satellite, Sputnik, into orbit. He'd sent dogs into space. He'd crashed an unmanned craft into the surface of the moon. And just weeks before, he'd pulled off another big step, blasting a capsule into space with a very special traveler. The flight had gone smoothly. The passenger, in a helmet and bright orange flight suit, had parachuted down near a village in the Ural Mountains. He'd hit the snow and collapsed, arms and legs splayed at odd angles.

Startled villagers raced to the fallen figure. Was this another Frank Powers? Another American sky pirate? Just in case, one man bent down and punched the stranger in the head.

Nothing. No reaction.

Soldiers sped up in cars, jumped out, and shoved everyone back from the body. But then the soldiers just stood there, blocking access. They didn't even bother to see if the guy was still alive.

He wasn't. He never had been. The space traveler was Ivan Ivanovich, an amazingly lifelike mannequin built specially for this final dress rehearsal. Scientists had filled his hollow limbs with test subjects, including mice, guinea pigs, and reptiles. The animals all came through the flight in fine shape. This was also a test of the capsule's communication system. Could a human voice be heard from space? Ivan wasn't up to the challenge of talking, so the designers had proposed adding a recording of a person singing.

Soviet security officers objected, knowing Americans would be watching and listening. "The West will think the cosmonaut has lost his mind, and instead of carrying out his mission he's singing songs!"

They compromised, using a tape of a choir; no one would think there was a choir up there. They also added a recording of a woman reading a recipe for borscht. All systems worked perfectly.

Korolev had been following news of the U.S. space program. The Americans were a lot less secretive than the Russians and were clearly close to sending the first human into space—by far the biggest prize yet in the space race. But the Soviets were about to get the first shot. Korolev and his team were now ready to strap a pilot into a tiny capsule atop an R-7 and blast him into space.

Hopefully. Of the last sixteen R-7 launches, eight succeeded. Eight failed.

That night, in a cottage near the launch pad, a twenty-seven-year-old fighter pilot named Yuri Gagarin lay still in a wooden bunk, pretending to be asleep. Never in his life had Gagarin been more in need of a good night's sleep. But that wasn't going to happen. Not tonight.

Two years before, Gagarin had been selected as one of two thousand candidates for a job that did not yet exist—cosmonaut, the Russian term for astronaut. They'd all been prodded and tested, examined inside and out, and given fiendishly difficult tasks such as solving math problems while wearing headphones through which a friendly voice whispered incorrect answers.

The two thousand candidates were cut to twenty. Then the tests got hard.

How would cosmonauts handle the massive g-forces they'd face on top of an accelerating rocket? To find out, the men were belted into a centrifuge, a tiny capsule at the end of a long spinning arm. Like a carnival ride from hell, the capsule whipped the pilots around and around until they felt they were being crushed, until their field of vision shrank to a narrow tunnel, until they couldn't move a muscle under the strain, couldn't breathe or even blink.

How would men react to the weightlessness they would experience in orbit? To find out, they took turns riding a specially adapted elevator in Moscow's tallest building. As the elevator car free-fell thirty stories, the candidates floated up from the floor for a moment. No one knew how a longer period of weightlessness would affect the human body.

What about the loneliness a cosmonaut might feel in space? Could a human handle such utter isolation without going insane? To test this, scientists locked the cosmonauts in isolation chambers for up to ten days at a time. After a short while inside, the candidates had no idea what time it was, whether it was day or night, whether anyone was listening to them when they talked.

Yuri Gagarin did everything well. He was competitive and cool-headed, focused and serious, but quick with a joke to cut the tension. That he could bend his athletic five-foot-three-inch frame into tight spaces was also a plus.

In the end, it came down to two candidates, Gagarin and Gherman Titov. Gagarin was selected to attempt the first space flight, with Titov as backup. They had the exact same training. Either could make the flight.

After a final day of preparation, the two cosmonauts had come back to their cottage by the launch pad ready to rest. But the doctors had been in their room. Wires snaked out of their mattresses and through a hole in the wall that hadn't been there before. The doctors were obviously going to monitor them all night from the next room, seeing who tossed and turned, who got the better night of sleep.

Gagarin could still be replaced. That's why he lay still in his bunk. If he fell asleep, he might move around, making the doctors think he wasn't sleeping well. So he refused to nod off.

Gherman Titov, a few feet away, was doing the exact same thing.

Around 3:00 a.m., Sergei Korolev stepped into the cottage, gestured for the doctors to be silent, and tiptoed down the hall to the cosmonauts' bedroom. He cracked open the door and peeked in.

A lovely sight. His handpicked boys seemed to be sleeping like babies.

Three hours later Gagarin, Titov, and Korolev sat together for a breakfast of Soviet space food—brown paste from a tube.

Gagarin said, "It's been ages since I've had anything so tasty!"

The cosmonauts stripped to their underwear, and doctors attached sensors all over their bodies. A team of technicians helped both men into bright orange pressure suits and helmets. One team member held out a piece of paper for Gagarin to sign. Not an official form—he wanted the man's autograph.

Gagarin and Titov were driven to the launch pad. Titov had held out hope that some last-second glitch with Gagarin's equipment would let him, Titov, make the historic flight. Now all he could do was wish Gagarin luck. The two friends attempted to kiss each other on the cheek in the Russian tradition. Their helmets banged together.

Gagarin rode an elevator 150 feet up to the top of the launch pad. A small capsule, Vostok 1, sat atop the R-7 rocket. The crew helped him through the hatch. They strapped him into the seat and plugged in his oxygen and pressure hoses. The cramped cabin had three small portholes, radio equipment, and instrument panels. It was a lot simpler than the MiG fighter jet Gagarin was used to flying, and that was by design—he wasn't supposed to touch the controls.

Scientists were genuinely worried about what they called "space madness." Even after all the testing, they had no idea how a human would handle the stress of space flight, so they'd rigged everything to work automatically. Gagarin could take manual control only by typing in a special three-digit code—a code he wasn't

supposed to know. In case of emergency, the code would be radioed up from ground control.

One of the technicians, Oleg Ivanovsky, broke the rules at the
last moment.

"Yura," he whispered, using Gagarin's nickname, "the numbers are three, two, five."

Gagarin flashed that reassuring smile everyone had come to
love. Korolev had already told him.

"Complete silence in the control room!" Anatoly Semyonov
announced into his microphone. "Cease all conversations!"

He immediately felt like an idiot. No one was talking but him.

Semyonov, one of Korolev's top rocket scientists, started the
countdown. In their bombproof control bunker—protection
against the very real possibility that the rocket would explode and
land on them—Sergei Korolev and his team sat at consoles watching screens and gauges. Doctors could see that Gagarin's blood
pressure was normal. Temperature normal. His pulse, incredibly,
was a steady sixty-four. Over the radio they could hear the man
whistling a pop song. Whistling!

"One minute to takeoff!"

Sergei Korolev tried, without success, to hide the strain in his
voice.

"One minute to takeoff," he told Gagarin over the radio. "You
heard?"

"I read you."

Gagarin's pulse rose to 109. He was human after all.

"During the launch you need not answer me," Korolev said.
"Answer when you can, though, as I'm going to be transmitting
details."

"I read you," Gagarin responded. "I feel fine and am ready to go."

"We're boosting pressure, and the cable mast has been removed."

"I felt it. I can hear the valves working."

"Ignition beginning. Pre-stage . . . intermediate stage . . . main stage . . . Lift off!"

White flames burst from the base of the R-7. An almost musical blend of roars and rumbles filled the capsule as Gagarin felt the rocket beneath him trembling, fighting gravity, and lifting off the ground.

His pulse hit 157.

"Poyekhali!" he shouted—Russian for "Let's go!"

Yuri Gagarin in his space capsule

OVER AMERICA

"T-PLUS SEVENTY," SERGEI KOROLEV SAID into his microphone in the control room.

A thousand things had to go right to get seventy seconds into the launch without something blowing up. But no one was celebrating yet.

"I read you," Gagarin answered. "I feel excellent. Continuing the flight. G-load increasing."

"T-plus one hundred. How do you feel?"

"I feel fine. How about you?"

Typical Gagarin. Sitting atop 250 tons of burning kerosene and liquid oxygen, his face flattened by a g-load that would cause an ordinary human to pass out—and he asks how the other guy is doing.

The R-7's four booster rockets fell away two minutes into the flight, their fuel spent. The central rocket burned another three minutes, then dropped off. Ten minutes after takeoff, Vostok blasted through the atmosphere and into space.

The team in the control bunker leaped from their seats, cheering, hugging, many with tears in their eyes.

Gagarin's ship sped forward at about 18,000 miles per hour while also being pulled down by Earth's gravity. This balance, perfectly calculated by Korolev's team, caused the ship to follow a curved path around Earth—an orbit. Inside Vostok, Gagarin felt himself lifting up from his seat, held in only by the straps. He made a note in his flight log with a pencil, then opened his writing hand. The pencil floated beside him in the capsule.

"Weightlessness has begun," he reported. "It's not at all unpleasant."

We can all picture astronauts floating in their ships, but the cause is surprising—it's not a lack of gravity. At Vostok's top altitude, 200 miles above Earth, the pull of gravity is about 90 percent as strong as it is on the planet's surface. Weightlessness is caused by the fact that an object in orbit is essentially in a free fall. Vostok was free-falling— not *toward* Earth, but *around* it. Gagarin felt weightless because he and his ship were falling at the same speed.

"The flight continues well," he said. "The machine is functioning normally. Reception excellent. Am carrying out observations of the earth. Visibility good. I can see the clouds. I can see everything. It's beautiful!"

His mother thought he was on a business trip.

Gagarin hadn't wanted his mom to worry. A few days before the mission, he told her he'd be away for a while on a work trip.

"How far?" Anna Gagarina had asked her son.

"Very far."

Now, at home, she was sweeping the floor. Her grown daughter was getting ready for work. Her grandson sat at the kitchen table doing homework.

The front door flew open. Her daughter-in-law Maria, Yuri's brother's wife, charged in, panting after the run from her house. "Why is the radio off? They're talking about Yura!"

Anna froze. "Tell me, what is it," she asked, her face draining of color. "Has he crashed?"

"Yura's alive!" Maria shouted. "He's in space!"

They turned on the radio, and there it was, a government announcement going out to the entire world: "The world's first satellite ship, Vostok, with a human on board was launched into an orbit around the Earth from the Soviet Union. The pilot cosmonaut of the spaceship satellite Vostok is a citizen of the Union of Soviet Socialist Republics, Major of Aviation Yuri Alekseyevich Gagarin."

"Feeling cheerful," Gagarin reported from orbit. "Am continuing flight, at present over America."

He thought about the American astronauts, imagining their surprise—and envy. He thought about his mother, wondering if she knew yet where he was. Gagarin flew from daylight into darkness as he rounded the side of Earth opposite the sun. Then, as he completed the orbit, he became the first person ever to see a second sunrise on the same day.

It was time for reentry. Vostok's braking rocket fired, a small rocket that slowed the ship down, allowing gravity to pull it back toward Earth. The next few minutes were second only to takeoff in terms of potential for disaster. Gagarin had to hit the layer of gases surrounding Earth at just the right angle. If he entered the atmosphere at too steep an angle, the friction caused by the ship speeding through the air would burn up both ship and passenger.

If he came in at too shallow an angle, his ship would bounce off the atmosphere like a stone skipping off the surface of a pond.

Vostok hit the atmosphere at the correct angle—but Gagarin could tell that something was wrong. A small equipment capsule that was connected to Gagarin's capsule by electrical cables had failed to separate. Still attached, the two capsules began spinning around each other. There was nothing Gagarin could do. He felt himself being pressed into his seat, the g-load rising beyond what he'd been trained to handle.

In the control room, Korolev had no idea this was happening. There was no way to communicate by radio with a ship speeding through the atmosphere.

Gagarin's spinning capsule heated to a glowing red. He heard the sound of cracking metal. His vision went fuzzy. He fought to stay conscious.

And then, suddenly, the spinning stopped.

The heat of reentry had melted the cables to the equipment capsule. Gagarin's craft stabilized and dropped smoothly into sunlight and blue sky. He ejected into the cold air. His parachute opened. He recognized the view from practice jumps. The Volga River. A railroad bridge. One hundred and eight minutes after takeoff, Yuri Gagarin's feet touched down on the soft dirt of a recently plowed field.

A woman and a young girl stood beside a calf, staring at the stranger in the bright orange suit.

Gagarin pulled off his helmet. "I'm a friend, comrades! A friend!"

The woman had been listening to the radio earlier that morning. She asked, "Can it be that you have come from outer space?"

Gagarin smiled. "As a matter of fact, I have!"

*　　*　　*

The first American statement on one of the towering achievements in all of human history was this:

"It's 3 in the morning, you jerk!"

A reporter had called NASA for a reaction to the big news from Russia. Annoyed to be woken from a cot in his office, the press officer John Powers pointed out the time.

The reporter pressed for a statement.

"If you're wanting something from us," the spokesman snapped, "the answer is we are all asleep."

And he hung up.

All over the country, below headlines in massive type about Gagarin's triumph, were brief articles with headlines such as "Puts Snooze Before News."

Military helicopters arrived just moments after Gagarin landed. He was whisked to a nearby air base and handed a phone.

"Tell me, how did you feel in flight?" Nikita Khrushchev asked. "What's space like?"

"I felt fine," Gagarin reported. "I saw the earth from a great altitude. I could see seas, mountains, big cities, river and forests."

"Let the world look on," said a triumphant Khrushchev, "and see what our country is capable of, the things our great people and our Soviet science can do."

Gagarin agreed. "Now let the other countries try and overtake us."

"Exactly!"

John Kennedy paced in his office that morning, asking, "What can we do? How can we catch up?"

This was a man who could barely stand to lose a game of touch football. He'd been known to knock over the pieces of a board game that wasn't going his way. Losing to Khrushchev, in front of the whole world, was infuriating. Besides, the space race was about a lot more than bragging rights. This was a technology race, a race to build machines capable of carrying heavy payloads at high speeds over long distances. A capsule into space one day. A bomb over the ocean the next. This was the Cold War.

Maybe the Americans should set their sights on beating the Russians to the moon, Kennedy suggested. But that was a problem for another day.

When the president talked to the press that afternoon, they seemed more interested in another pressing issue—Cuba. Whispers of a secret invasion force were getting louder, a reporter pointed out. How far was the United States prepared to go to help overthrow Fidel Castro?

"Well," Kennedy began, "first I want to say that there will not, under any conditions, be an intervention in Cuba by United States armed forces."

This was misleading, at best. Yes, the soldiers about to invade the Bay of Pigs were not American. But it was an operation planned by the U.S. military and the CIA, and funded by American taxpayers. If the plan worked, Kennedy figured, all would be forgiven.

In Havana, Fidel Castro took careful note of Kennedy's words. The American president was being very careful to say there would be no invasion by "United States armed forces."

He did not say there would be no invasion.

THE BAY OF PIGS

AT PUERTO CABEZAS, NICARAGUA, FOURTEEN hundred men boarded six rusting ships and set out to sea.

Pepe San Román and Erneido Oliva, the brigade's commanders, were professional soldiers—both in their late twenties, both ex-officers in the Cuban army. This was not typical of the group. The fourteen hundred volunteers ranged in age from sixteen to sixty-one. There were teachers, musicians, artists, mechanics, doctors, a few priests, and some experienced soldiers. Students made up the largest group.

Many of them had supported Fidel Castro at first.

Less than four years before, in November 1956, Castro and a force of eighty-one rebels had sailed from Mexico to Cuba, determined to retake their homeland from a corrupt dictator, Fulgencio Batista. Castro waded onto land and stumbled through a swamp to a hut.

"Have no fear," he declared. "I am Fidel Castro, and we came to liberate the Cuban people."

Batista's soldiers sped to the scene, and the ensuing firefight reduced Castro's force to twenty-one. Twenty-one against the dictator's force of forty thousand troops. Still, Castro was confident of success. And he had the rare ability to make others believe in his vision.

The rebels fled into the rugged Sierra Maestra and, very slowly, began to gather strength. In fiery speeches in forest clearings, Castro vowed to take control of Cuba and distribute the country's riches to the people—a modern-day Robin Hood. For decades, Cuban elites and wealthy Americans had been exploiting the island, gobbling up the richest sugar farms, the most profitable utilities and casinos. Batista helped it all happen, while pocketing millions. Those days, Castro promised, would soon be over.

Thousands of men and women joined the movement over the next two years. In quick guerrilla strikes, they hit Batista's forces, then slipped back into the mountains. The dictator panicked. In the first hours of 1959, he stuffed suitcases full of stolen cash and hopped on a plane to the Dominican Republic. Cheered on by massive crowds, Fidel Castro marched triumphantly into Havana.

Then, like all successful revolutionaries, Castro faced the harder challenge of improving life for the people. As promised, he built new schools and health clinics. As promised, he seized farmland owned by American companies and distributed the land to Cuban farmers. He seized American-owned businesses, putting them under control of his new government. The U.S. government struck back by imposing a trade embargo on Cuba, blocking the sale of Cuban sugar in the United States—a devastating blow to Cuba's economy.

This is where the Soviet Union stepped in.

Khrushchev offered to buy Cuban sugar. He offered to send the Cubans shipments of Soviet oil. Castro accepted—and began a drift toward Soviet-style communism, the very opposite of the freedom and independence his revolution had promised. He jailed political opponents by the thousands. He confiscated privately owned businesses, censored the media, and canceled elections. Many Cubans fled their country, most settling in Miami.

Now, in six rusting ships, fourteen hundred of those Cubans were sailing back home. The little force reached the Bay of Pigs just before midnight on April 16.

The captains cut their engines two thousand yards from the beach. Five men climbed into rubber rafts and paddled toward shore to mark the landing site with lights—and immediately discovered a major flaw in the plan.

The CIA had told them to expect a sandy approach, but the water here was clogged with razor-sharp reefs. Navigating the coral slowed the men down, leaving them exposed. Two soldiers driving past on a routine patrol stopped short when their jeep's headlights swept over five men in the shallow water near shore. Both sides opened fire.

The one advantage of landing at night—the element of surprise—was gone.

At an air base near Havana, Captain Enrique Carreras was sleeping in the cockpit of his plane—ready for action at a moment's notice. This hand-me-down British Sea Fury constituted a significant portion of Cuba's entire air force. Carreras, Cuba's top fighter pilot, was woken and called to the phone.

Invaders were hitting the beach at the Bay of Pigs, Castro told him. The Cuban army was on its way, but the air force had the most important job.

"Chico," Castro said, "you must sink those ships for me."

Carreras understood. Without the supplies on their ships, the rebels could not hold the beach.

The secretary of state came to the door in his bathrobe.

It was 4:30 a.m., and the CIA's Charles Cabell had come to Secretary of State Dean Rusk's door with an update—and an urgent request.

The battle was on at the Bay of Pigs, Cabell told Rusk, but the landing was taking longer than expected. The men weren't going to be out of the water by daylight. They'd be sitting ducks. U.S. Navy planes on the aircraft carrier *Essex* were ready to go. They could provide air cover, Cabell suggested, give the men a chance to unload their supplies and get off the open beach. All they needed was the president's okay.

Rusk agreed to wake Kennedy. He got the president on the line, then handed the phone to Cabell. The general made his case.

Kennedy listened without comment. He asked Cabell to hand the phone back to the secretary of state. Kennedy's first word to Rusk said it all:

"No."

As the sun rose at the Bay of Pigs on April 17, hundreds of men fought through chest-high blue-green water, lugging guns and radios and cases of ammunition, stumbling on coral, facing a steady barrage of bullets as they struggled up to the beach.

Pepe San Román splashed onto the sand, knelt, and kissed the ground. Then he heard a sound he'd dreaded—the roar of engines in the sky. Castro only had a few planes, but here they were at the worst possible time, unopposed, dropping low and strafing San Román's men in the water and in their open landing crafts.

At the controls of his Sea Fury, Enrique Carreras dove toward one of the invaders' boats and fired a rocket straight through its deck. Fires burst out, and men jumped into the water as the boat went down.

Carreras took aim at another boat, one sitting heavy in the water, loaded with supplies for the invasion. The crew saw him coming.

"Sea Fury!" they shouted, "Sea Fury!"

Carreras blasted a hole in the boat, igniting barrels of fuel and crates of ammunition. The ship exploded, blowing a massive black mushroom-shaped cloud hundreds of feet into the bright blue sky.

At the White House, John Kennedy listened to the latest updates from Cuba. The news was bad and getting worse. After the two supply boats went down, the others fled out to sea, taking their cargo of ammunition, food, and medical supplies. Castro's soldiers had started to arrive in large numbers, pinning the invaders on the beach.

Kennedy knew that he was seen as young, untested. The Bay of Pigs was his first major act on the world stage. He *needed* it to succeed.

Was it time to send in American forces? Where would *that* end? With all-out war in Cuba? Occupation of the entire island? What if the Soviets stepped in to defend their allies? What if they retaliated by attacking an American ally somewhere else in the world? The goal of the operation was to overthrow a pesky communist dictator, not to ignite World War III.

Kennedy picked up the phone and called his most trusted adviser, the U.S. attorney general—and the president's younger brother—Bobby Kennedy. The president told Bobby, "I don't think it's going as well as it should."

* * *

In Moscow, Nikita Khrushchev celebrated his sixty-seventh birthday. He could not have asked for a nicer present than the Bay of Pigs.

Back in 1956, when Hungarians began demanding freedom, Khrushchev had quite literally crushed the rebellion beneath the treads of Soviet tanks. That, in his mind, was how a leader behaved.

"I don't understand Kennedy," Khrushchev said to his son. "What's wrong with him? Can he really be that indecisive?"

Early the next morning, Pepe San Román and Erneido Oliva stood in a tiny building on the beach, studying maps taped to the concrete walls.

Day one had been a success, in some ways. The brigade had captured a long beachhead. But how were they going to fight their way inland? Castro's planes owned the sky. His troops and tanks blocked the roads. After fierce fighting all night, the invaders were nearly out of ammunition. Without fresh supplies they were doomed.

The CIA's plan called for the invaders to escape to the mountains if things went wrong on the beach. Looking at their maps, San Román and Oliva could see another mistake the Americans had made. The Escambray Mountains were near the original invasion site.

Here, at the Bay of Pigs, eighty miles of roadless swamp lay between them and the mountains.

The president spent most of the day in the Oval Office, hiding from the press and hoping for good news that he knew wasn't coming. After reading one update from Cuba, he shook his head and said, "We really blew this one."

After dinner, an aide reminded Kennedy that it was time to dress for the White House's congressional reception that evening. A formal gala was the last thing Kennedy was in the mood for, but twelve hundred guests were on their way. The president went upstairs and put on a tuxedo and white bow tie.

He and Jackie made a grand entrance to the ball, gliding down the stairs as a Marine band played "Hail to the Chief." They danced together in the East Room, smiling and laughing. People who didn't know better thought the president was having a wonderful time.

Near midnight, Kennedy and a few top officials slipped away to the West Wing to hear the latest from the CIA's Richard Bissell. There was nothing new, Bissell reported. The invading force was trapped on the beach.

U.S. Navy Admiral Arleigh Burke jumped in. "Let me take two jets and shoot down those enemy aircraft."

"No," Kennedy said. "I don't want to get the United States involved in this."

"Hell, Mr. President, we *are* involved!"

Burke was right, of course. But Kennedy worried about getting *more* involved, about how quickly the violence could escalate. The only other option Kennedy could see was to abandon those men on the beach. Accept defeat. Take the political beating that would go with it.

After three hours of back-and-forth debate, Kennedy stopped talking in the middle of a sentence, opened the door to the Rose Garden, and walked out. From inside the Oval Office, Kennedy's aides watched the president, in his long dress coat, pace back and forth on the wet grass.

Ken O'Donnell, Kennedy's appointment secretary, said, "He must be the loneliest man in the world tonight."

* * *

In the morning, backed up to the water at the Bay of Pigs, Pepe San Román radioed his CIA contact.

"Have you quit?" he demanded. "Aren't you going to support me anymore?"

The CIA promised to send back the supply ships as soon as they could. But time ran out. Castro's forces closed in, raining shells on the exposed beach.

"I have nothing to fight with," San Román reported to the Americans. "Taking to the woods. I cannot wait for you."

San Román's surviving fighters fled into the swamp. They were rounded up by Castro's forces, loaded into trucks, and driven as prisoners to Havana.

"We look like fools to our friends," wrote a *New York Times* columnist, "rascals to our enemies and incompetents to the rest."

In public, Kennedy accepted blame for the Bay of Pigs disaster. Privately, he seethed at what he saw as lousy advice from the CIA and military leaders.

"How could I have been so far off base?" he ranted to an adviser. "How could I have been so stupid to let them go ahead?"

First there was Gagarin's flight. Then the Bay of Pigs. Two epic defeats in less than a week, and John Kennedy took it very personally. Bobby Kennedy had never seen his brother so shaken, so down on himself.

On April 22, Kennedy flew to Camp David, where Dwight Eisenhower joined him for a private talk.

"No one knows how tough this job is," Kennedy confided as they walked in the woods, "until after he has been in it a few months."

Eisenhower said, "Mr. President, if you will forgive me, I think I mentioned that to you three months ago."

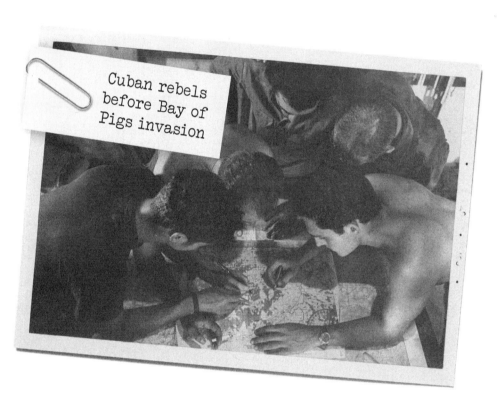

Cuban rebels before Bay of Pigs invasion

Rebel fighters
after capture
in Cuba

THE HEADLESS SPY

IN HIS PRISON CELL IN the Soviet Union, the American U-2 pilot Francis Gary Powers fantasized about the following foods:

1. Banana splits
2. Hamburgers
3. Salad

He never knew it was possible to miss salad.

In Pound, Virginia, Frank Powers's father was trying to figure out a way to get his son home. He'd even consulted the lawyer who worked in the office above his shoe repair shop.

"Hey, listen," Oliver Powers began, "have you heard of Rudolf Abel?"

The lawyer, of course, knew of the Soviet spy.

"Well, he's pulling time in Atlanta," Oliver said. "I'd like to see if he's willing to be exchanged for my son."

Together, they drafted a letter to Rudolf Abel and mailed it to the federal penitentiary in Atlanta.

Soon after, two government agents in dark suits came to visit. They told Oliver Powers to stop writing letters to enemy spies.

Actually, President Kennedy was open to the idea of a prisoner trade. It looked terrible to let an American pilot rot in a Russian prison. But any negotiations with the Soviets over an Abel-for-Powers trade would need to take place at a level far above Oliver Powers and his lawyer.

In the meantime, the battle for secret information remained a vital front of the Cold War. As the Soviets celebrated with Yuri Gagarin, and Fidel Castro crowed about his glorious victory at the Bay of Pigs, a Soviet official named Oleg Penkovsky boarded a flight from Moscow to London. Penkovsky, a colonel in Soviet military intelligence, was offering to share the Soviet Union's most guarded military secrets with the Americans and the British.

Possibly. Possibly, his offer was part of an elaborate Russian trick.

Until CIA agents could question the man in private, there was simply no way to know.

Oleg Penkovsky had entered the story nearly a year before—or tried to, anyway.

In the summer of 1960, on a warm, rainy night in Moscow, two American students were approaching a bridge over the Moscow River when Penkovsky walked up.

"I beg you to help me," he said.

The man was Russian, speaking choppy English. He was in his forties, his red hair beginning to gray. He reached into his jacket and took out an envelope.

"Do not open it," the man said, "and do not keep it overnight in your hotel. Go immediately to the American embassy with this letter. Your government will be grateful for this information."

One of the Americans, Eldon Ray Cox, asked the man for his name. The Russian handed over the envelope, turned, and walked away.

The Americans weren't sure what to do. The Soviets were infamous for planting evidence on tourists. Then they'd "discover" the evidence and use it to blackmail the visitors. Worried about being entrapped, Cox's friend went back to their hotel.

Cox sensed the man at the bridge was genuinely desperate for help. He got in a cab and asked to be taken to the American embassy.

In the embassy the next morning, several American officials stepped into the "bubble"—a large soundproof box suspended by wires from the ceiling. This was the only place Americans could talk with any confidence that Soviet listening devices could not pick up the conversation.

They opened the envelope the student had brought to the embassy the night before. Inside was a typed letter in Russian. An embassy official translated aloud:

"It is your good friend who is turning to you, a friend who has already become your soldier-warrior for the cause of Truth, for the ideals of a truly free world."

The writer said he had thought carefully about his decision. He was ready to take a step from which there could be no return.

"I have at my disposal very important materials on many subjects of exceptionally great interest and importance to your government."

The letter did not specify the exact nature of the materials. But it did include a hand-drawn map of a suggested dead-drop location: the entryway of a Moscow apartment building where a package could be hidden behind a radiator. There was also a photograph. It showed a man in a Soviet military uniform with the rank of colonel, standing beside an American officer, also a colonel.

There was a hole in the photo were the Soviet colonel's head had been.

The letter and photo were sent to the CIA's new headquarters in Langley, Virginia, where they landed on the desk of Joe Bulik, the officer in charge of America's secret operations inside the Soviet Union. Bulik needed answers to two questions:

1. Who is this guy?
2. Is he for real?

Question one could be attacked with detective work. Suppose the figure in the photo, the one with his head cut off, was the letter writer. With a little digging, Bulik identified the American standing beside the headless man as an officer who had served in Turkey in the mid-1950s. Bulik checked agency files for photos of Soviet military officials who'd been stationed at the Soviet embassy in Turkey at that time.

There was only one. Oleg Penkovsky. A known member of the GRU, the Soviet military intelligence agency.

The next step was simple. Bulik had agents track down the two American students who'd met the mystery man in Moscow. The students were shown photos of ten Soviet military officials and told to point to the man they'd met at the bridge. Both immediately picked out Oleg Penkovsky.

That was easy. Almost too easy.

Was Penkovsky a setup?

To answer that, the CIA would need to get some material from Penkovsky and test its validity and its worth. If Penkovsky was a loyal Soviet agent trying to deceive the CIA, he'd hand over what spies call "chicken feed"—secret information that is true, but not truly valuable. But what if he was the real thing? It was too tempting a possibility to ignore. The CIA had *never* had a high-ranking source inside Soviet intelligence.

The agency assigned Penkovsky a code name, Hero. A young agent, code-named Compass, was sent to Moscow with the mission of making contact. As cover, he worked as a janitor in a building where many American embassy officials lived—but apparently the KGB didn't buy it. They followed Compass everywhere he went. There was no chance to approach Penkovsky. No chance to use the dead-drop he'd suggested. After a few months of frustration, Compass made a desperate move.

Oleg Penkovsky was home with his wife when the phone rang. He answered. A voice began speaking in terribly garbled Russian. The voice switched to English. Penkovsky's English wasn't good enough for a phone conversation. He made out a word or two, nothing more. He knew any phone in Russia could be tapped.

He hung up. Wrong number, he told his wife.

Compass was out of ideas.

Smart enough to admit they needed help, the CIA turned to MI6—British foreign intelligence, an agency so secret the government refused to admit it even existed.

The Brits had a clever idea. They had an agent named Greville Wynne, a salesman who traveled often to Eastern Europe and the Soviet Union on legitimate business. Wynne flew to Moscow and arranged a meeting with Oleg Penkovsky. The British businessman made what sounded like a perfectly innocent offer, inviting the Soviets to send a delegation of government officials to Britain for a friendly tour of British steel mills and factories. Penkovsky presented the idea to his bosses, and they liked it. They told Penkovsky to personally lead the Soviet delegation—and to be sure to take every opportunity to steal Western technology.

So far, MI6's plan was working perfectly.

Now, in late April 1961, with Kennedy reeling from the Bay of Pigs and desperate for some good news, Greville Wynne drove to London Airport to meet his Soviet visitors.

Oleg Penkovsky came through customs carrying two large suitcases, flanked by the six other members of his delegation. Wynne had cars waiting to drive them to their hotel. Penkovsky went up to his room—a private room, which was essential to the plan.

Moments later, Wynne knocked on the door. Penkovsky let him in, shut the door, and finally allowed himself to smile.

"I can't believe it, Greville," he said in English, grabbing Wynne by the shoulders. "I just can't believe it!"

Wynne detailed the next step. There would be a formal dinner for the delegation, good food and drink. Then, after everyone was in bed and the hallways were empty, Penkovsky would be expected in room 360.

In room 360, two agents of MI6 waited with Joe Bulik and a second CIA man, George Kisevalter, who had experience running Soviet agents. They'd arranged a couch and chairs around a coffee table and set out a few bottles of wine.

Penkovsky showed up right on time. He took a seat.

"What do we speak, what language?" Kisevalter began in Russian. "How's your English?"

"My English stinks," Penkovsky said. "Let's speak Russian."

The Soviet officer lit a cigarette. "Well, gentlemen, let's get to work."

Penkovsky began with his own story. He was an only child, raised by a single mother. He'd graduated from Kiev Artillery School at age twenty, just as World War II began, and fought his way across Europe in an anti-tank regiment, sustaining serious wounds from a shell fragment that fractured his jaw and knocked out six teeth. After the war he applied for military intelligence training, joined the GRU, and rose to the rank of full colonel.

Penkovsky described his job. He gave details of how the GRU was organized. He named Soviet agents working in Europe. He talked for over three hours.

"I wish that your governments, and I consider them both my governments, trust me as their own soldier," he said.

Then he went to his room to get some sleep.

The American and British agents looked at each other—stunned and absolutely convinced. That was no chicken feed they'd just heard.

The two CIA men carried the wine bottles they'd emptied during the meeting out to the street and dropped them in a trash can. No need for anyone on the hotel staff to think anything interesting had happened that night in room 360.

LIGHT THE CANDLE

EARLY ON THE MORNING OF May 5, in Cape Canaveral, Florida, a man in a white-and-silver space suit sat in a tiny capsule, hemmed in by panels of gauges and switches. This was Navy-pilot-turned-astronaut Alan Shepard. Three weeks after Yuri Gagarin's launch, the United States was about to attempt its first manned space flight.

And, unlike the Soviets, the Americans were going to do it on live television.

Eventually.

Shepard had been strapped into his seat for four hours. The countdown kept stopping as technicians made final checks. At fifteen minutes to takeoff, they paused again to wait for clouds over the launch site to float past. Shepard didn't think he could make it. He'd been trained to handle any emergency—except this.

"Gordo!" he said over his headset.

Fellow astronaut Gordon Cooper answered from the control room. "Go, Alan."

"Man, I gotta pee."

"You what?"

"I've been in here forever," Shepard said. "Check and see if I can get out quickly."

"Hold on."

Cooper checked with the scientists. The answer was no.

Shepard said, "Tell 'em I'm going to let it go in my suit."

"No!"

Cooper reminded Shepard that his body was covered with sensors and electrical wires; he'd short-circuit the system.

So turn off the juice for a minute, Shepard suggested.

After some discussion, the technical team agreed.

"Okay, Alan. Power's off," Cooper reported.

None of this conversation was included in the official transcript NASA would later release to the media. Nor was Shepard's clearly audible "*ahhhhhh.*"

Oxygen flowing through the astronaut's suit dried it quickly. Now totally focused on the job ahead, he lost patience when there was yet another delay.

"Why don't you just fix your little problem," Shepard said, "and light this candle."

Evelyn Lincoln watched the countdown on a black-and-white television in her White House office. A tall white rocket with UNITED STATES painted down its side stood on the launch pad. At the very top was the astronaut's little black capsule. The countdown hit two minutes.

Lincoln stepped into the Cabinet Room, where Kennedy was

in a meeting. She leaned over the president's shoulder. "Two minutes."

"Two minutes to launch," Kennedy announced to the group.

He stood and walked into Lincoln's office. He'd been nervous about this launch for days. That was America on that Florida launch pad. Not just an American astronaut, but American technology, American pride. The country—and Kennedy personally—had been taking a pounding. Gagarin. Bay of Pigs. Could he handle another loss now? With the whole world tuned in?

Vice President Lyndon Johnson, Secretary of Defense Robert McNamara, and Secretary of State Dean Rusk crowded around the TV. Kennedy watched, arms folded, as the countdown hit zero.

The rocket lifted off the ground and shot smoothly into the sky.

Shepard's flight was not quite like Gagarin's. He didn't orbit earth—he sped 116 miles up, reached space, and arced back through the atmosphere. The capsule's parachute opened, and he splashed down in the ocean. The whole thing was over in fifteen minutes.

An assistant press secretary stuck his head into Lincoln's office and said, "The astronaut is in the helicopter."

Kennedy smiled. He could finally relax.

"It's a success," he said.

A badly needed one. Cheers echoed through the West Wing.

The next day, Oleg Penkovsky flew home from London. It had been a successful trip, in more ways than one.

Penkovsky had spent his days with his fellow Russians, touring British factories and watching presentations about products the Soviets might like to buy. After each tour, a member of the

Soviet delegation would slip back into the factory to photograph the equipment.

The British pretended not to notice. It was all part of the plan.

At night, back at the hotel, the British treated their guests to big dinners and endless drinks. After everyone went to bed, Penkovsky would sneak down to room 360.

In a series of late-night meetings, with tape recorders rolling, Penkovsky shared secret details about Soviet weapons technology. He revealed Khrushchev's plans in the case of nuclear war. He looked at photos of Soviet missiles taken at various May Day parades and identified each one, explaining its capabilities.

The United States and Britain had *never* had a source of information like this.

Why was he betraying his country? From a complex mix of motives, it seemed. He wanted to save the world from Khrushchev. He was disillusioned with Soviet life, the lack of freedom, the constant fear.

"The people are afraid to do anything," he said, "because if they open their mouths they will lose even the little bit they have."

He wanted a better life—nice clothes, money in the bank. He shamelessly produced a shopping list, including a sheet of paper on which he'd traced the feet of his wife and daughter, so he'd be sure to bring home the right size shoes.

Also, he reveled in the role of Cold War spy, a real-life James Bond. He looked forward to receiving the personal thanks of Queen Elizabeth and President Kennedy.

"You could throw me on a U.S. airplane to Washington, D.C.," he suggested at one meeting. "I could meet the president and fly right back."

"Okay, Oleg, someday."

When his plane landed in Moscow, Penkovsky collected his

two large suitcases. They were stuffed with electric razors, cigarette lighters, stockings, lipstick, perfume, and one set of false teeth. It was illegal to bring all this Western loot into the Soviet Union, but Penkovsky breezed through customs without a search—the goodies were for his bosses, and they made sure he wasn't bothered. Taking advantage of this, Penkovsky sneaked in a tiny Minox camera, a favorite device of fictional spies. And real spies.

On May 8, after a routine day at work in Moscow, he ducked out to a phone booth and dialed a number he'd been given by his new friends in London. He let it ring three times, then hung up. He waited one minute, dialed the same number, let it ring three times, and hung up.

Five rings would have signaled that something was wrong.

Three rings meant "All is well."

A week later, in Ottawa, Canada, John Kennedy made the terrible mistake of trying to plant a tree.

It was a ceremonial planting, meant to symbolize the friendship between two great nations, and Kennedy, in the spirit of the event, grabbed a shovel. He scooped a mound of dirt—and felt an explosion in his back. By the time he made it back to Air Force One, he could no longer walk without help.

This was Kennedy's life. There were days when his back ached relentlessly. And then there were the bad days.

But the timing of this injury was awful. Kennedy was about to head to Vienna, Austria, for a meeting with Nikita Khrushchev. The young president had not exactly made a great first impression on the world. He felt intense pressure to show the Soviet leader that he was smart and tough, that he could not be bullied.

Hobbling around the White House on crutches, Kennedy prepped for the summit by reviewing major issues of the Cold

War. Spies, Cuba, the space race, the arms race—they were all connected, all part of the larger struggle to stop the expansion of Soviet power. And there was still another front in the global war, one likely to spark the next superpower clash: the German city of Berlin.

In the last year of World War II, American and British forces had fought their way into Germany from the west. The Soviets battled in from the east. The Allies crushed Germany between them, forcing its surrender, but could not agree on what should happen next. The result was that Germany was divided in two.

With U.S. support, West Germany became a free country with democratic elections. In East Germany, the Soviets installed a communist dictator who took his orders from Moscow. Germany's capital city, Berlin, was also divided. West Berlin was part of free West Germany. East Berlin was part of communist East Germany.

This might have worked, except for one thing—Berlin was 110 miles *inside* of East Germany. West Berlin was essentially an island of freedom inside an oppressive police state.

Not surprisingly, every year more than 100,000 people moved across the border from East Berlin to West Berlin. This was a growing crisis for East Germany. The country's population was draining away. Nikita Khrushchev ranted often about this, threatening to seize the entire city and unite it under communist rule.

Kennedy vowed to defend the freedom of West Berlin. But how? The Soviets could pour millions of soldiers into Germany. The United States was four thousand miles away. Realistically, the only way to stop a Soviet invasion would be with hydrogen bombs. But that would mean World War III. The ultimate failure.

As Eisenhower had warned, there were no easy answers.

On the plane to Europe, pain raging in his back, Kennedy

studied Khrushchev's speeches. He read a psychological analysis done by the CIA. Khrushchev was a showman and a gambler, agency doctors concluded. He liked to joke around, but often used this talent to deceive, to disguise his intelligence and ruthlessness—to set opponents up for the strike.

It was good stuff, very helpful. Kennedy was feeling confident. He knew the issues cold—and besides, when did he ever meet someone he couldn't charm?

As his private train car rolled east toward Vienna, Nikita Khrushchev read the KGB's files on John Kennedy. The American president was a child of wealth and privilege. He'd used his father's money and connections to get ahead in politics. He was well-read and intelligent, but young and unproven. It's quite possible he could be intimidated.

Khrushchev's plan exactly. After all, he'd outlasted Stalin. He'd outmaneuvered his rivals. He'd crushed freedom movements in Eastern Europe. His side in the Cold War was on a winning streak. If Berlin was at the center of the chessboard, he had superior forces in and around that key square.

"Berlin is the testicles of the West," Khrushchev was fond of saying. "Every time I want to make the West scream, I squeeze on Berlin."

VIENNA

"KHRUSHCHEV WILL BE HERE ANY minute," Kennedy told his doctor early on the afternoon of June 3. "You'd better give me something for my back."

In an upstairs bedroom at the U.S. ambassador's residence in Vienna, the president's doctor gave him an injection to dull the pain. Kennedy was wearing the stiff back brace that he hid beneath his suit on bad days. He hoped this would be enough to get him through.

A few minutes later, a black limousine rolled to a stop on the gravel driveway in front of the building. Khrushchev jumped out, grinning. Kennedy willed himself to hop youthfully down the stairs toward the car. Photographers surrounded the leaders as they shook hands, both hatless in the light rain.

"I'm glad to see you," Kennedy said through an interpreter.

"The pleasure is mutual."

"Another handshake!" photographers called out.

More than fifteen hundred reporters had come to Vienna,

making this the most closely watched meeting of leaders the world had ever seen. The two men shook hands again. Still smiling for the cameras, Khrushchev told Kennedy he had helped swing the American election.

"How?" Kennedy asked.

Khrushchev explained: he could have released Powers, the American pilot, right before the election. That would have helped Kennedy's opponent, Vice President Nixon.

Kennedy, smiling for the cameras, said, "Don't spread that story around."

Just a little friendly banter.

Or was it? With Khrushchev, it was hard to be sure.

Inside, the leaders sat at a long table with their teams of aides and translators. Kennedy began by trying to outline his main point—that in the age of the Super, the United States and the Soviet Union must figure out how to compete with each other without allowing Cold War tensions to escalate to World War III.

Khrushchev jumped in, instantly angry. Communism was going to spread around the world, Khrushchev argued. The Americans could not accept this—*that* was the cause of Cold War tensions. To prevent war, the United States would have to back down. "The Soviet Union supports its ideas and holds them in high esteem," Khrushchev said. "It cannot guarantee that these ideas will stop at its borders."

Kennedy calmly explained that he understood that point of view—but still, the two powers must not push each other toward war.

And why, Khrushchev demanded, was that the Soviets' responsibility? When would the United States learn that not everyone could be bullied?

"There was a man who bossed his son," Khrushchev said. "Then his son grew up, but the father didn't realize it and took him by the ear. 'Look here, father,' said the son, 'I'm grown up. I have children of my own. You can't treat me the way you used to.'"

"We have grown up," the Soviet leader added, in case anyone had missed the point of his little story. "You're an old country. We're a young country."

They went back and forth all day, Kennedy on the defensive, Khrushchev hammering away. Take Cuba, Khrushchev scolded, take the Bay of Pigs. Was that the Americans' idea of easing Cold War tensions?

"That was a mistake," Kennedy said.

A mistake—who admits mistakes? Sensing weakness, Khrushchev pressed even harder. Kennedy came out of the room looking pale. He limped upstairs to the living quarters.

"How did it go?" Evelyn Lincoln asked.

"Not too well."

The president was as furious with himself as he was with Khrushchev.

"He treated me like a little boy," Kennedy fumed. "Like a little boy!"

"This man is very inexperienced, even immature," Khrushchev told aides after the meeting. "This young man thinks that, backed by the might of the United States, he can lead us by the hand and make us dance to his tune."

Later that evening six hundred guests gathered for a dinner gala at Vienna's glittering Schönbrunn Palace. An orchestra played Mozart. Waiters in white gloves carried cocktails on silver trays. Everyone turned to watch John and Jackie Kennedy walk in— John wearing a hand-cut tuxedo (with his back brace underneath),

Jackie dazzling the crowd in a sleeveless pink sequined gown. Nikita Khrushchev walked up in his baggy business suit with his wife, Nina, who sported a dark silk dress.

"Mr. Khrushchev," shouted a photographer, "won't you shake hands with Mr. Kennedy for us?"

Nikita turned to Jackie, grinning, "I'd like to shake her hand first."

A bit later, when Jackie Kennedy made her way to a sofa, Nikita Khrushchev sat down beside the first lady and treated her to a barrage of jokes and boastful stories. She played along, mentioning Strelka, one of the dogs the Soviets had sent to space and brought safely home.

"I see one of your space dogs has just had puppies," Jackie said. "Why don't you send me one?"

Nikita threw back his head and laughed.

Nina watched from a nearby couch.

John walked over and nearly sat in her lap.

"He got halfway," noted a *New York Times* reporter, "when he discovered to his horror he was about to sit on Mme. Khrushchev. The President of the United States quickly shifted to a chair and smiled an apology."

It was that kind of day for John Kennedy.

Talks resumed the next morning in a conference room at the Soviet embassy.

Kennedy tried to set a new tone, bringing up an issue the two powers might see eye-to-eye on—the need to stop testing nuclear bombs. Both sides understood that these tests caused radioactive fallout that threatened the entire world. Neither the United States nor the Soviet Union had tested bombs in nearly three years. So why not, proposed Kennedy, sign a treaty to ban tests permanently?

Khrushchev vowed the Soviets would not be the first ones to resume testing—then waved away the idea of a treaty.

The real danger, he said, "the bone in my throat," was Berlin.

East Berlin was now losing a thousand people a day. The best-educated youth and the most highly skilled workers were being lured away by the West. It was time for the entire city, East and West, to come under the control of East Germany.

The United States, Kennedy responded, would never abandon West Berlin. Freedom around the world, including in West Berlin, was what the Americans had fought for in World War II.

But the Soviets, Khrushchev shot back, had paid a *far* higher price for victory in World War II than anyone. The Americans and British were proud, rightfully, of their role in saving the world from Adolf Hitler. But of the three big Allied powers—the United States, Britain, and the Soviet Union—the Soviets took 95 percent of the casualties in the war with Germany. And it was personal—one of Khrushchev's own sons, Leonid, was killed in the war.

Kennedy pointed out that his older brother, Joe, had also died fighting in Europe.

Khrushchev was unmoved. "If the U.S. wants to start a war over Germany, let it be so," he said, waving his arm. "If there is any madman who wants war, he should be put in a straitjacket!"

They broke for lunch. Then the combat continued.

Kennedy circled back to his original point—that both sides had to step back from the cliff's edge before it was too late.

"We can destroy each other," he said.

"Yes, Mr. President, I agree."

So don't seize West Berlin, Kennedy cautioned. Don't force us to act.

"Force would be met by force," Khrushchev warned. "If the U.S. wants war, that's its problem."

And that's how the summit ended, with the Soviet leader promising to take action in Berlin by December. "And if there is any attempt to interfere with these plans," warned Khrushchev, "there will be war."

"Then there will be war," Kennedy said. "It's going to be a very cold winter."

The president returned to the U.S. ambassador's residence with a hat—and he hated hats—pulled low over his forehead. He dropped onto a couch and let out a long sigh.

"How was it?" asked *New York Times* reporter James Reston, who'd arranged to interview Kennedy after the meeting.

"Worst thing in my life," Kennedy said. "He savaged me."

Khrushchev, meanwhile, was in the mood to dance.

Back in Moscow a few days later, the Soviet premier attended a garden party at the Indonesian embassy. He joked, he sang, he banged on drums. When the musicians broke into a traditional Russian folk tune, Khrushchev showed off his moves on the dance floor while the crowd surrounded him, clapping in time with the music.

TIME TO START

SOON AFTER COMING HOME FROM Europe, John and Jackie Kennedy were sitting in the Oval Office when the Soviet ambassador to the United States stepped into the room flanked by two members of his staff. In one staffer's arms was a fluffy white puppy.

The president stared at the dog, then turned to his wife when he heard her gasp.

"I was only trying to make some conversation," she whispered.

The Soviet ambassador introduced Pushinka, daughter to Strelka, who had orbited earth in a Soviet spacecraft. Pushinka, the ambassador explained, was a generous gift from Nikita Khrushchev to the Kennedys. Of course, the dog was also a poke in the eye—an adorable reminder of Soviet victories in the space and rocket race.

Kennedy thanked the ambassador. Then he sent the

puppy to a military hospital to be checked for hidden listening devices.

She came back clean.

In the Ministry of Defense building in Moscow, Oleg Penkovsky shut himself in a room of secret files. He jammed a chair under the doorknob. He took out his mini Minox camera, opened a folder with technical specs of Soviet missiles, and began snapping pictures.

On the afternoon of July 2, Penkovsky took a break from the office and walked to a nearby park. He strolled along a tree-lined path, taking in the details—retired people on benches, mothers and children, vendors selling ice cream. She'd be here somewhere, he knew. Anne, that was the code name. He'd seen a photo of her back in the London hotel. An English woman, thirty-two, with dark hair. She'd have a baby boy in a carriage and two young daughters.

There she was, sitting on a bench, the girls playing nearby. He walked past without making eye contact. Too many people around.

A few minutes later it began to rain. A lucky break. People started leaving the park.

Penkovsky walked back to the woman. He stopped at the carriage and smiled at the baby. He pulled a small box of colorful vitamin C drops from his pocket and held it out to the mother—for the girls, he gestured.

She nodded thanks and slid the vitamins under the baby's blanket.

Anne's real name was Janet Chisholm. A former employee of MI6, she spoke Russian and French and was married to Ruari Chisholm, a diplomatic officer at the British embassy. Supposedly. His real job was head of the MI6 station in Moscow.

The Chisholms were used to surveillance. They'd found listening devices hidden in the walls of their Moscow apartment.

House cleaners openly went through their drawers. Janet fired the first one she caught, but what was the point? They were working for the KGB, she realized. They'd just send someone else. It was not an ideal environment in which to try to collect documents from a Soviet spy. But MI6 needed *someone* to take the risky role of courier. Janet Chisholm stepped up.

The first meeting had gone well. She led her daughters back to their apartment with a vitamin box full of Soviet secrets under her baby son's blanket.

Two days later, on July 4, Oleg Penkovsky was called into his boss's office.

And given a promotion.

Everyone was impressed with the intelligence he'd brought back from London, Penkovsky was told. He should plan more of these "friendly tours" to cities in the West.

Penkovsky promised to get right on it.

He was now in the rare position of being a double agent. Both sides trusted him. Both sides were sure he was working for *them*.

"You know," John Kennedy told his guests, "they have an atom bomb on the third floor of the embassy."

The president had invited a few friends to dinner. Knowing his love of spy novels, they figured he was joking about the Soviets having an actual fission device hidden in the Soviet embassy in Washington.

Kennedy wasn't joking. The Soviets had sneaked in the parts, he said, and assembled them in the embassy attic.

"If things get too bad and war is inevitable, they will set it off and that's the end of the White House and the rest of the city. That's what I'm told."

Kennedy was almost certainly wrong about there being a bomb in the city—it's probably another example of the big eyes of fear. But the fact that he believed it tells us a lot about his state of mind in the summer of 1961. The Cold War was heading in a terrifying direction.

"Ever since the longbow," he said that summer, "when man had developed new weapons and stockpiled them, somebody has come along and used them. I don't know how we escape it with nuclear weapons."

On July 10, in the Oval Hall of the Kremlin, Nikita Khrushchev spoke to a large group of party leaders, military officers, and atomic scientists. It was time, Khrushchev had decided, for the Soviet Union to resume testing hydrogen bombs.

The Soviets were behind America in terms of the might of their arsenal. The ongoing embarrassment of East Berlin was also a factor. How could they convince the world of the wonders of communism when people were leaving by the thousands? Something had to be done to strengthen the Soviet position.

Khrushchev announced his decision. It was not up for discussion.

Andrei Sakharov, the physicist who led the Soviet hydrogen bomb program, borrowed a piece of paper from a scientist next to him. More tests, he wrote, and ever more powerful bombs, would only make the world more dangerous for everyone. He passed the note to Khrushchev.

Khrushchev glanced at it. Then at Sakharov.

An hour later, they took a break for wine and caviar. Khrushchev stood to make a toast.

"Sakharov writes that we don't need tests," he began, holding up the piece of paper. "But Sakharov goes further. He's moved beyond science into politics. Here he's poking his nose where it doesn't belong."

Powerful men stared down at their plates. Andrei Sakharov was utterly alone.

"Leave politics to us—we're the specialists," the premier continued, growing louder and redder as he worked himself up. "You make your bombs and test them, and we won't interfere with you; we'll help you. But remember, we have to conduct our policies from a position of strength. We don't advertise it, but that's how it is! There can't be any other policy. Our opponents don't understand any other language."

Television lights shined on the president's desk. The air-conditioning was off. The Oval Office was quiet, bright, and sweltering. John Kennedy sat at his desk, sweating through his makeup, waiting to address the nation.

Kennedy did not yet know that the Soviets were about to resume nuclear tests, though that would have fit in with his theme for the evening—Berlin, Khrushchev's constant threats, and the danger of nuclear war.

West Berlin, Kennedy told the American people, was "the great testing place of Western courage and will." The Soviets already controlled a billion people and a huge chunk of the globe. If the United States were to retreat from Berlin, the communists would move closer to world domination. "We do not want to fight," he said, "but we have fought before."

Kennedy announced that he would ask Congress for more defense spending. Planes with hydrogen bombs would be on alert at all times. "An attack upon that city," he said of West Berlin, "will be regarded as an attack upon us all."

Which brought him to the larger point he needed to discuss.

"In the thermonuclear age, any misjudgment on either side about the intentions of the other could rain more devastation in several hours than has been wrought in all the wars of human history." In this frightening new world, each American had a new responsibility: know what to do in case of nuclear war. Do your part to help the country live on. "In the event of an attack," Kennedy said, "the lives of those families which are not hit in a nuclear blast and fire can still be saved—if they can be warned to take shelter and if that shelter is available."

Give yourself a chance. Make a plan. Stock up supplies. Build shelters.

"The time to start," he said, "is now."

Americans, who had been listening to warnings about nuclear war for ten years, got the message. The sales of shovels shot up after Kennedy's speech. Also canned food, bottled water, guns, and Geiger counters to measure radiation. People dug holes in their yards or carved out shelter spaces in basements of homes and apartment buildings. "If war never comes," a *Life* magazine article suggested, "children can claim it for a hideaway, father can use it for poker games, and mother can count on it as a guest room." The government's Civil Defense department printed millions of posters and pamphlets, urging every American to prepare for the worst.

Some families built their bunkers in secret, worried that neighbors might come knocking. "When I get my shelter finished," announced one man in the suburbs of Chicago, "I'm going to mount a machine gun at the hatch to keep the neighbors out."

A civil defense official in Las Vegas, Nevada, recommended the formation of a five-thousand-man militia—not to fight

Russians, but to beat back Californians who might arrive once the bombs began to fall.

"The United States is openly preparing for war," Radio Moscow beamed to the world shortly after the president's speech. "If a third world war breaks out, no ocean will protect America. It is very dangerous to play with fire in the age of hydrogen bombs and ballistic rockets."

The Soviet Union, meanwhile, went on openly preparing for war.

Tens of thousands of government officials worked to teach the entire population what to do if the Americans attacked. Average Soviet citizens had no money for private bunkers, so the focus was on building public shelters in the basements of large buildings. If the warning sounded, Soviet civil defense planners explained, up to two million people could fit into the subway tunnels under Moscow.

In early August, Walter Ulbricht, the dictator of East Germany, traveled to Moscow to meet with Nikita Khrushchev about the ongoing crisis in Berlin. Ulbricht proposed a way to solve the problem once and for all. He just needed backing from Moscow.

Khrushchev agreed to the plan. "When would it be best for you to do this?" he asked. "Do it when you want. We can do it at any time."

Ulbricht proposed starting on August 13.

Khrushchev chuckled. In the West, he pointed out, the number thirteen was considered unlucky.

"For us," he added, "it would be a very lucky day indeed."

Escape from
East Berlin

THE BERLIN WALL

"MOTHER, GO AWAY. IT'S SUNDAY."

It was early on the morning of August 13 and Harry Seidel was sleeping—or trying to—in the East Berlin apartment he shared with his mother, wife, and baby son.

Harry's mother shook his shoulder again. "You must get up. They've closed the frontier."

"They've what!"

He shot out of bed and ran to the radio. It was true—the East German police were blocking the border to West Berlin. It had to be done, the government claimed, to protect the citizens of the East from the evil capitalists of the West.

Seidel threw on his riding clothes and rolled his racing bike to the front door.

"Where are you going, Harry?" asked Rotraut, his wife.

"To think," he said. "And to look."

Harry Seidel got on his bike and pedaled toward the border.

Just two years before, he'd been one of the top young cyclists in East Germany. The government paid him to train and race, prepping him for the 1960 Olympics in Rome. But when pressed by officials, he refused to take steroids. Or to join the Communist Party. The training money evaporated. Seidel took a job delivering morning newspapers in West Berlin. He was one of about eighty thousand East Berliners who crossed the border every day for work—though that would not be possible now.

As he rode through the city on this warm summer morning, Seidel saw Soviet-made tanks blocking intersections. He watched soldiers and police unrolling barbed-wire fences across streets connecting East and West Berlin. In an instant, the barriers separated people from their schools and jobs, their friends and families. Seidel saw a man in the West, with tears in his eyes, staring through barbed wire at a two-year-old boy holding the hand of an old woman in the East. "Please," the man kept saying. "Please do something. It's my son."

The West Berlin police could do nothing.

But maybe Harry Seidel could.

John Kennedy was sailing off the coast of Cape Cod when he got the news from Berlin. He hurried back to shore and called the White House from his family's vacation home.

The president's worst fear was that the Soviets and East Germans were seizing West Berlin, in which case he'd have only minutes to decide whether or not to respond with nuclear bombs. But that did not seem to be the case. He was relieved.

"It's not a very nice solution," Kennedy said. "But a wall is a hell of a lot better than a war."

*　　*　　*

Thousands of West Berliners lined the border, some just curious, some throwing stones over the barbed wire at East German police, taunting them with insults:

"Pigs!"

"Nazis!"

The police fired back with canisters of tear gas. U.S. Army helicopters hovered overhead, just watching. The fence was on East German territory. Short of invasion, there wasn't much the Americans could do.

In some spots, apartment buildings lined the border between East and West, and people jumped out windows in the East and landed in the West. When East German police began boarding up lower-story windows facing the West, people climbed to higher floors. West Berlin firefighters raced to the scene and held out nets to catch people as they jumped to freedom. Ida Siekmann, a fifty-nine-year-old nurse, died after leaping from a third-story window, becoming the first person to die attempting to escape from East Berlin.

The first to be killed by police was a twenty-four-year-old tailor named Günter Litfin, who jumped fully clothed into Berlin's Spree River and tried to swim across the water separating East and West. East German police on a bridge opened fire. Litfin raised his hands in surrender. The police shot him through the neck. Then they went to his mother's apartment and trashed the place, tossing clothes from drawers, slicing open mattresses, smashing appliances.

"Your son has been shot dead," they told her. "He was a criminal."

In the days after August 13, the East Germans fortified the border with watchtowers and bright floodlights—just like a prison.

They began replacing the barbed wire fences with permanent slabs of concrete.

Nikita Khrushchev was pleased with the way things were working out.

Kennedy had sent fifteen hundred more U.S. troops into West Berlin, but the Soviet leader saw that for what it was, a symbolic show of support for the West. The Soviets moved in more troops and tanks—and nothing happened. For all his big talk about supporting freedom, Kennedy did not seem eager to fight in Berlin.

"To use the language of chess," Khrushchev said of these maneuvers, "the Americans had advanced a pawn, so we protected our position by moving a knight."

The Soviet position, Khrushchev concluded, was stronger than ever. And he saw an important lesson here. The American president, in times of crisis, could be forced to back down.

But almost immediately, the Berlin Wall began to backfire on Khrushchev. Thanks to people like Harry Seidel.

A few nights after the wall went up, Seidel found an unlit spot along the banks of the Spree. He pulled in a deep breath and dove in. The river here was two hundred yards wide. He swam silently beneath the surface, coming up for air halfway across.

And nearly hitting his head on an East German police boat.

The boat's searchlight swept across the empty black water. Over the sound of the boat's chugging motor, Seidel heard one of the officers say, "Let's go. Nothing to see here."

Seidel slipped under the water and made it across to the West.

He'd promised Rotraut he'd find a way to get her and their baby across. He got right to work, watching the East German guards, learning their schedules and routines, looking for soft spots.

The border around West Berlin was nearly a hundred miles long. The East Germans were building walls across the most heavily populated areas but stuck with fences in other places. Two fences, usually, with a wide patch of empty ground between the two. The death strip, as it became known. Anyone caught in this no-man's-land would be shot on sight.

Seidel picked a remote section of fencing. He waited for guards to take a dinner break, then crept forward and clipped the first wire, crawled across the death strip, clipped the bottom of the second fence, and wriggled back into East Berlin. He hurried down a dark road to a nearby café, hoping to use the pay phone to call his wife.

A bunch of off-duty East German police were drinking beer at the bar.

"Hello, comrade," one called to Seidel, "been digging a ditch?"

Harry looked down at his muddy clothes. An obvious flaw in his plan.

"Been stuck under my truck for the past two hours," he improvised.

"Where's the truck now? I didn't hear you arrive."

"Still there, stuck," he said, pointing down the road. "Two hours and I can't get a squeak out of it."

"What'll you do, then?"

Have a schnapps, Harry said. Then call a tow truck.

"Best of luck," a policeman said.

Harry bought the drink, went to the phone, and dialed. His wife picked up.

"Get ready quick," he said. "I'm coming for you."

Rotraut crushed up a sleeping pill, put some of the powder into a bottle, and fed it to her baby son, Andre. She pulled on black pants and a black sweater and tied a black scarf over her blond hair.

Harry met Rotraut at their apartment building. He led the way back to the spot where he'd cut the barbed wire. Hearing the sound of motorcycles approaching, they flattened themselves against the wall of an abandoned cottage. Andre's eyes were wide open, but he was fast asleep.

The police drove slowly past.

"Let's go," Harry whispered.

They sprinted to the wire. Rotraut crawled through. Harry handed her the baby, then followed. They dashed across the death strip, under the second wire, and ran a hundred yards into West Berlin before daring to stop.

On August 30, Nikita Khrushchev announced to the world that the Soviet government had decided, "with a heavy heart," to resume nuclear tests.

Khrushchev, as always, blamed the Americans.

"The United States and its allies are spinning the flywheel of their military machine ever faster," charged the official Soviet statement, "fanning up the arms race to unprecedented scope, increasing the strength of armies, making the tension of the international situation red-hot."

The Soviets had been caught unprepared by Hitler in World War II. "Like twenty years ago," the statement continued, "ominous clouds of war are once again overhanging the approaches to our motherland."

This time the Soviet Union was ready. Soviet scientists were designing new superbombs, more powerful than anything ever tested. And they had rockets—as Yuri Gagarin's flight showed the world—to deliver these bombs to any spot on the globe.

*   *   *

"F***ed again," John Kennedy said to his brother when he heard the news. Hadn't Khrushchev promised in Vienna that the Soviets would not be the first to restart nuclear testing?

"I want to get off," Bobby Kennedy said.

"Get off what?"

"Get off the planet," Bobby said.

In a secret lab in the Ural Mountains, the Soviet physicist Andrei Sakharov and his team devised a new kind of hydrogen bomb. They named it Big Ivan. Its yield, they calculated, would be in the range of one hundred megatons.

A one-hundred-megaton bomb would create a fireball larger than the state of Maryland.

HUMAN RACE

JOHN KENNEDY WAS TAP-TAP-TAPPING HIS front teeth with the back of his thumb. Close aides recognized the habit. It meant he was either bored or angry.

He was not bored.

At Kennedy's request, U.S. Army General Lyman Lemnitzer, chairman of the Joint Chiefs of Staff, had come to the Cabinet Room to give a briefing on the nation's nuclear arsenal, and how it might be used in time of war. Lemnitzer set up thirty-eight charts on easels and brought the president up to speed.

Pentagon planners had selected more than a thousand priority targets in the Soviet Union, as well as Eastern Europe and communist China, mainly military bases and cities. In case of war, explained Lemnitzer, the goal was to hit every single target multiple times. In one highly coordinated operation, the United States would launch weapons from bombers, submarines, and missile bases in America and Western Europe. The attack would kill an estimated 285 million people—not counting deaths from radioactive fallout. Those figures would depend a lot on the wind.

This was when Kennedy started tapping his teeth.

Of course, Lemnitzer pointed out, the Soviets were sure to respond. American cities would suffer as well. "Under any circumstances," he said, "it would be expected that some portion of the Soviet long-range nuclear force would strike the United States."

Kennedy asked how many Americans would die in this all-out superbomb exchange scenario.

Seventy million was the guess. About half the country.

On his way out of the meeting Kennedy muttered, "And we call ourselves the human race."

Harry Seidel cycled the long wall around West Berlin. It was a great way to stay in shape—and study the enemy. Back in the bedroom he shared with Rotraut and Andre, he made notes on a big map of Berlin taped to the wall.

"Their Achilles' heels," he liked to say.

Seidel was free, but it wasn't enough. More than a million people were still separated from their families by the Berlin Wall. The East German government cracked down on what little freedom citizens had, offering rewards to people for spying on their neighbors, for reporting any criticism of the government, any escape plans. Children were given cash for informing on friends and family. Police won medals for shooting escapers. Seidel's own mother had been thrown in jail as punishment for his escape. He'd get her out one day, he vowed. Meanwhile, he continued finding weak spots in the border and leading people under the wire.

Escape got harder as East Germany replaced the barbed-wire fences with solid walls and tall watchtowers. East Berliners responded creatively—some took a newfound interest in scuba diving and mapped out underwater routes to freedom. Students calling themselves the Travel Bureau guided escapers from East to West through the city's maze of sewer pipes. A train driver named Harry Deterling picked up twenty-four friends and relatives along the train's usual route through East Berlin. As the train neared the border, where it normally stopped, Deterling accelerated. East German guards jumped out of the way as the train tore into the West at fifty miles per hour.

These escapes put the Berlin Wall at the heart of the Cold War. And not in a good way, from Nikita Khrushchev's perspective. In the center of Europe were two cities, one free and one imprisoned. East German authorities could claim that the wall was meant to protect their citizens from "terrorists" in the West, but no one believed it. Khrushchev had hoped the Berlin Wall would be a symbol of Soviet strength. Instead, it became a stark symbol of what was at stake in the Cold War. When communists take over, they lock you behind a wall.

Harry Seidel did his part to keep the pressure on. On one of his scouting rides through Berlin, he saw a young man in the West talking across the death strip to a young woman in the East. He watched East German guards hit the woman and drag her away.

"Bastards!" the man howled, grabbing the barbed wire with his bare hands.

Seidel jumped off his bike.

The man turned to him, tears running down his face. "We were going to be married in October."

"You will be married in October," Seidel said. "I'll be your best man if you like."

"But how can we?"

"Give me your address. I'll be in touch."

Seidel went home and put on two layers of clothes, a track suit over a dress suit. After dark, he crawled under the fences into East Berlin, took off the top layer, stashed it for later, and walked down the street in the clean suit. He picked flowers and carried them in a bouquet, as if on his way to visit relatives.

After a successful night's work, he got back to his apartment in West Berlin early the next morning. He pulled off his muddy track suit and told his wife, "I'm going to be best man at a wedding."

Janet Chisholm wore a Russian fur hat and carried a shopping bag, blending in with the crowd on the sidewalks of Arbat Street in central Moscow.

She opened the door to a secondhand shop. A bell on the door jingled as she stepped inside. She began browsing shelves filled with silverware, pottery, clocks, paintings.

This was Chisholm's system for contact with her Soviet source. She would be at specific spots in the city at particular times on certain days of the week. When he had material to drop off, he knew where to find her.

Oleg Penkovsky came into the shop. He looked around a bit, then left.

Chisholm followed him to a small side street. He turned into the doorway of an apartment house. She held back, making sure he wasn't followed, then entered. As they exchanged a few pleasantries in Russian, sounding like acquaintances but not close friends, he handed her an envelope.

She rode the trolley to her apartment. Her husband came home for lunch. They spoke of everyday things as they ate. He took the envelope back to his office at the British embassy and put it in a diplomatic pouch—a sealed bag that, by international agreement, all embassies can use to ship confidential material back home. Penkovsky's envelope was soon on its way to London.

A week later, while Chisholm and Penkovsky chatted in an apartment house lobby, an old woman came slowly down the stairs. The two spies grabbed each other in a romantic embrace, hiding their faces. The woman looked away. Oleg slipped a pack of cigarettes, with three film cartridges inside, into Janet's shopping bag.

One miniature roll of film at a time, Soviet military secrets leaked out of Moscow and made their way to London and Washington. At the White House, CIA officials kept President Kennedy informed of the intelligence—the product, as spies call it. Kennedy was never told the spy's real name; that would be an unnecessary security risk. The important thing was the product. Frank Powers and the other U-2 pilots had given the government a view from above the Soviet Union. This new source was offering a view from *inside*.

The president knew the information was useful. In fact, it would turn out to be even more vital than he could have guessed.

On October 30, 1961, a Soviet long-range bomber flew to 34,000 feet and released Big Ivan over an island in the Barents Sea. A huge parachute opened, giving the bomber time to escape. The bomb detonated, as planned, at just over 13,000 feet.

Concerned about the fallout from such a massive blast, Sakharov's team had removed some of the nuclear fuel, lowering the bomb's yield to fifty megatons—still, by far, the largest human-made explosion in history. Ivan's initial flash was visible for six hundred miles. The blast wave knocked over buildings one hundred miles away, broke windows in Finland and Norway.

No target was big enough for such a weapon. This was a tool not of war, but of terror.

*   *   *

Big Ivan's message was heard in America, loud and clear.

"There is no escaping the fact that nuclear conflict would leave a tragic world," declared the opening pages of *Fallout Protection*, a U.S. government booklet published by the millions in late 1961. "The experience would be terrible beyond imagination and description."

But not to worry! If you happened to survive the burst of heat and the shock wave, there was plenty you could do! Remove clothing that may have been contaminated by radiation, the booklet suggested. Wash your skin and hair. Fill sinks and tubs with clean water.

Then get into your shelter—you did prepare a shelter, right? A well-stocked shelter must have first aid supplies, a radio, flashlights, extra batteries, and cases of canned food. "Select familiar foods," the booklet advised. "They are more heartening and acceptable during times of stress."

And don't forget a can opener.

What about the problem of human waste? "The most elemental device is a metal pail with a tight cover."

The goal is to stay alive for two weeks. After two weeks, the worst of the radioactive fallout will have settled back to the ground. Check your radio often. The government, if it exists, will let you know when it's safe to come out.

In public, President Kennedy encouraged Americans to take this stuff seriously.

When *Life* magazine published a special issue with designs for fallout shelters, Kennedy added a note saying, "I urge you to read and consider seriously the contents of this issue."

In private, he was already losing enthusiasm for civil defense. With the destructive power of the weapons the Soviets were now building, the whole idea of planning for life after nuclear war seemed like a cruel joke.

On a rainy afternoon in Washington, Kennedy met with Jerome Wiesner, his top science adviser. Kennedy had ordered the resumption of underground testing of H-bombs in September, and he wanted a better understanding of the dangers of fallout. How, he asked, would the fallout impact Americans? How would it impact children all over the world?

"It comes down in rain," Wiesner said.

Kennedy pointed to the Oval Office window. "You mean there might be radioactive contamination in that rain out there right now?"

"Possibly."

The president stared out at the Rose Garden. Aides said they'd never seen him look so depressed.

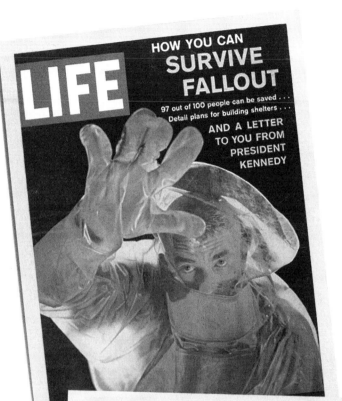

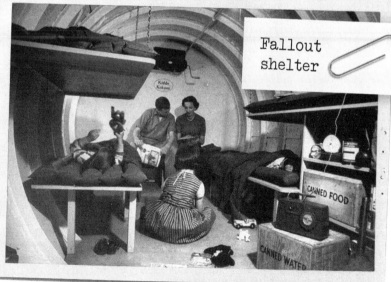

Fallout
shelter

OUT OF THE EAST

HARRY SEIDEL SAW IT RIGHT away—in Berlin, escape tunnels would have to run backward.

Throughout history, people have tried to dig their way *out* of prisons. In East Berlin, Seidel realized, you'd have to dig your way *in*. The dreaded Stasi, the German secret police, had agents and informers everywhere. No tunnel that started in the East could stay secret for long. Start in a basement in the West, though, and you'd have a chance to break through.

For his first attempt, Harry Seidel picked a spot where the Berlin Wall ran down the center of a narrow road. The buildings on either side of the wall were less than a hundred feet apart. Seidel took sick leave from his newspaper delivery job, packed tools and a week's worth of bread and cheese, and moved into the cellar of a building on the western side of the wall.

A few carefully selected men and women slipped in and out to help. Seidel quickly developed a system. Flashlight in hand, one worker at a time crawled to the front of the narrow tunnel, loosened earth with a small shovel, and piled it into large metal bowls one of the diggers had brought from his butcher shop. Another volunteer pulled the full bowls back on a rope, dumping the dirt into a corner of the cellar.

The space was damp and freezing. Everyone caught colds. As they worked their way forward, diggers passed out from lack of oxygen and had to be dragged back by their heels. Harry Seidel worked twelve hours at a time. His strengths as a cyclist—strong muscles, pain tolerance, and massive lung capacity—made him the ideal tunneler.

Harry knew he'd passed under the Berlin Wall when he began to hear East German police talking on the street above. After four days of digging, his spade hit brick.

He poured a little sulfuric acid on the mortar between two bricks. Fifteen minutes later, he was able to work the tip of a screwdriver through the softened mortar. He peered into a cellar in the East, not knowing who was on the other side.

One of the team had slipped into the East to gather people for the escape—but they easily could have been caught or followed. Seidel was relieved to see his friend and a group of passengers, as he began to call them, waiting in the cellar.

He removed enough bricks to open a small hole. Fifty-six men, women, and children wriggled into the tunnel and crawled to the West.

Someone must have informed on the escapers, because the police found the tunnel four days later. By then Harry Seidel was back to delivering newspapers, like nothing had ever happened.

* * *

When Francis Gary Powers walked back from the bathroom on the evening of February 7, 1962, he was surprised to see a KGB colonel at the door of his prison cell.

"How would you like to go to Moscow tomorrow?" asked the colonel.

"Why? What's happening?"

The man walked away without offering an explanation.

Frank's cellmate Zigurd thought it was good news. They were going to send him home! Powers was not so sure. But then a guard opened the door and dropped a suitcase on the floor. He told Powers to start packing.

Early the next morning, guards led Powers out of the prison. He looked back at the tiny window of his cell. Zigurd, in blatant violation of prison rules, was standing on a cabinet, looking down. The two had spent every day together for a year and a half. They had become close friends. They knew they would never see each other again.

The KGB colonel got into a car with Powers. A driver took them to the station, and they boarded a train. Powers tried asking questions about what was happening, but the colonel would say nothing. They reached Moscow by afternoon. A car was waiting, and Powers allowed himself to believe he was about to be driven to the American embassy and set free.

The car drove directly to the Lubyanka prison. Powers was marched to a familiar hallway and locked in a cell two doors down from where he'd been held while awaiting trial. The mattress was a little softer. Could that be interpreted as a good sign?

The next morning, he and the colonel drove to the airport. They got on a small plane with no other passengers. A fantasy flashed through Powers's mind—he could knock out the colonel, punch out both pilots, grab the controls . . .

The plane took off and flew west. A good sign, definitely.

In an underground cell at the U.S. military base in West Berlin, James Donovan had one last meeting with his client, Rudolf Abel.

In a Brooklyn courtroom three and a half years before, Donovan had argued that Abel should not be executed for spying. One day, suggested Donovan, American authorities might wish to trade the Soviet spy for someone in Soviet custody.

That day had come. John Kennedy had personally approved the trade of Rudolf Abel for Francis Gary Powers. Bringing Powers back home would not exactly change the course of the Cold War, but it would be a feel-good story for Americans. One small victory, at least.

Donovan entered Abel's cell, and they shook hands. Donovan asked whether Abel was worried about going home—the KGB would wonder if their spy had talked while in enemy custody.

"Of course not," Abel said. "I've done nothing dishonorable."

On the other side of Berlin, Frank Powers looked out the window of a moving car at a gray winter morning. He was cold, even in his overcoat and Russian fur cap. The car stopped, and a Soviet official in a well-cut suit got into the back seat.

They were going to drive to Glienicke Bridge, the man explained in perfect English. On the far side of the bridge was West Berlin. The Americans would bring their prisoner. Both groups would walk toward the middle of the bridge, where a white line marked the border between East and West. If all was in order, the exchange would be made.

"However," the Soviet official cautioned, "if anything goes wrong on the bridge, you are to return with us. Do you understand that?"

Powers nodded. It was a lie. He'd make a run for it if he had to. They'd shoot him, he knew. One way or another, he wasn't going back to prison.

They stopped at one end of the bridge. To Powers, the green steel span was a thing of beauty. Guardrails closed the road to traffic from both sides.

Soviet soldiers watched from the woods along the eastern shore.

American soldiers, dressed like fishermen in a clothing catalog, floated below in rowboats.

Flanked by Soviet officials, Powers carried his suitcase onto the bridge. Rudolf Abel, with a small American entourage, approached from the other side. Both groups stopped a few feet from the line.

A KGB man stepped over the line. He looked at Rudolf Abel. He told Abel to remove his glasses. He turned and nodded—yes, this was the right man.

At the same time, a CIA agent named Joe Murphy walked over the line to confirm the American's identity.

Powers nearly blew it, calling out, "Oh, hey, Charley!"

"Nope," Murphy said, "Try again."

Powers recognized the agent from the air base in Turkey. But he couldn't come up with the name.

Murphy gave him another chance. "What was the name of your high-school football coach?"

Powers's mind froze.

Murphy asked the prisoner for the names of his wife, mother, and dog. He got those right.

"You're Francis Gary Powers."

Both sides were satisfied. Powers and Abel avoided eye contact as they crossed each other in the middle of the bridge.

News of the successful trade reached the White House a little before 3:00 a.m., local time. John Kennedy was still up, hosting guests at a late-night party and awaiting updates from Berlin.

Kennedy wanted to get the good news out as quickly as possible. His press secretary, Pierre Salinger, jumped on the phone and started waking up reporters. Come to the White House for a press conference, he told them.

The reporters were nervous—why call in the middle of the night?

Salinger had to assure them that, no, World War III had not begun.

THE DECISION

OLEG PENKOVSKY STEPPED OUT OF a Moscow apartment house and watched a brown car drive slowly past, heading the wrong way down a one-way street.

Just moments before, in the building lobby, he'd handed a package of film to Janet Chisholm. Was this car following him? Following her? Had it just made a wrong turn?

The car swung around in a U-turn. Penkovsky glanced as it passed. In the back seat were two men in dark overcoats.

Janet Chisholm continued her routine through February 1962, and into March. Penkovsky did not show up for a single meeting. In case she was being watched by the KGB, Chisholm switched up her pattern in small ways, still going to the same parks and stores, but on different days, hoping to make her Moscow life appear normal.

If she saw the spy at any point, she knew to be on her guard. When a source suddenly goes silent, you must consider the possibility that he has been caught and forced to talk. Or that he has flipped and that the next time you see him, he'll be working for the other side.

Finally, at a cocktail party in late March, she spotted him.

About fifty people stood around in small groups in the apartment of a British diplomat, chatting and sipping drinks. Many Russian officials had been invited to drop by. Janet Chisholm, who was now pregnant with her fourth child, stood with her husband, Ruari, scanning the crowd—and there was Penkovsky, talking with a man from his office. She made brief eye contact with him. He went back to his conversation.

Ruari stepped into the next room, leaving Janet alone. Slowly, in no hurry, Penkovsky worked his way from group to group toward her. They greeted each other like casual friends. He was smiling, charming as ever. He noticed that she was pregnant.

"You must be feeling rather tired," he said. "Why don't you rest for a few minutes in the hostess's bedroom?"

A clever ploy to steal a moment alone? Or a trick to set her up, catch her in the act? Her instinct was to trust him.

She found the bedroom and lay down. Through the door, she could hear Penkovsky talking loudly with the woman whose bed she was now using.

"What a lovely apartment," he said. "Please show me around."

The bedroom door opened. The woman led Penkovsky in. As if startled by the sight of a pregnant woman in the bed, he offered sincere regrets for the intrusion. He turned to leave, his hands behind his back. One palm held a pack of cigarettes.

Chisholm reached out and took it. She stuffed it into her purse.

A few minutes later, apparently refreshed from her rest, she returned to the party.

The contents of the cigarette pack—several rolls of film and three letters—were sent to London. The photos on the film were of highly classified military documents. Penkovsky was still with them.

In the coded letters, he described the car he'd seen at his last meeting with Chisholm. From this point on, he suggested, they should meet only at public receptions, places they both had a reason to be. He added a personal note for Janet:

"Be careful. . . . They are watching you all of the time now."

That same week, in Berlin, Harry Seidel walked into an ambush.

Seidel's newest tunnel started in the basement of a café in West Berlin and led to the cellar of an apartment house in the East. He led a group of passengers through, then crawled back to the East. To keep the tunnel open for another day, he needed to go upstairs for a moment to make sure no one had left any evidence of the escape behind. A man named Horst, who lived in the building, spotted Seidel in the hallway. Horst recognized the famous cyclist—and escape artist. He told Seidel he wanted out. Be ready to go tomorrow, Seidel told him.

Horst informed the Stasi. They gathered upstairs.

The next night Seidel and a fellow digger, a young man named Heinz Jercha, crawled back to the apartment house to meet the next group of passengers.

"You always go upstairs first," Jercha said. "Let me go once."

Jercha flipped open the cellar's trap door and climbed out.

The Stasi opened fire.

Seidel grabbed Jercha by the hand, helping him stumble down the stairs. He was bleeding from the chest. Seidel slammed the cellar door shut. Bullets pierced the wood as he and Jercha dove into the tunnel. Seidel pushed Jercha forward, urging him to keep moving. As they reached the western side, other diggers pulled Jercha out of the hole. He was barely conscious.

"Get him into the car quick," Seidel ordered.

Jercha died on the way to the hospital.

This was a major story on both sides of the Berlin Wall. In the West, the diggers were heroes who'd risked everything to strike a blow for freedom. In the East, the official story was that Harry Seidel, a traitor and terrorist, had murdered Heinz Jercha.

Horst, the informant, was soon driving around East Berlin in his reward—a new car.

On May 31, at a crowded party at the British embassy in Moscow, Janet Chisholm met Oleg Penkovsky one last time. She slipped him a package of unexposed film. He gave her exposed film and a letter.

"I am sick and tired of all this," the letter said. Penkovsky knew he was running out of time. "Send film and a small pistol that can be conveniently carried," he wrote. "We will continue to work until the last opportunity."

He was right to be worried.

The KGB had begun to suspect Penkovsky. Resorting to a favorite tactic, they arranged a special vacation for the family living in the apartment above Penkovsky. While the family was enjoying a few days by the Black Sea, agents let themselves in, drilled holes in the floor, inserted cameras, and began watching their suspect.

Janet Chisholm flew home to Britain to have her baby. Like Francis Gary Powers, she was out of the game for now.

But the action continued.

In West Berlin, Harry Seidel lay awake for several nights after his friend's death. Then he started to plan a new tunnel.

In Hawaii, tourists gathered at night on the beach and looked to the southwest. Right on schedule, the sky above the horizon flashed white, then glowed green, pink, and red. The United States had resumed nuclear testing in the Pacific.

American kids began reading about new comic book heroes called the Incredible Hulk and Spider-Man. Both got their powers from nuclear blasts and radiation—no coincidence, given the state of the world.

At the Central Intelligence Agency, planners revived the plot to assassinate Fidel Castro. One idea was to poison his scuba gear with tuberculosis. Another was to find a very large and brightly colored shell, stuff it with explosives, and place it in the water where Fidel liked to dive.

John Kennedy, an avid reader of thrillers, tore through a new novel called *Seven Days in May*, in which the U.S. military tries to seize control from an ineffective president. It was fiction, of course, but there was one real-sounding passage that made Kennedy wonder, a detail about the football—the briefcase with nuclear commands.

"The book says one of those men sits outside my bedroom door all night," Kennedy said to General Chester Clifton, his top military aide. "Is that true?"

"No. He's downstairs in the office area," Clifton said. "He'll be upstairs—we've timed it many times—he can make it even if he has to run up the stairs and not use the elevator—in a minute and a half. If he knocks at your door some night and comes in and opens the valise, pay attention."

And in the Soviet Union, while walking along the Black Sea waterfront with his minister of defense, Nikita Khrushchev proposed an idea that would push the world to the brink of nuclear annihilation.

Khrushchev loved to escape to his villa by the sea. Except for one infuriating thing—under President Eisenhower, the Americans had begun building a nuclear missile base across the water in Turkey. When people came to visit, he'd hand them binoculars, point to the horizon, and ask what they saw.

Water. They saw water.

"I see U.S. missiles," he'd fume, "aimed at my dacha."

On this spring day in 1962, Defense Minister Rodion Malinovsky told the premier that the American missiles in Turkey were operational. They could deliver hydrogen bombs to Soviet territory in five minutes.

The feeling that the enemy was closing in was just one of many Cold War problems Khrushchev faced that spring. The Berlin Wall was becoming a real black eye. The United States continued to threaten Cuba; Fidel Castro was hearing rumors of new plots to bring him down. The Soviets were still behind the Americans in nuclear striking power. The Americans had bases all over Western Europe—and now there was a new one, right across the Black Sea in Turkey.

Something had to be done, Khrushchev decided. Something bold that could put the Soviet Union back on offense.

"Rodion," he said. "What if we throw a hedgehog down Uncle Sam's pants?"

PART 3
Eyeball to
Eyeball

SERGEI KHRUSHCHEV
Nikita's son and confidant

ARTHUR LUNDAHL
head of secret
National Photographic
Interpretation Center

ROBERT McNAMARA
U.S. Secretary of Defense

THOMAS POWER
U.S. Air Force
general/SAC
commander

DEAN RUSK
U.S. Secretary
of State

CAPTAIN VASILI ARKHIPOV
also known as "the man who saved the world"

ANATOLY DOBRYNIN
Soviet ambassador in the United States

DAVID SHOUP
Commandant of U.S. Marine Corps

McGEORGE BUNDY
U.S. National Security Adviser

CURTIS LeMAY
U.S. Air Force Chief of Staff

RUDOLF ANDERSON
U-2 pilot shot down over Cuba

THE PLAYERS

GRAVE ISSUES

SIXTY-SIX MILLION YEARS AGO, GIVE or take a few centuries, an asteroid about the size of Manhattan Island slammed into Earth near what we now call the Yucatán Peninsula of Mexico. This, scientists are pretty sure, is what wiped out the dinosaurs. The asteroid's impact blasted debris high into the atmosphere, creating a blanket of soot that blocked sunlight and caused the planet to cool by a global average of fifteen degrees Fahrenheit. The fossil record shows that about three-quarters of Earth's species, including all of the non-bird dinosaurs, went extinct.

In the second half of the twentieth century, scientists began to realize that human beings could do something similar to themselves.

Think of volcanic eruptions, they pointed out. Think of the blast of Mount Tambora, on an Indonesian island in 1815, the most powerful eruption in recorded human history. Tambora shot so much sunlight-blocking ash and gas into the atmosphere that snow fell in New York State in June the next year. Summer frosts damaged crops from North America to Asia, causing widespread famine, killing millions of people around the world.

A nuclear war could have the same effects—but worse.

The bombs would ignite massive fires, sending millions of tons of soot into the atmosphere. The planet would cool, likely for several years. Crops would fail. Humans, like the dinosaurs, would run out of food. The entire species could be wiped out. Scientists came up with a term for this terrifying scenario: nuclear winter.

In 1962, most non-scientists knew nothing of the possibility of nuclear winter. But that didn't really matter. The dinosaurs had never heard of asteroids, either.

Now in his second year as president, John Kennedy settled into a daily routine in the White House. After breakfast in bed with a stack of newspapers, he dressed in one of his hand-tailored suits and walked with his four-year-old daughter, Caroline, down the outdoor colonnade to the West Wing. Before lunch he'd swim laps in the White House pool, originally installed so Franklin D. Roosevelt could exercise muscles damaged by polio. Kennedy kept the water heated to ninety degrees to soothe his ailing back.

Of the books he read in the first half of 1962, one stood out: Barbara Tuchman's *The Guns of August*. Tuchman's book describes how the world's great powers, through a series of misunderstandings, stumbled into the First World War. Kennedy wanted everyone in his administration to read it, to ponder its chilling lessons. A student of history, he often quoted an exchange between German leaders from early in the war, as the horrific combat spiraled out of control.

"How did it all happen?" one of the men asked.

"Ah," the other said, "if only one knew."

There *had* to be a better answer than that.

Throughout human history, people had invented new weapons, taken sides, and fought. The weapons grew ever more deadly, but the pattern remained the same. Why? Was this inevitable? Could the pattern be broken? Just twenty-one years after World War I ended, World War II erupted, killing four times as many people. In World War III, there would be no slow mobilization, no moving troops around by ships or massing on muddy fields. It would all be over in a matter of hours.

John Kennedy's greatest fear was that he and Nikita Khrushchev were making the same mistakes as past leaders, bumbling down the same ruinous road. Kennedy couldn't shake the nightmare image of two people in rags, huddled in radioactive rubble, wondering how they got there.

"How did it all happen?"

"Ah, if only one knew."

"It is insane," Kennedy told aides, "that two men, sitting on opposite sides of the world, should be able to decide to bring an end to civilization."

Nikita Khrushchev put his hedgehog plan into action that summer.

Khrushchev announced he was sending agricultural equipment to his good friends in Cuba. Cargo ships sailed from Soviet ports, their decks crowded with tractors and other farming machines.

The real cargo was hidden in the holds below.

The convoys of Soviet ships continued across the Atlantic through summer and into the fall of 1962. American military planes circled overhead, taking pictures. As far as the pilots could see, the ships really *did* carry farm supplies.

But why did the Cubans suddenly need eighty shipments of tractors? And what was in the holds below deck?

In Washington, D.C., Republican senators demanded answers. Whatever Khrushchev was up to, was President Kennedy going to sit back and let it happen? Was he going to let Khrushchev get the best of him yet again? Senator Kenneth Keating went on television to charge Kennedy with being a "do-nothing president."

That hit where it hurt. Right up there with Kennedy's fear of nuclear war was his fear of appearing weak. He pointed out that there was no evidence the Soviet Union was sending offensive weapons to Cuba—but he added some tough talk to the mix.

"Were it to be otherwise," he said, "the gravest issues would arise."

Nikita Khrushchev was at his beach home on the Black Sea when he read Kennedy's statement. The "Were it to be otherwise" line was worrisome.

It was definitely otherwise.

The U.S. secretary of the interior, Stewart Udall, happened to be visiting Russia, and Khrushchev summoned him for a talk. Udall was flown to Sochi and driven by car to the premier's waterfront retreat. The luxurious stone villa had balconies overlooking the sea, a badminton court, and a swimming pool with a retractable glass roof.

Khrushchev and Udall changed into swimsuits and walked down to the gravel beach. Udall dove in off a pier. Khrushchev, who did not swim well, bobbed in a rubber tube. After a nice lunch by the pool, the Soviet leader got down to business. He informed his guest that he was tired of Americans acting as if they owned the world.

"War in this day and age means no Paris and no France, all

in the space of an hour," Khrushchev warned. "It's been a long time since you could spank us like a little boy—now we can swat your ass."

Then, as usual after a rant, Khrushchev softened his tone. He knew John Kennedy was under pressure at home. He assured his guest that he liked Kennedy and did not wish to embarrass him, especially not before the congressional elections coming up in November.

"Out of respect for your president," Khrushchev promised, "we won't do anything until November."

That performance, Khrushchev hoped, would buy him a little more time. He didn't need much.

"Soon the storm will break loose," he said to Oleg Troyanovsky, one of his top foreign policy aides, when they were back in the premier's office in Moscow.

Troyanovsky took the storm analogy one disturbing step further. "Let's hope," he said, "the boat will not capsize altogether."

Backyard
bunker drill

SPECIAL WEAPONS

WINTER ARRIVES EARLY ABOVE THE Arctic Circle. Near midnight on the night of September 30, 1962, four Soviet submarine commanders walked through thick fog along a wooden pier on Sayda Bay, an inlet of the Barents Sea. The men's boots crunched patches of snow as they approached a wooden shed guarded by armed soldiers.

Inside the windowless space, top commanders of the Soviet navy's Northern Fleet sat at a table. Coals glowed in a small stove in the corner, no match for the room's icy air. Admiral Leonid Rybalko, bundled in a wool hat and dark greatcoat, asked the submarine commanders to have a seat.

"Each of you has been entrusted with the highest responsibility imaginable," the admiral began. "Your actions and decisions on this mission could start or prevent a world war."

The commanders did not know where they were being sent, or why. But they'd seen crates of summer clothing loaded into their ships. They could guess. They'd watched cranes lowering torpedoes into their subs. This was normal. The unusual thing was that each ship got one torpedo with its nose painted purple. These, they were told, were the "special weapons." These were nuclear bombs.

Only one of the four commanders, Captain Nikolai Shumkov, had ever fired this type of weapon. In a test a year before, he'd launched a torpedo with a nuclear warhead and watched the fiery explosion through a periscope. The blast was ten kilotons, half the size of the American atomic bombs used in World War II.

So, yes, with such a weapon, a single submarine really could start the next world war. Which brought up the obvious matter of rules of engagement. Under what conditions, asked the commanders, were the weapons to be used?

Under direct orders from Moscow, answered Admiral Anatoly Rossokho. Or, he continued, under dire circumstances, such as being out of touch and under enemy attack.

"I suggest to you," he told the submarine commanders, "that you use the nuclear weapons first, and then you will figure out what to do after that."

"Once your face has been slapped," added another admiral, "don't let them hit your face one more time."

The four commanders huddled on the icy pier after the meeting. They lit cigarettes and kidded each other about who was going to look worst in shorts. They shook hands and wished each other good luck.

Captain Vitali Savitsky, in submarine B-59, was first to cast off his lines and cruise into the bay. Beside him in the open bridge cockpit was Captain Vasili Arkhipov, chief of staff of the four-boat brigade.

A little over a year before, in the summer of 1961, Arkhipov had been an officer aboard the Soviet navy's first nuclear-powered submarine, K-19. Driven by two fission reactors, this sub was a major advance for the Soviets. But construction had been rushed. Sixteen days into the mission, while the sub was 300 feet beneath the surface of the North Atlantic, a pipe carrying cool water to one of the reactors burst. Before the reactor could melt down and explode, volunteers crawled into the reactor compartment and welded together a backup cooling system. They saved the boat but paid a terrible price.

"Skin not protected by clothing began to redden," K-19's captain recalled of the heroic young men who'd made the repair. "Faces and hands began to swell. Dots of blood began to appear on their foreheads, under their hair. Within two hours we couldn't recognize them."

Of the 139 crew members, 8 died within days. Fourteen more, poisoned by radioactive steam that leaked out of the reactor compartment, would die within the next two years. The Soviet government covered up the tragedy, warning the survivors they would be imprisoned if they ever spoke of it.

Now, as the four Soviet submarines set out on their mission, the effects of K-19 were still being felt. Nuclear-powered subs could have hidden deep underwater for long periods of time — but the navy was still redesigning its nuclear subs. So, at this key moment, the Soviets had to rely on older boats powered by a combination of batteries and diesel engines. These diesel-electric subs could cruise underwater on battery power for up to forty-eight hours, but to recharge they needed to approach the surface, take in oxygen, and run their diesel engines. This would make them easier for the enemy to track.

Another impact of the K-19 disaster was that the horrific

images were still fresh in the mind of Vasili Arkhipov. As the brigade's chief of staff, Arkhipov could have served aboard any of the four subs heading out to sea. He just happened to be on B-59.

Vasili Arkhipov is not exactly a household name. It probably should be.

The second submarine to leave was B-36, under the command of Captain Aleksei Dubivko. Snow fell on the ship's black hull as it churned toward the open water. The officers pulled in a few last lungfuls of fresh air, then climbed down the bridge ladder and pulled shut the watertight hatch. The crew opened the boat's ballast tanks, allowing seawater to rush in. The sub's bow dipped, and the boat slid beneath the surface.

Dubivko walked through compartments crowded with pipes and valves, engines and batteries, sleeping bunks and stacks of supplies, busy young men at controls. He met his senior officers at a table piled with navigational charts for oceans all over the world—they didn't know which ones they were going to need. The first officer spun the dial of a safe, opened it, and pulled out an envelope marked TOP SECRET. Dubivko broke the seal and took out a stack of papers.

"Our brigade is tasked with a special mission for the Soviet Union," he read aloud, "which includes transiting the Atlantic in secret to a new home port in an allied country. The transit must remain undetected by enemy forces, and the submariners must arrive in Mariel, Cuba, by October 20."

The commanders of the other subs read the same orders. The sailors were excited to be headed to the sunny Caribbean. Best of all, the orders stated that crew members' families would be able to join them in Mariel, a long way from the Arctic.

Morale was high as they set out on their seven-thousand-mile journey. No one seemed to mind that there was one man aboard each boat who was not an experienced submariner. Probably a KGB man, the crew whispered. Anyway, he carried a pistol in a holster and slept beside a torpedo that, for reasons they could only guess, had its tip painted purple.

MILK RUN

OLEG PENKOVSKY WAS EXHAUSTED, SCARED, and all alone in a way only a spy could understand.

When the British salesman and MI6 agent Greville Wynne visited Moscow, Penkovsky slipped into Wynne's hotel room. He turned the radio up loud, gestured for Wynne to join him in the bathroom, and blasted the water in the sink and bathtub.

Then he slumped over and began to weep.

His bosses had canceled his last couple of trips abroad, Penkovsky explained. Maybe they suspected something. Maybe they *knew* something.

"I must go," he said, pulling himself together. "It looks bad if I hang around here."

Wynne passed on the bad news. The CIA produced a Soviet passport in the name of Vladimir Butov. The photo in the passport was of Penkovsky. At a Moscow party, an American embassy official slipped the passport to Penkovsky—he'd need it if it became necessary to make a sudden run for the border.

The team then prepared a letter for Penkovsky, thanking him for his vital work and assuring him that a bank account with $250,000 would be waiting when the time came for him to settle in the West. The letter also asked Penkovsky what Nikita Khrushchev was up to in Cuba. Did he know the purpose of all those shipments?

An American embassy official brought the envelope to a diplomatic gathering, the kind of party Penkovsky usually attended. Penkovsky did not show up.

As Soviet ships arrived in Cuba, Fidel Castro welcomed his new guests with open arms. Castro had liked Khrushchev's plan as soon as he heard it. He was a gambler, like the Soviet leader, and he enjoyed being center stage. This move would certainly put him there—and, he hoped, protect him from another American invasion.

"They could begin it," Castro told aides, "but they would not be able to end it."

Cuban soldiers helped the Soviets load their secret cargo onto eighty-foot trailers. Driving by night, police on motorcycles led slow-moving convoys down narrow back roads. At sharp bends in the road they stopped to tear down huts that were blocking the long trucks from making the turn. Cuban officers assured families who lost their homes that it was "for the sake of the revolution."

At selected spots in rural areas, Soviet soldiers began cutting trees, surrounding the clearings with barbed wire. Working twelve-hour days in the tropical heat, teams raced to pour concrete rocket-launching pads. General Issa Pliyev, the top Soviet commander in

Cuba, reported to Moscow that the work was going well. The new bases would be operational before the end of October.

On October 5, the first James Bond movie premiered in London. In the film, *Dr. No*, Bond battles a ruthless villain holed up on a Caribbean island with a secret weapon aimed at America.

At Edwards Air Force Base in California, Major Richard Heyser spent the afternoon of October 13 trying to get some sleep. He rolled out of bed early that evening, ate a big plate of steak and eggs, did his pre-breathing, made his last-chance bathroom stop, pulled on his pressure suit, and climbed into the cockpit of his U-2.

A U-2 flight had kicked the Cold War into a new gear in the spring of 1960. Now, in the fall of 1962, history was about to repeat. President Kennedy had approved an overflight of Cuba. He knew the risks, of course, but this was the only way to get a look at what was happening.

By early on the morning of October 14, Heyser was 72,500 feet above the island, snapping 928 photos through clear blue skies. He was over Cuban territory for just six minutes. The job done, Heyser banked north and brought his plane in for a smooth landing at McCoy Air Force Base in Florida.

"A piece of cake," he said of the flight. "A milk run."

The next day, in a darkened room in Washington, D.C., a team of photo analysts sat at light tables studying Heyser's U-2 images through microscopes. These analysts had seen plenty of aerial photos of Cuba. They recognized the usual mountains and forests, the sugarcane farms and baseball fields. But this batch of pictures showed something new.

A clearing in the woods. Trucks with trailers. Six long, thin objects on the trailers, covered by canvas. The objects were precisely sixty-seven feet long.

Sixty-seven feet. The analysts turned to their loose-leaf binders, the ones with Soviet missile specs — secret information provided by Oleg Penkovsky, though they did not know the source.

That's when they called in their boss.

Arthur Lundahl, head of the government's secret National Photographic Interpretation Center, stepped into the room.

"I understand you fellows have found a beauty."

Lundahl bent over one of the microscopes. He studied the images, then looked up at his staff.

"I think I know what you guys think they are," he said, "and if I think they are the same thing, and we both are right, we are sitting on the biggest story of our time."

Lundahl asked his staff to work through the night. He got on the phone to his boss, Ray Cline, at CIA headquarters in Virginia.

"Ray, our worst fears are coming to pass in Cuba."

"Are you fellows sure?"

"Yes, I am sorry to have to maintain it, but we are sure."

Cline passed the news up the ladder to McGeorge Bundy, Kennedy's national security adviser. Bundy took the phone call in the middle of a dinner party at his home.

"Those things we've been worrying about," Cline said, "it looks as though we've really got something."

"You're sure?"

Pretty sure, Cline said. They'd know more by morning.

It was Bundy's job to tell the president. He hesitated. This news was going to set off a crisis like nothing the world had ever seen.

Dinner guests were laughing in the dining room, enjoying an ordinary evening.

Bundy decided the news could wait until morning. Let the president get one last night of good sleep.

The four Soviet submarines cruised past the Azores, a group of islands about eight hundred miles off the coast of Portugal. The boats performed their daily ritual of coming up to shallow water, raising a radio antenna above the waves, and checking for new orders from the Northern Fleet commanders. There had been no word yet. There was nothing today.

It was unnerving to be so out of touch. Aboard the sub B-130, Captain Nikolai Shumkov gave his communications officer permission to break the rules and try to get some sort of update on world events. The young submariner put on his headphones and tuned in to an American radio station.

The announcer was in the middle of telling listeners about the exciting World Series between the San Francisco Giants and New York Yankees.

Baseball. A good sign. The world was not at war.

MEDIUM RANGE BALLISTIC MISSILE BASE IN CUBA

SAN CRISTOBAL

U-2 photo of missile site in Cuba

LAUNCH POSITION

MISSILE-READY TENTS

MISSILE ERECTORS

BULLFIGHTER

JOHN KENNEDY SPENT THE MORNING of October 16 in bed in his robe and slippers, reading glasses on, poring through a stack of newspapers. The headline that stuck out was in the *New York Times*:

EISENHOWER CALLS PRESIDENT WEAK
ON FOREIGN POLICY

At a Republican campaign dinner the night before, Dwight Eisenhower had contrasted his own performance with Kennedy's. "No walls were built," he said of his time in office. "No threatening foreign bases were established." Now, in less than two years, you had the Bay of Pigs, the Soviets sending the first man to space, the Berlin Wall—and this suspicious buildup in Cuba. "It is too sad to talk about," Eisenhower told the crowd.

It was an unwritten rule in American politics that former presidents did not attack current presidents. Well, so much for that.

McGeorge Bundy knocked on the door. He came in and told the president what the photo interpreters had found.

Kennedy's first response was to lash out at Khrushchev, as if his opponent had broken the rules of the game. "He can't do this to me."

He picked up the phone and called his brother. "We have some big trouble. I want you over here."

Bobby Kennedy charged into Bundy's office demanding to see the photos.

"Oh sh**! Sh**! Sh**!" he chanted, slamming fist and palm together. "Those sons a **** Russians!"

The president, the calmer of the brothers, stuck to his planned schedule for the day. Until he figured out how to react to Khrushchev's move, he wanted everything to appear normal. First up that morning was a visit from American astronaut Walter Schirra. Schirra was shown into the Oval Office with his wife and two kids. Kennedy took a seat in his rocking chair and smiled for the cameras. They chatted and posed, and then Kennedy led the children outside to meet his daughter Caroline's pony, Macaroni.

It was nearly noon before he was able to duck into the Cabinet Room with his top advisers for a briefing on developments in Cuba. Arthur Lundahl, the chief photo interpreter, opened a large black case and had begun sliding out photos when Caroline burst in for a visit.

Kennedy jumped up from his chair and put his arm around his daughter.

"Caroline, have you been eating candy?"

She didn't answer.

"Answer me," he said, smiling. "Yes, no, or maybe?"

He led her out of the room. When he came back, the smile was gone.

"Okay," he said, sliding into his chair. He flipped a switch under the table activating microphones hidden in the wall. A tape machine in the basement began rolling. Bobby Kennedy was the only other person in the room who knew of this secret recording system.

Lundahl set three black-and-white photos in front of the president. He handed Kennedy a magnifying glass.

"Sir," Lundahl said, "we've never seen this kind of installation before."

A football field—that was Kennedy's first thought. The images showed a clearing in the forest. Some kind of construction in progress. Long tube-shaped objects on trailers.

The tubes were Soviet R-12 rockets, Lundahl explained. They could fly into space. Or they could carry a hydrogen bomb to a target up to 1,300 miles away. The southeastern United States, including Washington, D.C., was well within range from Cuba.

"How do we know this is a medium-range ballistic missile?" Kennedy asked.

"The length, sir."

"The what? The length?"

"The length of it, yes."

Lundahl explained about the binders of data on Soviet missiles. Kennedy knew about the CIA's extraordinary source inside Soviet military intelligence. He still didn't know Oleg Penkovsky's name, but now, more than ever, the value of the spy's product was clear.

Kennedy studied one of the missiles with the magnifying glass.

"Is it ready to be fired?" he asked.

"No, sir," answered Sydney Graybeal, a CIA missile expert.

"How long have . . . ," Kennedy began. "We can't tell that, can we? How long before it can be fired?"

"No, sir."

Secretary of Defense Robert McNamara asked about warheads—any sign of H-bombs to go with the rockets?

Not yet, Graybeal said. If the warheads were on the island, the missiles could be ready to fire in a couple of hours.

General Maxwell Taylor, chief of staff of the U.S. Army, informed the group that the military was working on plans for an air strike on the missile base.

"How effective can the takeout be?" Kennedy asked.

"It'll never be 100 percent, Mr. President."

John Kennedy had spoken often of some sort of looming showdown with the Soviet Union, some eyeball-to-eyeball moment that would shove the future one way or the other. He hadn't realized it was going to happen so soon.

"I don't think we've got much time," Kennedy said. "We're gonna take out these missiles."

Still going through the motions of a normal day, Kennedy attended a White House luncheon with the crown prince of Libya, then kept an appointment to speak at a foreign policy conference for journalists at the State Department. Reporters in the audience thought the president seemed unusually tense. At the close of his remarks, Kennedy offered a glimpse into his frame of mind when he pulled a piece of paper from his pocket and recited a poem:

> *Bullfight critics row on row,*
> *Crowd the enormous plaza full,*
> *But only one is there who knows,*
> *And he's the one who fights the bull.*

That same day, in the Allegheny Mountains of West Virginia, a five-hour drive from Washington, construction crews finished a three-year job called Project X. The teams had cut into a hill beside the Greenbrier, a luxury hotel, and built a secret underground shelter for the U.S. Congress.

A long hallway in the hotel led to a door with a warning sign: DANGER: HIGH VOLTAGE KEEP OUT.

Behind that door was room for all 535 members of Congress, with meeting chambers and rows of metal bunk beds. To brighten up the space, workers attached window frames to the solid concrete walls and painted pleasant nature scenes inside the frames.

The crews were never told what they were building, or why it needed so many urinals, but it was obviously some kind of bomb shelter. Equally obvious was the fact that in the case of nuclear war, they would not be invited in.

PRETTY BAD FIX

JOHN KENNEDY AND HIS TOP advisers gathered again in the Cabinet Room on the morning of October 18. Over the coming days, the group would become known as the Executive Committee of the National Security Council—ExComm for short.

Arthur Lundahl set out new aerial photos of Cuba. These images, he explained, showed intermediate-range missile sites. The medium-range missiles, the ones they'd already known about, could hit targets within about 1,300 miles. These new intermediate-range missiles could hit targets as far as 2,800 miles away.

In other words, every city in the continental United States.

General Maxwell Taylor pointed out that there were likely other missile sites they hadn't found yet. An air strike could never be guaranteed to destroy them all.

Kennedy understood. The riskiest move he could make would be an air strike that left some of the missile sites intact. One danger was that those weapons could be fired at the United States.

Another was that once the shooting started, Khrushchev could use the opportunity to pounce elsewhere.

"What do we do when . . . ," Bobby Kennedy said, forming his thoughts on the fly. "I think he moves into Berlin?"

Secretary of Defense Robert McNamara jumped in. "Well, when we're talking about taking Berlin, what do we *mean* exactly? Do they take it with Soviet troops?"

"That's what I would see, anyway," President Kennedy said.

"I think there's a real possibility of that," McNamara agreed. "We have U.S. troops right there. What do *they* do?"

General Taylor said, "They fight."

"They fight," McNamara said. "I think that's perfectly clear."

"And they get overrun," Kennedy said.

"Then what do we do?" Bobby Kennedy asked.

"Go to general war," said General Taylor. "Assuming we have time for it."

President Kennedy asked, "You mean nuclear exchange?"

"Guess you have to," Taylor said.

A chilling reminder of just how quickly events could get out of control.

"Well, let me ask," President Kennedy began. "Is there any-one here who doesn't think that we ought to do something about this?"

This was the central question. It was followed by seven seconds of silence.

The president agreed with what the silence implied: they *had* to act.

He had already warned Khrushchev that the "gravest issues would arise" if the Soviets put missiles in Cuba. If he backed down now, if he just let the Cubans have their bombs ninety miles from

Florida, wouldn't that make the Soviets even bolder? Wouldn't they want to see what else they could get away with?

And there would be another price for inaction: Kennedy's political opponents would attack. They were already calling him soft, blaming him for everything from the Bay of Pigs to the Berlin Wall. Imagine how they'd pounce if he let the Soviets keep their missiles in Cuba.

With the stakes so high, maybe worries about approval ratings and elections should have played no part in the president's thinking. But this was the real world.

In spite of the enormous risks, Kennedy decided that the Soviet missiles had to go.

Spread out to avoid detection, the four Soviet subs reached the Sargasso Sea, off the southeast coast of the United States, on October 19. The crews had been looking forward to warm weather. This was not what they had in mind.

These boats were built for northern waters, where air-conditioning was unnecessary. They simply could not cope with tropical seas. The inside temperature rose to well over one hundred degrees, with 90 percent humidity. To conserve fresh water the men were allowed just two showers a week, and their own growing stench added a nauseating layer to the reek of diesel fuel.

As they did every day at the assigned time, the captains raised their antennas to check for messages from back home. For the first time in nearly three weeks, new orders came in: "Assume combat readiness and form a line west of the Caicos and Turks Island passages in the Caribbean Sea."

"What does this mean?" an officer aboard B-36 asked his commander. "Are we at war?"

"I don't know," Captain Dubivko said.

He decided to linger near the surface long enough for his English-speaking communications specialists to listen to a few minutes of news on the radio. The Americans were still talking about baseball. The Yankees had beaten the Giants in game seven of the World Series.

Air Force Chief of Staff Curtis LeMay was once asked how he would deal with Fidel Castro's Cuba.

"Fry it," he said.

He was not necessarily speaking figuratively.

During World War II, General LeMay had played a key role in crushing Japan by planning the firebombing of Tokyo and dozens of other Japanese cities. During the Korean War, LeMay called for use of atomic bombs on communist North Korea—a proposal rejected by the White House. He built the U.S. Air Force's Strategic Air Command—with its bomber fleet, flight crews, hydrogen bombs, and missiles—into the most powerful military force in human history.

LeMay's view of the Cold War was driven by the assumption that the Soviet Union and the United States were on a collision course. At some point, he believed, the United States was going to face a choice: surrender to the Soviet Union or destroy it. The American military had the lead in planes and bombs. That lead was shrinking. Therefore, it was logical to fight sooner rather than later.

In the mid-1950s, before the U-2 flights began, LeMay had several times ordered Air Force planes to make reconnaissance flights over Soviet territory—without President Eisenhower's knowledge or permission. It is not clear whether he was trying to gather intelligence or provoke war.

"Well," he told the crew of one plane, "maybe if we do this overflight right, we can get World War III started."

The pilots figured it was a joke. They hoped it was.

On October 19, at 9:45 a.m., Curtis LeMay and the chiefs of staff of the U.S. Army, Navy, and Marines met with Kennedy and his top aides in the Cabinet Room.

General Maxwell Taylor reported that the chiefs were in full agreement. They recommended an immediate air strike on the missile sites in Cuba.

Kennedy agreed that a passive response would be a mistake. But an air strike came with so many dangers. What if some of those missiles in Cuba were ready to fire? If the strike didn't destroy all of the missiles, some could be launched at American cities. And what if, while the Americans were fighting in Cuba, the Russians rolled over U.S. forces in West Berlin? Kennedy did not have enough troops and tanks in Europe to stop a Soviet advance.

"Which leaves me only one alternative, which is to fire nuclear weapons," Kennedy said. "Which is a hell of an alternative."

There was one other option to consider: a blockade. Dozens of Soviet ships were still at sea, on their way to Cuba. American ships could block access to the island. The blockade would be lifted only when Khrushchev agreed to bring his missiles back home.

But there were terrible dangers there, too. A blockade, like an air strike, was an act of war. Besides, what if a Soviet ship refused to stop? The Americans would have to fire, and events could easily escalate from there. Worst of all, the Soviets already had missiles in Cuba, and maybe nuclear warheads, too. A blockade would give the Soviets time to finish work on their missile sites.

"I don't think we've got any satisfactory alternatives," Kennedy said.

General LeMay rejected that view. Khrushchev, he argued, had blundered by picking a fight in a part of the world where America was stronger. "I'd emphasize," LeMay told the president, "a little strongly perhaps, that we don't have any choice except direct military action."

Kennedy refused to accept that he had no options. He refused to accept that war with the Soviet Union was inevitable. There had to be *some* way to confront the Soviets, to eventually defeat them, without killing hundreds of millions of people.

Normally, LeMay at least tried to hide his contempt for the young president. That was out the window now. A blockade was weak, he charged. It would only invite the Soviets to attack. It was the act of a coward.

"In other words," LeMay said, "you're in a pretty bad fix at the present time."

"What did you say?" Kennedy snapped.

"You're in a pretty bad fix."

The president exhaled a frosty laugh. "Well, you're in there with me. Personally."

The military chiefs continued talking after Kennedy and his advisers left the room. They did not realize they were being recorded.

Marine General David Shoup congratulated LeMay. "You pulled the rug right out from under him."

At the same moment, Kennedy ranted in the Oval Office. "These brass hats have one great advantage in their favor. If we listen to them and do what they want us to do, none of us will be alive later to tell them that they were wrong."

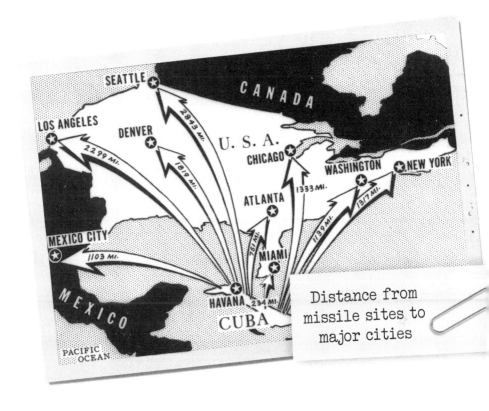

Distance from missile sites to major cities

YOUR MOVE

UNDECIDED ON HOW TO HANDLE Cuba, John Kennedy flew to the Midwest on October 19 and gave a series of campaign speeches.

In Washington, ExComm members continued to meet in secret. Kennedy wanted a unanimous recommendation, but the team was divided between advising a blockade or an air strike. Curtis LeMay continued to push for a surprise bombing raid, followed by an invasion of Cuba.

Reporters noticed lights burning in important offices all night—a sure sign something unusual was going on.

There was still no word from Oleg Penkovsky.

Every morning an American agent checked for a fresh chalk mark on a specific lamppost on Kutuzovsky Prospekt, a busy Moscow street. Penkovsky had been told to mark the post as a signal that he'd loaded the dead-drop he suggested in his original note to the Americans.

There was nothing on the pole.

Every moment an agent sat by the phone. Penkovsky had been given an emergency number. He knew to call from a pay phone. It could be assumed that the KGB was listening. Penkovsky was to say nothing. He was to blow three times into the phone, then hang up. He was to wait one minute, then do the same thing again. He understood the seriousness of this signal. It would be taken to mean that the Soviet Union was about to launch a nuclear strike.

The phone did not ring.

On the morning of October 20, White House press secretary Pierre Salinger met with reporters outside a Chicago hotel. He reviewed the schedule of President Kennedy's campaign speeches that day, then went up to Kennedy's suite and was surprised to find his boss still in pajamas, unshaven. White House physician George Burkley stood beside the president's bed.

"I have a temperature and a cold," Kennedy announced. "Tell the press I'm returning to Washington on the advice of Dr. Burkley."

Salinger thought the president looked fine.

Kennedy picked up a pen and pad and wrote: "99.2 degrees temperature. Upper respiratory infection. Doctor says he should return to Washington."

"There," he told Salinger, holding out the paper. "Tell them that."

The reporters were already on their buses outside the hotel. Salinger called them out to break the news. An hour later, he and Kennedy were on their way back to Washington aboard Air Force One.

"Mr. President," Salinger asked, "you don't have that bad a cold, do you?"

Kennedy said, "I've had worse."

Hundreds of Soviet soldiers gathered in a forest clearing in central Cuba. Many of the men went shirtless in the hot sun, their military pants chopped into cutoffs.

"We have completed the assignments of the first stage," an officer told the group. The missile base was combat ready. The crews had built concrete pads, assembled eight missile launchers, and aimed them north. On trailers, hidden under canvas sheets, lay R-12 rockets. "We may die a heroic death," the officer proclaimed, "but we won't abandon the people of Cuba!"

The men cheered and fired guns into the air.

"Gentlemen, today we're going to earn our pay," Kennedy said as he walked into the White House.

The president really *had* planned to give campaign speeches that day—until his brother called early that morning. ExComm was hopelessly divided, Bobby reported. The press was starting to ask questions. The president needed to get back to town and make the final decision himself. Today.

In the White House's second-floor Oval Room, air strike and blockade proponents battled it out for three hours. Either action would push the world closer to war.

"There isn't any good solution," Kennedy said. "Whichever plan I choose, the ones whose plans we're not taking are the lucky ones—they'll be able to say 'I told you so.'"

Assuming they'd be around to say it.

Anyway, there was no point in going back and forth any longer.

Kennedy made his decision. He stepped onto the balcony and looked out at the Washington Monument. It was a beautiful fall day.

Fourteen years earlier, First Lady Bess Truman had been standing in the Blue Room of the White House, welcoming guests to a formal tea, when she noticed an odd sound coming from above. A sort of glassy tinkling. She looked up.

The massive chandelier hanging from the ceiling was swaying, its crystals clinking together.

Why? The windows were closed. There was no breeze.

Mrs. Truman gestured to a White House usher, J. B. West, and whispered, "Would you please find out what is going on upstairs?"

West ran up to the living quarters. "What's going on up here?" he asked Alonzo Fields, the head butler.

"The boss is taking a bath," Fields said, "and he asked me to get him a book from the study."

That's all it took—the butler's footsteps. The two men felt it as they walked around. The entire floor was shaking.

Bess Truman came up just after her husband got out of the tub. "I was afraid the chandelier was going to come right down on top of all those people!"

"And I would have come crashing through the ceiling," Harry Truman chuckled, greatly amused by the image of arriving at the tea party in only his reading glasses.

It had been obvious for years that the White House needed work. Pictures on the wall tilted on their own. Dropped objects rolled down dips in the hardwood. And one evening, when Bess and Harry's daughter, Margaret, sat down at her grand piano, a back leg of the instrument plunged through the floor, sending a snow of plaster dust into the dining room.

That did it. The Trumans moved out. Construction crews gutted the building.

The renovation provided an opportunity to add a new feature to the White House — an atomic bomb shelter. The Cold War was starting. The White House was the bull's-eye on target America. The new basement shelter had a four-inch-thick door, Army cots and canned food, a direct phone line to the Pentagon's bomb shelter, and a shower to wash off radioactive fallout.

John Kennedy knew about the shelter, of course, though he'd never thought much about it. Now, standing on the White House balcony, gazing out at the Washington Monument, Kennedy wondered if he would be the first president to need the bunker.

His brother and a few others came out to join him.

"We are very, very close to war," John Kennedy said. Then, trying to cut the tension with a little dark humor, he added, "And there's not room in the White House bomb shelter for all of us."

At the National Photographic Interpretation Center, CIA photo interpreters continued working around the clock. On the evening of October 21, they found something new: a nuclear warhead storage bunker. There was no way to know what, if anything, was locked inside.

American tanks, artillery, and thousands of soldiers headed to Florida by truck, railroad, and airplane. The American press speculated about the meaning of these developments.

Nikita Khrushchev tried not to. He had made his move. Now it was Kennedy's turn. As they walked in Moscow, Sergei asked his father for an update.

All Khrushchev could say was, "We have to wait."

* * *

On October 22, at 4:00 a.m. Washington time, the White House press secretary, Pierre Salinger, packed clothes into a bag and left home without waking his wife and children. He didn't think he'd be coming home anytime soon.

At the White House, Salinger called reporters together. He confirmed their suspicion that the country was facing a major crisis. He told them that President Kennedy would explain everything to the American people in a televised address.

"We have just submitted to the networks a request for a half hour of time at seven tonight," Salinger said.

A reporter attempted a joke. "Do you think they will give it to you?"

Salinger was not laughing. "I have a feeling they will," he said.

In Moscow, where it was afternoon, Sergei Khrushchev stood in the hall of the family home, watching his father talk on his direct line to the Kremlin. Sergei could not tell what the conversation was about. Only that it was unpleasant.

When the call was over, Sergei and his father went for a walk. Winter had already come to Moscow. Snow lay in drifts against the bottoms of buildings.

"In Washington they've announced that the president will deliver an important speech tonight," Khrushchev said. "They've probably discovered our missiles."

"What will happen?"

"I wish I knew."

The situation was bad, even more dangerous than the Americans realized. Some of the medium-range missiles in Cuba were ready to fire. There were enough warheads already on the island to demolish several American cities. Perhaps Kennedy knew this. But he had no way of knowing that Soviet commanders in Cuba also had dozens of short-range nuclear weapons—tactical weapons, designed to devastate enemies on the battlefield. If the Americans attacked, Soviet commanders could wipe out the invading force before it got off the beach. And there were four Soviet submarines in the area, each with a nuclear torpedo that could destroy an entire enemy fleet.

When they came home from their walk, Khrushchev went to his special phone without removing his coat.

"Call the members of the Presidium," he ordered. "Ask them to meet me in the Kremlin in one hour."

On his way out the door the Soviet leader told his son, "Don't wait up for me."

"Khrushchev will *not* take this without a response, maybe in Berlin or maybe here," Kennedy told ExComm members that afternoon. "I think we've done the best thing, at least as far as you can tell in advance."

Secretary of State Dean Rusk urged everyone to buckle in. "This is going to go very far," he said, "and possibly very fast."

At 5:00 p.m., congressional leaders filed into the Cabinet Room for a briefing. Kennedy quickly outlined the situation and explained his planned course of action.

Senator Richard Russell objected, calling for an all-out invasion of Cuba.

"We decided that was not the wisest first move," Kennedy said. "And you would, too, if you had more time to think about it."

Another senator jumped in to demand an immediate invasion.

It was so easy to talk tough—when you weren't the one who had to make the decisions. Kennedy stood up, unable to hide his irritation.

He said, "I gotta go and make this speech."

THE CUBAN MISSILE CRISIS

EVELYN LINCOLN MADE HER WAY through the clutter of cameras, cables, and bright lights in the Oval Office. She stepped up to President Kennedy's desk and held out a brush. Kennedy took it, ran it through his hair, handed it back.

"Thirty seconds," someone said.

Kennedy stacked the papers of his speech. He sat a bit stiffly in his chair, partly due to the back brace under his freshly pressed suit. Also, he was about to take the world to the brink of nuclear war.

The director gave the on-air signal. The president looked into the camera, his face showing both strain and determination.

"Good evening, my fellow citizens."

Kennedy explained that Soviet missiles had been discovered in Cuba. The missiles gave the Soviets the ability to strike the United States in minutes with devastating force. Those missiles, he demanded, must be removed.

"The 1930s taught us a clear lesson," he said, referring to

the way Germany and Japan had begun grabbing territory before World War II. "Aggressive conduct, if allowed to go unchecked and unchallenged, ultimately leads to war."

All over the country, Americans were crowded around television sets in homes, in bars, in department stores. No president had ever spoken to so many people at once.

"We will not prematurely or unnecessarily risk the costs of worldwide nuclear war in which even the fruits of victory would be ashes in our mouth," Kennedy told the world. "But neither will we shrink from that risk at any time it must be faced."

The U.S. military, he continued, was going to enforce "a strict quarantine" on Soviet ships headed to Cuba. The word *quarantine*, he'd decided, sounded less warlike than *blockade*. The result was the same. "All ships of any kind bound for Cuba from whatever nation or port will, if found to contain cargoes of offensive weapons, be turned back."

Crews aboard U.S. Navy ships listened live on the radio.

So did English-language specialists aboard four Soviet submarines in the Caribbean.

"It shall be the policy of this nation," Kennedy warned, "to regard any nuclear missile launched from Cuba against any nation in the Western Hemisphere as an attack by the Soviet Union on the United States, requiring a full retaliatory response upon the Soviet Union."

He did not specify that "full retaliatory response" meant the utter destruction of every city in the Soviet Union. He didn't need to.

"My fellow citizens," Kennedy said, "let no one doubt that this is a difficult and dangerous effort on which we have set out. No one can see precisely what course it will take or what costs or casualties will be incurred."

*   *   *

As Kennedy spoke, the U.S. Strategic Air Command went to Defense Condition Three, or DEFCON 3.

DEFCON 5 is normal peacetime readiness, while DEFCON 4 is an increased state of readiness. At DEFCON 3, nuclear missile and bomber crews are ready to go in fifteen minutes.

DEFCON 2, one step short of war, had never been reached to this point in the Cold War.

DEFCON 1 means imminent nuclear war.

Pilots who happened to be on vacation drove through the night to get back to their bases. Flight crews were told there would be no more drills.

"If the buzzer blows," one officer explained, "it'll be the real McCoy."

An aide walked into the Presidium conference room at the Kremlin with a copy of Kennedy's speech.

"What have you got?" Khrushchev said, attempting a smile. "Read it out."

The aide translated key passages into Russian for the officials gathered at the long table. Khrushchev's first reaction was relief. A blockade was better than an immediate air strike, which could lead so quickly to all-out war.

Now it was his turn to move.

Should he just retreat? Bring home the missiles and let Kennedy have his way?

No, he quickly decided. That would be humiliating, both personally and for the Soviet Union. Just like Kennedy, he feared that appearing weak would only invite his enemies to attack.

Besides, the more he thought about Kennedy's demands, the angrier he got. The United States had missiles in Turkey. Why shouldn't the Soviet Union be able to have its own missile bases in Cuba?

Khrushchev dictated a rough draft of a defiant response to the Americans. Presidium members agreed to gather again at 10:00 a.m.

"Let's stay here until the morning," the premier ordered. "Foreign correspondents and intelligence agents are probably prowling around near the Kremlin. It doesn't pay to show that we're nervous. Let them think we're peacefully asleep in our beds."

"Well, it looks like war," Fidel Castro announced after Kennedy's speech. "I cannot conceive of any retreat."

The Cuban leader drove to the office of the newspaper *Revolución* and dictated a front-page story for all of his citizens to read in the morning. "The nation has woken up on a war footing, ready to repulse any attack," Castro declared. "Every weapon is in its place, and beside each weapon are the heroic defenders of the Revolution and the Motherland."

At their bases in the forest, Soviet missile regiments were on full alert.

In the waters east of Cuba, the commanders of the Soviet submarines knew Kennedy's blockade would bring a massive U.S. naval presence to the area. America's anti-submarine forces, known as hunter-killer groups, used planes, helicopters, warships, and nuclear-powered subs to track down enemy boats. If the Soviet subs hadn't been spotted yet, they would be soon. The captains had their orders. If attacked, they had permission to fire their special weapons.

On Tuesday morning, October 23, Nikita Khrushchev woke from a decent night's sleep on the couch in his office. Other Presidium members had made do with conference room chairs. The group met in the morning in wrinkled suits.

The officials approved Khrushchev's message to Kennedy. They agreed to raise the Soviet military's level of preparedness. Missiles based in the Soviet Union were to be armed with nuclear warheads. General Pliyev, the Soviet commander in Cuba, was authorized to use his short-range atomic bombs in the case of an American attack. The four submarines were to stay in position near Cuba. All ships on their way to Cuba were to continue to their assigned ports on that island.

The ship they were particularly anxious to get quickly into port was the *Aleksandrovsk*, a freighter carrying twenty-four hydrogen bomb warheads for intermediate-range missiles, along with forty-four tactical nuclear warheads. It was one sailing day from Cuba.

That morning in American schools, students practiced ducking under their desks, turning their heads away from windows. Teachers handed kids lists of items to stock in whatever shelter their families had prepared. World War III could begin at any time, teachers announced. If there was enough warning, students would be sent home.

Shoppers stripped shelves of canned food and bottled water, radios and batteries. Drivers waited in long lines at gas stations. Bank tellers noted a sharp decline in deposits. Vacationers fled from Florida. Caribbean cruise lines canceled trips. At television stations, which normally went off the air overnight, executives considered the radical idea of broadcasting news twenty-four hours a day. It wasn't possible; they simply didn't have the staff.

*   *   *

In the White House, CIA Director John McCone informed Kennedy and ExComm that the Navy was monitoring the movements of Soviet submarines east of Cuba. This was the first time Soviet subs had ever been spotted so close to the American coast.

Using sophisticated listening equipment, anti-submarine specialists were able to identify different boats by the sound of their propellers. These were Foxtrot class diesel-electric subs, fairly outdated by American standards. The Foxtrots had never been known to carry nuclear weapons.

So that was good news.

IF TIME PERMITS

KENNEDY AND HIS ADVISERS THEN turned to Nikita Khrushchev's letter—the Soviet leader's formal response to Kennedy's televised speech of the night before.

"Just imagine, Mr. President," the message began, "that we had presented you with the conditions of an ultimatum which you have presented us."

Khrushchev angrily rejected Kennedy's right to impose a quarantine, comparing Americans to lawless pirates. "The violation of the freedom to use international waters," Khrushchev charged, "is an act of aggression which pushes mankind toward the abyss of a world nuclear missile war."

It did not sound as if Soviet ships would be honoring the American blockade.

This fit with the latest intelligence. Ships were still cruising full speed toward Cuba. Eight would hit the quarantine line by tomorrow morning, just as Kennedy's order to stop ships went into effect.

"Okay," Kennedy said. "Now what do we do tomorrow morning, when this—these eight vessels continue to sail on?"

The CIA director said, "Shoot the rudders off 'em, don't you?"

"This is a problem," Secretary of Defense McNamara cautioned. "We want to be *very* careful."

The point was obvious. Once the shooting started, things could escalate quickly.

When the meeting ended, John and Bobby Kennedy stayed behind to talk in private. It's possible they forgot the tape was still rolling.

"How's it look?" Bobby asked.

"Looks real mean, doesn't it?"

"Well, there isn't any choice," Bobby said. The president *had* to confront Khrushchev head-on. "I mean, you woulda . . . you woulda been impeached."

"That's what I think," Kennedy said. "I woulda been impeached."

Bobby tried to assure his brother that whatever happened in the next few days, even the outbreak of war, would not be the president's fault. He couldn't quite find the words.

"You can't really . . . I mean, if it's gonna come, if you . . . it's gonna come."

"Will there be war?" Sergei Khrushchev asked his father when they walked in Moscow that evening.

Nikita Khrushchev looked exhausted. "It's one thing to threaten with nuclear weapons," he said, "quite another to use them."

In Havana, Fidel Castro delivered a ninety-minute televised rant against the United States and John Kennedy. "All of us, men and women, young and old, we are all united in this hour of danger," he concluded. "All of us, revolutionaries and patriots, will share the same fate. Victory will belong to us all. Victory or death!"

Soviet officials based in New York traded jokes about the words that would appear on their tombstones. "Here lie the Soviet diplomats," one suggested, "killed by their own bombs."

At the Pentagon, on a wall-sized map of the Atlantic Ocean, young men used long poles to plot the latest locations of American and Soviet ships. The U.S. fleet formed a long arc stretching from Puerto Rico to the tip of Florida, blocking the path to Cuba. The Soviet ships were heading for the line.

After spending the day hidden 200 feet below the surface, the Soviet submarines rose to shallow depth to recharge their batteries in the dark. The captains peered through the boats' periscopes. They could see American planes patrolling overhead.

Very early on the morning of October 24, just hours before the blockade went into effect, the freighter *Aleksandrovsk* pulled into the port of Isabela de Sagua, Cuba. Take every bomb ever used in the history of war. Multiply that explosive force by three. That's what was aboard the *Aleksandrovsk*.

"So you've brought us a lot of potatoes and flour," Soviet General Anatoly Gribkov joked to the ship's captain.

The captain had no idea who was allowed to know about his cargo. "I don't know what I brought," he said.

"Don't worry," said the general. "I know what you brought."

Americans left for school and work that Wednesday morning not knowing if they would be coming home.

A weather forecaster in Columbus, Ohio, predicted: "Low today, 48: high, 4,800."

Memphis, Tennessee, police stopped a man trying to pry up a manhole cover with a crowbar. He told the cops he was looking for somewhere to hide.

People walked the streets with portable radios to their ears.

They bunched in front of TV displays in store windows. Announcers reviewed the air raid alarms that would be used in case of emergency. A steady tone meant an attack was one hour away. A rising and falling tone meant the bombs were already in the air.

Clear enough. But most people had nowhere to go.

A small minority of Americans had built home shelters. Most people didn't have the space, didn't see the point, or couldn't afford their own bunker. Many public buildings were marked with black-and-yellow FALLOUT SHELTER signs, but most of these spaces were not stocked with food, water, or medicine. Some had cases of "survival crackers"—bulgur wheat blocks with an estimated shelf life of three thousand years. Others had drums of water that were supposed to become toilets when they were emptied. The country simply had not taken civil defense very seriously. Now it was too late.

"Iowa is not ready for a nuclear attack," announced the state's civil defense director.

As if striving to say something even less helpful, New York's top civil defense official said, "As far as shelters for the majority of our citizens is concerned—of course, we don't have any."

Asked what Chicago residents should do in case of attack, the state's civil defense director said, "Take cover and pray."

"Shelters? There are none around here that I know of," a Los Angeles police officer told a desperate caller. "If you find one, let me know."

General Thomas Power—*he* had a shelter.

At the Air Force's Strategic Air Command headquarters in Omaha, Nebraska, the SAC commander marched down a concrete ramp into the earth. Armed guards let him through a set of thick steel doors, and he continued deeper underground.

General Power had fought alongside Curtis LeMay in World

War II. Like LeMay, he believed that only the threat of over-whelming force could save Americans from the Soviet Union.

"Why do you want us to restrain ourselves?" he'd erupted at Kennedy advisers when they'd questioned the military's plans to launch thousands of bombs in one massive attack. "Why are you so concerned with saving their lives? The whole idea is to *kill* the bastards! Look, at the end of the war, if there are two Americans and one Russian, we win!"

General Power walked through another set of steel doors into SAC's cutting-edge command center. Busy specialists sat at panels of buttons and switches. The darkened space was lit mainly by the Big Board—a massive wall of screens displaying maps plotting the positions of SAC planes and enemy forces.

Power had two special telephones at his desk, one gold and one red. The red phone put him in direct touch with SAC wings all over the globe. The gold phone was his direct link to the president. It had to be answered within six rings, no matter what.

Power activated the red phone. A buzzer sounded at over two hundred bases, alerting personnel that the commander was on the line.

"This is General Power speaking," he began. "I am addressing you for the purpose of reemphasizing the seriousness of the situation this nation faces."

Power was broadcasting in the clear, rather than encoding his message. He knew the Soviets were listening. He *wanted* them to hear.

With a confrontation at the quarantine line only hours away, Power raised SAC's state of readiness to DEFCON 2 for the first time in history. One step short of nuclear war.

"Review your plans for further action," the commander

continued. "If you are not sure what you should do in any situation, and if time permits, get in touch with us here."

And if time didn't permit? Power did not need to say the words. Pilots had their assigned targets.

Air Force flight crews jumped into planes and flew to civilian and military airfields all over the country, dispersing bombers so that no Soviet attack could hit them all. Sixty B-52s, loaded with hydrogen bombs, circled the outside edges of the Soviet Union—above the Arctic Ocean north of Greenland, above the Mediterranean Sea, above the western coast of Alaska. Until further notice, crews would fly twenty-four-hour shifts, refueled in the air, ready at a moment's notice to proceed to their targets.

"They're trying to intimidate us," Nikita Khrushchev said.

This was an accurate observation.

At the White House, key staffers were handed envelopes marked TO BE OPENED IN EMERGENCY. Inside was a card with instructions on where to go to meet a helicopter in case of evacuation—essentially, a ticket out of town. A ticket for one.

Evelyn Lincoln felt a moment of doubt. As committed as she was to the president, would she really leave her husband behind?

Kennedy aide Larry O'Brien wanted to know what would happen to his wife. He was assured that she'd be given a special sticker to put on her car. In case of emergency evacuation, people in other cars would have to get out of her way. It said so on the sticker.

"Is this a joke?" O'Brien asked.

Not a joke. Absurd, but not a joke.

At an Army base in Harrisburg, Pennsylvania, an elite helicopter squadron waited on high alert with one assignment. If called upon, they would land on the White House lawn, pull the president out of the bomb shelter, and whisk him to the underground command center at Mount Weather. In case Washington had already been hit, the soldiers would don radiation suits, smash down the bunker door, and wrap the president in protective clothing before heading out. A special briefcase with all of Kennedy's medications was packed and ready. The president's bed at Mount Weather even had a special mattress for his bad back.

At the Greenbrier, in West Virginia, the bomb shelter for Congress was stocked with food for sixty days. Most members of Congress had no idea the place existed. They were not trusted to keep the secret.

Soviet ships continued on their course to Cuba. A fleet of American ships blocked their path. Four Soviet submarines monitored the situation from below.

In Atlanta, a police officer directed traffic with a radio held to his ear.

"No," he updated passing drivers. "They haven't met the Russian ships yet."

The Big Board
at SAC
headquarters

BLINK

AN AMERICAN REPORTER WALKED AROUND central Moscow, trying to gauge the mood on the street. He found a range of emotions: fear, anger, and most of all, grim determination. It was less than twenty years since the end of World War II. The Russians had endured devastation of their homeland far beyond anything most Americans could even imagine. If necessary, people told the reporter, they would do so again.

"War? I've been there," a cab driver said. "I am used to fighting."

An elderly woman put it more bluntly. "Your friend Kennedy is lucky he's not here. We'd tear him to pieces."

In the White House Cabinet Room, CIA Director John McCone reported that work at the missile sites in Cuba was continuing around the clock. More warhead storage buildings had been located. The Soviet military stood at an increased stage of readiness.

Two large ships suspected of carrying weapons, the *Kimovsk* and the *Yuri Gagarin*, would be at the quarantine line in an hour. They were being escorted by four Soviet submarines. The American ships were in position and had their orders to intercept.

The president's face tightened as he listened to these updates. His hand covered his open mouth. Everything he'd been dreading was coming together in one terrible moment.

And the next step—whatever it was going to be—was out of his control.

"How did it all happen?"

"Ah, if only one knew."

Bobby Kennedy looked across the table to his brother. The two locked eyes for a long, private moment. Bobby knew exactly what his brother was thinking: *Was there something further that should have been done? Or not done?*

Some of the group began discussing procedures for stopping and searching Soviet ships when John McCone broke in.

"Mr. President," he said, "I have a note just handed to me."

All conversation stopped. All reading and note taking stopped.

"Soviet ships currently identified in Cuban waters—I don't know what that means—have either stopped or reversed course," McCone said, holding up a sheet of paper.

Several people gasped.

Someone said, "Phew!"

Secretary of State Dean Rusk raised the obvious question. Ships stopped—but were they heading *to* Cuba, or away from it?

The note didn't say, McCone answered.

"Why don't we find out," Kennedy suggested.

McCone left the room. A few long minutes passed. He came back in.

"Whadda ya have, John?" Kennedy asked.

"The ships were all westbound, all inbound for Cuba," McCone said. "They either stopped them, or reversed direction."

"We're eyeball to eyeball," said Dean Rusk, "and I think the other fellow just blinked."

Was that right? Had Khrushchev just blinked?

Maybe. Maybe not. An immediate confrontation at sea had been avoided, at least. That was something.

But the crisis continued.

And, over the next seventy-two hours, a series of moves and countermoves, mistakes and misunderstandings, would bring the most terrifying moments yet. If a novelist put some of this stuff into a fictional thriller, the reader would be justified in throwing the book aside and shouting, "Come on, that would never happen!"

But it did happen. It's how the world nearly ended.

For instance: In Alaska, at the height of the crisis, the U.S. Air Force's early-warning radar system picked up what looked very much like a Soviet missile attack.

Actually, it was a spaceship on its way to Mars.

Sergei Korolev, the brilliant rocket scientist behind Sputnik and Yuri Gagarin's flight, had long dreamed of sending an unmanned probe to the red planet. Now, with American bombers stalking the borders of Soviet territory, he launched the rocket. The craft made it through the atmosphere but then blew up, showering fragments—which looked like missiles on American radar screens—back to Earth.

Only after racing to calculate the trajectories of the fragments could Air Force personnel report that the flying objects were not coming over the North Pole toward American cities.

At Baikonur Cosmodrome, Korolev's team prepared another rocket for launch, ready to try again.

No, they were not really following the news.

New orders came in from Moscow: get the Mars probe off the next rocket and attach a 2.8 megaton warhead.

The four Soviet submarines, with their special weapons, remained on patrol in the warm waters east of Cuba. It was far too hot to cook. The crews lived on pickled vegetables and one cup of water per day.

Missile teams in Cuba spent a rainy night practice-loading dummy warheads on their rockets. The real hydrogen bombs were removed from storage bunkers and loaded onto trucks. Convoys drove through the night, at a maximum speed of twenty miles per hour, toward the missile sites.

American bombers continued circling their spots along the Soviet border. If the order to attack was to come, it would be in the form of a six-character string of letters and numbers sent by radio from Strategic Air Command in Omaha. Working independently, two crew members in each plane would compare the code to the codes in sealed envelopes they'd been given before takeoff. If everything matched, the plane would proceed to its assigned target.

Late that night, in a Washington, D.C., bar, two American reporters talked about the possibility of being sent to cover a potential American invasion of Cuba.

"It looks like I'm going," one of the reporters said.

He meant he was going *if* there was an invasion.

The bartender, a Russian informant, missed that second part. He reported to his contact, a KGB agent, that the American reporter was on his way to Cuba to cover the war.

The agent rushed to the Soviet embassy with this alarming news. Ambassador Anatoly Dobrynin encoded the message using a one-time pad. He called the telegraph company, Western

Union, which sent a bicycle messenger. After picking up the note, the messenger cycled around town, picking up other telegrams, before returning to the office.

Incredibly, with the world on the brink of annihilation, this is how information was sent between Washington and Moscow.

The bartender's tip had not yet reached the Kremlin when Presidium members gathered the next morning, Thursday, October 25. Nikita Khrushchev opened with a joke.

"The Americans have chickened out," he said, chuckling. "It seems that Kennedy went to sleep with a wooden knife."

Nothing. Crickets.

Soviet officials were used to Nikita's pithy proverbs, but no one got this one.

"What do you mean, 'wooden'?" asked the deputy prime minister.

"They say," Khrushchev explained, "that when someone goes bear hunting for the first time, he takes a wooden knife with him—so it is easier to clean his pants."

Now it made sense. Sort of. Another day had passed without an American attack on Cuba. President Kennedy had blinked.

Maybe. Maybe not.

Kennedy was still insisting the Soviet missiles had to be removed from Cuba. And it was Khrushchev who had ordered his ships to turn around. All part of the plan, Khrushchev insisted. There were plenty of missiles and warheads already in Cuba. He was merely buying time to get everything set up.

That evening, as he walked with his son near their home, the Soviet leader let his guard down. The missiles, he told Sergei, might have to come home.

Sergei was shocked. Why the sudden retreat? Why even consider such a humiliating step?

Khrushchev talked about the pressure President Kennedy must be under. The U.S. military was surely pushing him to take those missiles out by force. That must not be allowed to happen.

Here was the key. Here was a confession he dared make only to his son. The missiles in Cuba had always been a bluff.

The goal was to give the Americans a taste of their own medicine, to make them live with a bit more fear. That would even out the global balance of power. The Soviets could refocus on driving the Americans out of Berlin, and the march to Cold War victory could continue from there. The flaw in the plan was that if the Americans attacked in Cuba, Khrushchev had no real answer. What should he do, fire the missiles? That would be the end of everything. He could go on the offensive in Berlin, where he was stronger. But that would also quickly escalate to nuclear war.

And yet, if the Americans attacked Cuba, how could he *not* answer?

Like Kennedy, Khrushchev was under constant pressure to be tough, to never back down. If the Presidium and military leaders lost confidence in him, they'd yank him from power, even throw him in jail. Like Kennedy, he had to balance fears about his own future with the danger of blowing up the world.

When they got back home, Khrushchev sat in his favorite chair. He sipped tea with lemon and flipped through the newspaper. Finally, he walked up the stairs to bed.

At Duluth Airport in northern Minnesota, a few minutes after midnight, an Air Force guard spotted some sort of dark figure climbing a fence around a building that housed vital radar equipment. The guard fired at the intruder, then ran to sound the alarm.

The alarm was connected to other bases and airports all around the Great Lakes region. At Volk Field in Wisconsin the wrong alarm sounded. Instead of the sabotage siren, a louder horn woke everyone—the order to launch bombers immediately. Pilots, who'd been sleeping in their flight suits, jumped into their planes and warmed up the engines. The planes were already loaded with H-bombs. Crews taxied onto the runway, believing war had already begun.

As the first jet was about to take off, a jeep sped onto the runway, flashing its headlights to get the pilot's attention. An officer jumped out of the jeep and explained to the pilot that they'd checked with Duluth. The United States was not at war.

Back at Duluth Airport, soldiers searched for the saboteur. They inspected the damaged fence he'd tried to climb. They found footprints leading to and from the perimeter of the airfield.

Someone recognized the shape of the prints. They were the tracks of a black bear.

On Friday morning, October 26, the Presidium listened to the latest intelligence from America. Troops were openly massing in Florida. American politicians, the press, people on the street—everyone was talking about a U.S. invasion of Cuba.

It was at this point that the message arrived from the KGB source in Washington, the intelligence from the bartender who'd overheard newspaper reporters saying they were leaving soon to cover the war. Nikita Khrushchev had heard enough.

"Nadezhda Petrovna," he called out to his stenographer.

She said, "I'm ready."

Anti-aircraft
missiles on a
Florida beach

KNOT OF WAR

"I'M GETTING MORE CONCERNED ALL the time," CIA Director John McCone told President Kennedy that afternoon in Washington.

Some Soviet ships had turned back, but so what? Two more missile complexes in Cuba would be ready to fire by the end of the day.

The blockade was not working.

"We're not gonna get them out with the quarantine," Kennedy said of the missiles.

The military leaders were still demanding an air strike, followed by an invasion. But that would give the Soviets time to fire whatever missiles the air strike had missed.

"So," Kennedy summarized, "it still comes down to a question of whether they're going to fire the missiles."

Ten days after the missiles had first been found in Cuba, the president was circling back toward his original position: the U.S.

military was going to have to go in and take them out. And the longer they waited, the more dangerous the job became.

"It's very evil stuff they've got there," McCone said. "They'll give an invading force a pretty bad time."

The Soviet submarines had been ordered to go down fighting. One by one, they would get their chance.

Captain Nikolai Shumkov brought his submarine to shallow depth for a quick recharge. At sea for nearly a month, B-130 had lost two of its three diesel engines. Its batteries could barely hold a charge. Of most immediate concern, they were being tracked by anti-submarine forces, the U.S. Navy's dreaded hunter-killer groups.

With American ships closing in, Shumkov dove the sub to 450 feet. But they were in the net. The steady ping of the enemy's sonar waves bouncing off the boat's metal hull made it all too obvious.

A depth charge exploded in the water outside the sub. Then several more. Most likely, the Americans were just trying to force him to surface. They could use bigger bombs, Shumkov knew, if they were trying to destroy him.

Still, hadn't those admirals back at Sayda Bay told him not to let his cheek be slapped?

A charge landed directly on the hull, exploding with a deafening roar, violently tossing the entire boat.

Nikolai Shumkov knew the power of his nuclear torpedo. He'd tested one, seen it explode. Whatever fleet the Americans had up there would be wiped out. He and his crew would be killed, too. He had no way of knowing what was happening in the world and no more time to think.

The captain gave the order to surface. If World War III had not already begun, he would not be the one to start it.

The boat broke the surface. A crewman opened the hatch to

the bridge cockpit. Shumkov climbed up the ladder and stood in the fresh air, taking in the amazing sight. He was completely surrounded by American ships.

An American destroyer began flashing a message using a bright lamp. The sub's communications officer knew the code.

"They're asking us 'Do you need assistance?'"

Shumkov had to laugh. "Sure," he said. "How about a couple diesel engines, a ton of fresh water, and some green vegetables?"

Then he added, "Don't send that."

Nikita Khrushchev's urgent message to John Kennedy followed the usual route. It was dropped off at the American embassy in Moscow, translated into English by the American staff, encoded, sent by telegraph to the State Department in Washington, decoded, and delivered by hand to the White House.

The process took twelve hours.

"This reads as if he wrote it himself," Llewellyn Thompson said, "without consultation or editing." Thompson, the former ambassador to the Soviet Union, knew Khrushchev well. "He's worried. He seems to be under a lot of strain."

Kennedy read the letter for himself. It was long and emotional, oddly personal. A few passages jumped out.

"If indeed war should break out," Khrushchev wrote, "then it would not be in our power to stop it, for such is the logic of war. I have participated in two wars and know that war ends when it has rolled through cities and villages, everywhere sowing death and destruction."

Then Khrushchev made a stunning proposal. If Kennedy promised not to invade Cuba, the Soviets would withdraw their missiles from the island.

"Mr. President, we and you ought not now to pull on the ends of the rope in which you have tied the knot of war, because the more the two of us pull, the tighter that knot will be tied. And a moment may come when that knot will be tied so tight that even he who tied it will not have the strength to untie it."

Could this be it? The way out of the crisis?

Or yet another Khrushchev deception?

Kennedy needed time to think about it.

Nina Khrushcheva called the Kremlin to check on her husband. Nikita told her he would not be home that night. He spent a restless night on his office couch.

Fidel Castro couldn't sleep either. At 2:00 a.m., he drove to the Soviet embassy in Havana and woke the ambassador, Aleksandr Alekseyev. Convinced the Americans were about to attack, Castro began dictating a desperate message to Nikita Khrushchev.

Alekseyev cut in. His Spanish was excellent, but he wanted to be sure he had not misheard. "You want to say," the Russian asked, "that we should be the first to deliver a nuclear strike?"

"No, I don't want to say that directly," Castro said. "But the situation is developing in such a way that it's either we or they. If we want to avoid receiving the first strike, if an attack is inevitable, then wipe them off the face of the earth."

Appalled, Alekseyev took down the message. He began the time-consuming process of sending it to Moscow.

Khrushchev awoke that morning—Saturday, October 27—feeling a little bit better. He had lived through another night. He showered, shaved, ate breakfast, and sat down with the Presidium to write a new letter to the American president. A letter with new demands.

And forget the twelve-hour route to Washington, he decided. This letter would be broadcast on Radio Moscow. The whole world would hear it. Then the pressure would be back on Kennedy. Let *him* make the next difficult move.

It was midnight in Alaska. At Eielson Air Force Base, near Fairbanks, U.S. Air Force Captain Chuck Maultsby took off in a U-2 and flew north, soaring past the north coast of Alaska and out over the Arctic Ocean. His mission was to monitor recent Soviet atomic tests by collecting air samples from near the Soviet border.

Obviously, someone should have thought to postpone this flight. Someone should have pointed out that it could wait until the world wasn't one tiny mistake from calamity. But no one did.

Still, it should have been fine. Chuck Maultsby was an experienced pilot. He was not supposed to come within one hundred miles of Soviet airspace.

The trouble began as he approached Earth's magnetic north pole. The needle of his compass started to swing and spin, unable to point north since north was straight down. Expecting this, the pilot was prepared to navigate as sea captains had done for centuries, using star charts and a sextant. But he was not prepared for the aurora borealis—the northern lights. This awesome display of flashing color is caused by charged particles streaming out from the sun and colliding with atoms in the atmosphere above the North Pole. Maultsby couldn't get a clear view of the stars through the dancing streaks of green.

With no landmarks below, no compass, no sextant, Maultsby did the right thing. He turned around.

Only the angle of his turn was, understandably, just a little bit off.

At a radar station in the far northeast corner of the Soviet Union, crews watched their screens for signs of an American attack. It would likely begin with U.S. bombers coming over the North Pole, taking the shortest route to Soviet cities. Early that morning the radar operators picked up an unidentified plane as it sped down from the pole and crossed the border of the Soviet Union.

FINAL OFFER

AT THE WHITE HOUSE, SATURDAY morning began with a glimmer of hope as Nikita Khrushchev's "knot of war" letter was read and discussed in the Cabinet Room.

"He's scared," said Robert McNamara.

President Kennedy nodded. He was the only person on earth who fully understood exactly *how* scared the Soviet leader was.

The good news was that Khrushchev was offering to remove his missiles from Cuba in exchange for an American pledge not to invade. He seemed to be backing down. The group had just begun discussing the proposal when an aide ran in with breaking news from the Associated Press.

Kennedy read aloud from the slip of paper. "Premier Khrushchev told President Kennedy in a message today he would withdraw offensive weapons from Cuba if the United States withdrew its rockets from Turkey."

The Soviet leader, apparently, had just made this statement on the radio.

Several people began talking at once. What just happened? In yesterday's letter, Khrushchev had proposed removing Soviet missiles from Cuba in exchange for Kennedy's promise not to invade. Now he was demanding the Americans remove their missiles from Turkey. Had Khrushchev changed his position overnight?

"It's very odd, Mr. President," said McGeorge Bundy, the national security adviser.

"I think we have to assume," Kennedy said, aggravation in his voice, "that this is their new and latest position."

"How can we negotiate with somebody who changes his deal before we even get a chance to reply?" McNamara asked.

"There must have been an overruling in Moscow," Bundy said.

Others guessed, correctly, that Khrushchev's first offer had been made in a state of panic and that this new one was written in a calmer frame of mind. In any case, most of the advisers were in agreement—the president should *not* make the trade. He must *not* give in to Soviet pressure. To do so would weaken the United States in the eyes of its allies, and the entire world.

Easy enough to say. Harder for the one who has to decide.

"I'm thinking about what—what we're going to have to do in a day or so," Kennedy said.

Say they struck in Cuba. Say the Soviets fired their missiles. There'd be no turning back. And Khrushchev's Cuba-for-Turkey trade would start to look mighty good.

"We have a problem."

These were the words Lieutenant Fred Okimoto heard as he was shaken from sleep at Eielson Air Force Base in Alaska. The man standing over his bed explained that Chuck Maultsby's U-2 was lost, possibly somewhere over Soviet territory.

Okimoto hurried across the dark base to the U-2 hangar. He climbed the stairs to the small office where he'd plotted Maultsby's route and prepared his star charts. Now he had to figure out a way to get the pilot home—with no way of knowing precisely where the airplane was.

The navigator looked out the window, thinking. The sky above central Alaska was black. But a band of dim red light was just visible above the hills to the east. This gave Okimoto an idea.

He got Maultsby on the radio and asked if the pilot could see the sunrise.

"Negative," Maultsby said.

Not good. That meant the plane was very far west, hundreds of miles inside Soviet airspace.

"Turn left 15 degrees," Okimoto instructed the pilot.

Maultsby heard the transmission, faintly. He was also picking up a much stronger signal from a nearby radio station. Russian folk music played in his headphones. Maultsby felt his lungs tighten. His ears pounded with the sound of his own rushing blood.

The terrible thought in his mind was *I'm the next Francis Gary Powers.*

Shortly after noon, Secretary of Defense Robert McNamara drove across the Potomac to the Pentagon. For a week he'd been sleeping just a few hours a night on a cot in his office. He was utterly exhausted.

McNamara walked into the "tank," a war room with a huge world map on the wall. The Joint Chiefs were all there, finalizing plans to destroy the Soviet missiles in Cuba.

What exactly was the plan? McNamara asked.

Start with a massive air strike, General Curtis LeMay explained, followed quickly by a full-scale invasion. "Attacking Sunday or Monday," he said.

Today was Saturday.

A worried McNamara wanted to know whether they could take out the missiles without killing a lot of Russian soldiers at the missile bases.

LeMay grunted. "You must have lost your mind."

At this tense moment, news came in from Alaska. A U-2 had strayed over Soviet airspace and was being chased by six Soviet fighter jets. Khrushchev must be thinking, *Why now?* Why would the Americans send in a spy plane now, unless it was some sort of last-second reconnaissance before the bombers swept in?

The blood drained from McNamara's face as he shouted, "This means war with the Soviet Union!"

The president had just finished his lunchtime swim when the secretary of defense called with the U-2 news. Kennedy wasn't a shouter. All he could do was laugh, as if this were just too much to believe.

Now would be a good time to get on the phone to Moscow. Let Nikita Khrushchev know his country was not about to be wiped off the map.

If only that were possible.

It was maddening, it was *crazy*, but all the president could do was hope the Soviets did not overreact to the U-2 overflight. Here was yet another painful illustration of just how little control Kennedy had over all the different ways that war could begin.

Fred Okimoto's directions saved Chuck Maultsby. And maybe everyone.

After nearly ten hours in the air, his fuel running out, Maultsby put his plane down on a strip of ice at a government radar station in Kotzebue, on the western edge of Alaska. He popped open the canopy but could not stand on numb and frozen legs. Radar operators had to help him out of the cockpit. The pilot's first request was for a little privacy.

"My bladder was about to burst," he'd later say. "So I excused myself and shuffled to the other side of the U-2."

Word of the pilot's safe return came as a tremendous relief to Kennedy. But there was to be no letup now.

As soon as the ExComm members gathered, more bad news arrived. A pilot named Rudolf Anderson, flying a U-2 mission over Cuba, had not returned. Nothing more was known.

The team turned to the thorny question of how to respond to Khrushchev's two different messages. They needed to decide by tonight. Kennedy made the point that no matter what they wound up proposing, this would be the final offer. If Moscow did not agree right away to remove the missiles, the American military would do the job.

The group rushed to put the ultimatum into words. People kept calling out edits, word changes, criticisms of each other's sentences. Everyone was tired and on edge.

"I just think somebody . . . ," Kennedy started, then began again. "We're gonna have to decide which letter we send."

"Why don't we try to work it out," Bobby Kennedy suggested, "without you being there to pick it apart?"

Only Bobby could have said that.

Now it was Captain Vitali Savitsky's turn to make the ultimate decision.

As Kennedy's team met in Washington, the commander of the Soviet submarine B-59 was 1,000 feet below the surface of the sea, penned in by a U.S. hunter-killer group. The torturous ping of enemy sonar waves echoed relentlessly through the boat. The temperature rose to 120 degrees, 140 in the engine compartment. Drenched in sweat, crewmen gasped for air as oxygen levels fell and carbon dioxide levels rose closer to the lethal zone every time someone exhaled.

Depth charges began exploding all around the sub. The captain could not be certain if they were meant to warn him or to kill him.

"I will *never* surface!" Captain Savitsky vowed to his crew.

To be forced to the surface would be humiliating. And worse, a violation of orders, which could have awful consequences if he ever made it back home. But that left limited choices. The sub's batteries were so low that they were making barely three miles per hour. Escape was impossible.

Charges began to hit the boat directly, clobbering the hull like a hammer on a pail. Men were literally falling down from lack of oxygen. Furious, convinced he was under attack, Captain Savitsky called for the officer in charge of the nuclear torpedo.

"Should I ready the special weapon?" the officer asked.

"Affirmative," Savitsky ordered. "Ready tube number two."

Russian B-59 submarine during Cuban missile crisis

FIRST SHOT

KENNEDY AND HIS TEAM WERE still debating how to respond to Khrushchev when an aide came in and handed a note to Robert McNamara.

"The U-2," McNamara said. They all knew he meant the plane that had gone missing over Cuba. "The U-2 was shot down."

Kennedy sounded stunned. "The U-2 was shot down?"

"Yes, it was found shot down."

"Was the pilot killed?" Bobby Kennedy asked.

General Maxwell Taylor looked over the brief report. "The pilot's body is in the plane," he said.

Rudolf Anderson was the first person to die in the Cuban missile crisis. Yet again, an event outside Kennedy's control had shoved the world closer to the edge of the cliff.

"How do we—" Kennedy began.

"How do we interpret this?" McNamara said, finishing the president's sentence.

Khrushchev *knew* the surveillance planes were unarmed. Why shoot one down? Why now? Was it some kind of signal? Was it too late to negotiate?

"They've fired the first shot," said one of McNamara's assistants.

Kennedy agreed. "We are in an entirely new ball game."

The group was angry, eager for revenge. General Taylor called for an immediate strike. At the very least, they had to take out the antiaircraft weapons that had hit the American plane.

"We ought to go in at dawn," McNamara agreed.

Yet again, Kennedy resisted making a snap decision.

When they took a short break, Robert McNamara stepped outside. Looking up at the streaks of color in the sky above Washington, he wondered whether this was the last sunset he'd ever see.

And that was without knowing what was happening in the Caribbean.

Captain Savitsky's torpedo crew loaded their purple-tipped weapon into B-59's firing tube number two. Standard procedure was that two officers needed to authorize the firing of the weapon—the captain and the boat's political officer, a representative of the Soviet government. Each had a unique key. The keys had to be used together to unlock the firing mechanism for the special weapon.

Captain Savitsky and the political officer pulled out their keys.

On any other sub, that would have been enough. The torpedo would have been launched. The American fleet would have been blown apart beneath a boiling mushroom cloud. Then what? President Kennedy had warned that any Soviet attack would be met with "a full retaliatory response."

The reason this didn't happen is that Vasili Arkhipov, chief of staff for the four Soviet subs, just happened to be aboard B-59. Arkhipov had survived the K-19 nuclear submarine disaster the year before. He'd gained experience keeping cool under impossible pressure. He'd seen the horrors of radiation poisoning up close.

"No!" Arkhipov now commanded. "The conditions for firing have not been met."

"Maybe the war has already started up there!" Savitsky shouted. "We're gonna blast them now! We will die, but we will sink them all—we will not become the shame of the fleet!"

Another explosive hit the hull, throwing men to their knees. A seal ruptured and green seawater sprayed in.

Vasili Arkhipov remained calm. Taking Savitsky by the arm, he said, "You can't do this."

"Prepare to fire tube number two," Savitsky ordered.

Arkhipov refused to yield. The American Navy had more powerful bombs than the ones they were dropping, he argued. They could have already sunk the sub if they'd wanted to. If B-59 fired its special weapon, *they* would be the ones to start the war.

Savitsky held Arkhipov's glare for a long moment.

"Cancel attack," Savitsky finally said. "Prepare to surface."

It was after midnight in Moscow. Nikita Khrushchev was home, sitting in his favorite chair with a glass of tea—and no idea that a man he'd never heard of had just saved the world.

Still, he could feel things slipping out of control.

That U-2 flight over Soviet territory had set off alarms, causing some terrifying moments. And Khrushchev had just gotten word that a different U-2 had been shot down over Cuba. He'd never authorized that. A local commander had simply decided to take a shot. What would happen if the Americans retaliated? There would be no way for Khrushchev to keep a lid on the violence from six thousand miles away.

More bad news arrived. Foreign policy aide Oleg Troyanovsky, who was spending the night at the Kremlin, called to say a letter from Fidel Castro had just come in, a truly unhinged message. Castro wanted Khrushchev to know that Cuba was about to be attacked. Troyanovsky read the key sentences over the phone: "It would seem the appropriate time to think about putting a permanent end to such a danger. No matter how difficult and terrible this decision is, in my opinion there is no other solution."

"What?" Khrushchev gasped, horrified. "Is he proposing that we start a nuclear war?"

"Apparently."

Any hope of getting some rest that night was gone. Khrushchev told Nina and Sergei he'd be meeting with Presidium members in the morning at Novo-Ogaryovo, a government retreat outside the city. He suggested they go to the family dacha nearby. It might be a good day to be out of Moscow.

Jackie Kennedy and the kids were spending the weekend at their country home in rural Virginia, out of the Washington, D.C., fallout zone. The president called to check in with them, then met in the Oval Office with only his closest advisers.

The group had put together a formal letter from Kennedy to Nikita Khrushchev. Kennedy agreed to the proposal in Khrushchev's "knot of war" letter—the Soviets would remove their missiles from Cuba, and the United States would give, as the letter put it, "assurances against an invasion of Cuba." It was a tough letter, demanding an immediate halt to all work at the Cuban missile sites. There was no mention of the demand in Khrushchev's second letter, the removal of American missiles from Turkey.

This was Kennedy's last shot to resolve the crisis without war. With that in mind, he had a special assignment for the person he trusted most, his brother Bobby. There was a second part of Kennedy's message to Khrushchev. One that could not be put into writing.

Bobby understood. He picked up the phone and called the Soviet ambassador, Anatoly Dobrynin.

Dobrynin walked into Bobby Kennedy's office at the Justice Department thirty minutes later, bracing for an outburst of Bobby's famous temper. But the ambassador could see right away that Bobby was in no mood to trade punches. He looked like he hadn't slept in days, looked more scared than angry.

"We are under very severe stress," Bobby began. He gave Dobrynin a copy of Kennedy's letter to Khrushchev. The text was being released to the press, so it would arrive in Moscow without the usual delay. He emphasized the central point: if Khrushchev did not remove the missiles, the Americans would.

"The danger of war is great," Bobby said. "It's going to be hard to stop this process. The generals are itching for a fight. They want to go. The situation might get out of control, with irreversible consequences."

Dobrynin asked if this was a threat.

"A statement of fact," Bobby said.

"And what about Turkey?" Dobrynin asked.

This was a delicate issue. This was why Bobby wanted to meet, to deliver a private message about the American missiles in Turkey. The president would remove them, Bobby said. In four or five months, they'd be gone. But the president would never admit in public to making this offer. This part of the deal had to remain secret, or it was off the table. The Soviet leader had one day to decide.

"Time is running out," Bobby said. "We mustn't miss our chance."

John Kennedy and aide Dave Powers were sitting in the White House living quarters having a late supper of roast chicken when Bobby walked in.

"How did it go?" the president asked.

Message delivered, Bobby reported. He grabbed a chicken leg and summed up the meeting. He did not sound optimistic. Dave Powers continued nervously chowing down.

"God, Dave," Kennedy joked. "The way you're eating up all that chicken and drinking up all my wine, anybody would think it was your last meal."

Powers said, "The way Bobby's been talking, I thought it *was* my last meal."

MOSCOW TIME

SUNDAY AT 10:00 A.M., NIKITA Khrushchev's car stopped in front of Novo-Ogaryovo, a two-story mansion in a birch forest.

"What's new?" Khrushchev asked Oleg Troyanovsky as he got out of the car.

"There's a letter from Kennedy," the aide said. "During the night it was broadcast on American radio."

"Let's go in. We'll look at everything there."

Top officials took seats at a long dining room table, set at each place with folders of key documents. According to the latest intelligence reports, the United States was ready to launch an attack in the Caribbean, most likely later today or tomorrow.

The premier did not open with a joke. No talk of wooden knives.

Troyanovsky read President Kennedy's letter aloud. Kennedy was offering to promise not to invade Cuba in exchange for the removal of the Soviet missiles. The president's message ended with a warning. "The continuation of this threat," Troyanovsky recited in a slow, steady voice, "would surely lead to an intensification of the Cuban crisis and a grave risk to the peace of the world."

The room was silent. Khrushchev looked around the table, waiting for opinions.

Presidium members studied the contents of their folders, shuffling papers they'd seen many times. No one wanted to go first.

Khrushchev understood. He'd gotten them into this mess. He was the one who would have to say the painful words.

"We find ourselves face to face with the danger of war and of nuclear catastrophe, with the possible result of destroying the human race," he told the group. In an act of true bravery, an act that required far greater courage than aiming missiles or threatening war, he said, "In order to save the world, we must retreat."

A ten-minute drive away, Sergei Khrushchev paced from room to room in the family dacha, wondering what the Presidium was doing.

His mother sat watching TV. He couldn't understand how she could be so calm.

Sergei called his father's office at the Kremlin to ask for an update.

"They're still at the meeting, which is not being held here," an official told him. "We don't know when it will end."

Knowing he shouldn't, Sergei dialed the number of the government dacha down the road. He quickly thought up an absurd excuse—he'd ask whether his father would be coming home for lunch.

A soldier picked up the phone and informed Sergei that the Presidium meeting would probably not be over by lunchtime.

"What's new?" Sergei asked.

"Nothing."

The soldier hung up.

Sergei turned on the radio. Music, routine news. He left the radio on, just in case.

At Novo-Ogaryovo, the group had just begun discussing Kennedy's proposal—it was not *too* bad, at least they got *something* for the missiles—when Oleg Troyanovsky was called to the telephone in the hallway. He came back with a page of handwritten notes. A telegram, he explained, had just come in from Ambassador Dobrynin in Washington.

"Read it," Khrushchev said.

This was Dobrynin's report about his brief meeting with Bobby Kennedy last night. The key point was President Kennedy's secret offer to remove the American missiles from Turkey.

"So," Khrushchev said, "what do you think?"

More silence.

Khrushchev worked out his ideas aloud, as if speaking to himself. Kennedy was pleading for help. The president added this Turkey detail to say, *Please accept my public offer before it's too late.* Why did this part of the deal have to be secret? Obviously, Kennedy was thinking of politics, thinking of his image. He wanted the world to believe he'd "won" the showdown. Well, Khrushchev could live with that. Look what he got from the Americans—a pledge not to invade Cuba *and* the removal of the missiles in Turkey.

Everyone agreed. The mood in the room lightened. It looked as if the crisis was finally over.

The phone in the hall rang again. The door opened, and an officer gestured to General Semyon Ivanov, a top military official. Ivanov stepped out to take the call. He came back in with news.

According to American newspapers, President Kennedy would be addressing the nation on television today at 5:00 p.m.

"At five o'clock whose time?" Khrushchev demanded.

Ivanov checked his notes. "Moscow time."

Ten in the morning in Washington. This was seriously alarming. Presidents did not make televised speeches on Sunday morning. Kennedy must have something of vital importance to tell the American people. What could it be, but an announcement that U.S. forces had begun their attack in Cuba? Kennedy's military men must have won out. They would get their invasion after all.

How long before this point of no return? A few hours? He shouted orders to Defense Minister Malinovsky, to be immediately relayed to Soviet commanders in Cuba: "Allow no one near the missiles. Obey no orders to launch!"

Malinovsky hurried out of the room.

Now he needed to get a message to Kennedy. There was no time for the usual coded telegrams. Turning to his stenographer, he said, "Let's begin, Nadezhda Petrovna."

A Presidium member named Leonid Ilychev dashed out of the mansion with a stack of hastily typed pages. He jumped in a black government car, and the driver sped out of the forest and onto the busier roads leading into the city. Swerving through traffic, honking his horn at red lights—which was illegal in Moscow—the driver pulled up to Moscow's Radio Center building. Ilychev jumped out while the car was still moving.

Radio officials were waiting in the lobby.

"Which floor?" Ilychev shouted as he ran into the elevator.

The rickety cage creaked slowly up—and stopped between two floors.

Radio officials gathered outside. They assured Ilychev that the repairman had been called.

No time, Ilychev said, sliding his papers through a crack between the doors.

Moments later, the pages were in the hands of Yuri Levitan, the Soviet Union's most famous news broadcaster. It was Levitan's deep voice that first announced the victory over Hitler, the death of Stalin, Yuri Gagarin's space flight. He looked over the pages, clearing his throat. He asked for a few minutes to practice with the text, but Leonid Ilychev, who'd made it out of the elevator, insisted it had to be now.

"Attention, this is Radio Moscow," Levitan said into the microphone. "We have the following important announcement."

Presidium members listened live on a radio in the dining room at Novo-Ogaryovo.

"Dear Mr. President," Levitan began. "I have received your message of October 27. I express satisfaction and thank you for the sense of proportion you have displayed and for realization of the responsibility which now devolves on you for the preservation of peace throughout the world."

Nikita Khrushchev nodded in agreement with his own words.

"The Soviet government," continued the announcer, "has issued a new order to dismantle the arms you describe as offensive, and to crate and return them to the Soviet Union."

Sergei and Nina listened at the family dacha.

Well, that's it, Sergei thought. *We've retreated!*

"I regard with respect and trust the statement you made in your message of October 27, that there will be no attack, no invasion," read Levitan. "In that case, the motives which induced us to render assistance of such a kind to Cuba disappear."

Tape machines rolled at the American embassy in Moscow. Russian-speaking diplomats made quick translations of the message.

"If we, together with you, and with the assistance of other people of good will, succeed in eliminating this tense atmosphere, we should also make certain that no other dangerous conflicts which could lead to a world nuclear catastrophe would arise."

It was a sunny Sunday morning in Washington, unusually warm, with highs expected to reach the low sixties. National Security Adviser McGeorge Bundy was eating breakfast in the White House when an aide ran in with the text of Khrushchev's announcement.

Bundy grabbed the phone and called up to the president's bedroom.

"I feel like a new man now," Kennedy said. "Thank God it's all over."

The world heard the news on the radio that morning. White House advisers cheered in their cars on their way to work. Evelyn Lincoln missed it at first. She was driving with her husband, Abe, but with the radio off, enjoying what they feared were a last few moments of peace.

"Wasn't it great about the news?" a staffer asked when Lincoln walked into the West Wing.

"It sure was," she said, not wanting to admit she had no idea what everyone was so happy about.

Bobby Kennedy missed it, too. He'd promised to take his daughters to a horse show that morning. He was pulled from the stands to take a call from the White House.

General Curtis LeMay was sure this was another one of Khrushchev's tricks. The thought of Kennedy accepting the deal enraged him. "This is the greatest defeat in our history," LeMay howled, pounding a table. "We should invade today!"

In Havana, the newspaper editor Carlos Franqui dialed Fidel Castro's number. "Fidel," Franqui began, "what should we do about this news?"

"What news?"

Franqui hesitated, realizing Castro hadn't heard yet of Khrushchev's decision. There was a long silence. Castro asked if the editor was still on the line.

Franqui told him the news.

"Son of a *****!" Castro roared. "Bastard! ***hole!"

Franqui heard a boot kicking a wall and what sounded very much like shattering glass.

In the dining room at Novo-Ogaryovo, Nikita Khrushchev and the group waited anxiously for some response from the White House. An aide rushed in with a cable from Soviet agents in Washington: the KGB had just observed President Kennedy going into a church.

What was the meaning of this?

Presidium members debated the point. Was he praying for guidance in the coming war? Was it some kind of trick? But what sort of trick involves going to church?

All they could do was guess.

Finally, late in the afternoon, Kennedy's response to Nikita Khrushchev's offer was broadcast on American radio.

"I welcome Chairman Khrushchev's statesmanlike decision," Kennedy announced. "It is my earnest hope that the governments of the world can, with a solution of the Cuban crisis, turn their urgent attention to the compelling necessity for ending the arms race and reducing world tension."

The group passed around glasses of vodka and raised a toast.

Khrushchev stood up. "Why don't we go to the theater? We'll show the whole world that there's nothing more to fear."

Someone went to get a newspaper so they could see what was playing in Moscow.

What about President Kennedy's televised speech? The one newspapers had announced he'd be giving that day—the announcement that had pushed Khrushchev to immediately end the most dangerous crisis in human history?

That was just a big misunderstanding.

Television listings in American papers *did* include a John Kennedy speech at 10:00 a.m. Washington time. But it was only a replay of his speech from six days earlier, the Oval Office address in which he'd announced the crisis to the world. The Soviet agent who'd read the listing had failed to pick up on that important detail.

As they say, fear has big eyes.

John and Bobby Kennedy enjoyed a quiet moment together in the Oval Office.

The American press was already playing the missile crisis up as a victory for Kennedy, sweet revenge for the beating he'd taken from Khrushchev during his first year in office. The brothers saw it that way, too—but didn't want to crow too loud in public. What if Khrushchev got angry at being taunted and changed his mind? What if he told the world that Kennedy had secretly promised to remove American missiles from Turkey? That would make the resolution of the crisis look less like an American victory and more like a compromise.

What was wrong with a compromise? Nothing, really, but

Kennedy planned to run for reelection in 1964. He preferred the version of the story in which he made the other guy blink.

As the brothers reviewed the gut-churning events of the last thirteen days, Kennedy wondered aloud whether he'd just lived through the high point of his presidency. He talked about Abraham Lincoln, who'd gone to a play right after winning the Civil War—and everyone knows how that turned out. Something about the gory image appealed to Kennedy's dark sense of humor.

"This is the night I should go to the theater," he said.

"If you go," Bobby said, "I want to go with you."

Five days later, just as the world was beginning to calm down, a telephone rang in Moscow. It was the line with the emergency number given only to Oleg Penkovsky.

A CIA agent lifted the receiver and held it to his ear.

On the other end, someone blew into the phone three times— *puff, puff, puff*—then hung up.

Sixty seconds passed. The phone rang again. The code was repeated.

This signal was designed to be used in one case only. It meant the Soviet Union was about to launch a nuclear strike.

REMATCH

BEFORE BURSTING INTO A FULL-BLOWN panic, CIA agents in Moscow made some quick calls to sources around the country. The Soviet military was not at a heightened level of alert. There was no special activity at Soviet missile bases or airfields.

Maybe World War III was not about to begin after all.

An agent ran out to check the lamppost on Kutuzovsky Prospekt. It was marked with a gray chalk X—Penkovsky's signal that he'd loaded his dead-drop.

The job of unloading the box went to a twenty-five-year-old CIA agent named Richard Jacob. As a precaution, Jacob cut a slit in one pocket of his long raincoat. He walked along crowded Moscow streets, slipping in and out of stores, dry-cleaning himself on the way to the dead-drop location. He stepped into the dingy lobby of an apartment building, reached his arm behind the radiator, and grabbed a matchbox hanging by a wire.

As he turned to leave, four large men charged in and wrestled him out to a waiting car. In the struggle, Jacob managed to drop the matchbox through the slit in his pocket—a clever bit of tradecraft, but it didn't help. The Russian agents scooped up the box, drove Jacob to a police station, and dragged him into a room where three men in suits were waiting to question him.

Jacob pulled out his diplomatic ID, which showed that he was a secretary and archivist at the American embassy. No one was buying it.

"Secretary-archivist," demanded one of the interrogators, "or spy?"

The exact details of Oleg Penkovsky's arrest are still hidden away in classified Russian files. But we know that once the missile crisis began, the KGB considered it too dangerous to have Penkovsky on the loose. We know they picked him up on October 22—the day of John Kennedy's dramatic televised speech. And we know Penkovsky talked. At the very least, he talked about the dead-drop location, and he described the CIA's secret telephone signal.

Which raises the question: Why did the Soviets use the phone signal?

They wanted to set a trap, apparently. They wanted to see who would come to empty the box.

Fine, but what about the fact that the phone signal meant nuclear war was about to begin? What if the Americans in Moscow had relayed this information straight to the White House? What if Kennedy had initiated an American response?

There are two possible explanations, both disturbing:

1. The KGB knew the meaning of the signal but used it anyway. They were willing to risk igniting a whole new crisis to catch a low-level American agent and score points against their arch-enemies at the CIA.

2. The KGB did not know the true meaning of the signal. Penkovsky told them how it worked, but not what it meant. According to this theory, Penkovsky knew he was a dead man and decided to take the whole world down with him.

Option one seems more likely.

Either way, the eighteen-month mission of the most valuable spy the United States ever ran in Russia was over. Putting it in the merciless terms of the spy game, CIA Director John McCone noted, "This source will be of no further value."

A week later, in West Berlin, Harry Seidel decided to attempt his seventh escape tunnel.

Seidel's mother was finally out of prison in the East. He'd vowed to get her out, and this was his chance. Though he'd always planned and run his own digs, this time, in a hurry to free his mother, he joined an ongoing project. Starting in a landscaping shed in the West, the tunnel went down 9 feet and burrowed toward the yard of a farmhouse on the other side of the wall, 250 feet away. Seidel moved into the shed and worked with his usual furious dedication, going home only to wash his clothes.

Before leaving for the final push, Seidel kissed his young son, Andre, goodbye.

"Be a good boy," Seidel said, "and in two days from now you'll be sitting on your granny's lap."

On the night of the escape, November 14, the diggers got the "all clear" signal from the farmhouse. The family that lived there was in on the plan and would be among the night's passengers. Seidel, as always, volunteered to open the hole. Standing on the shoulders of another digger, he punched through the top layer of soil and peeked above the grass.

The passengers should have come right out, but there was

no movement in the house. The yard was dark and quiet. Seidel picked up a few crumbs of dirt and tossed them at a window. No response.

He threw a pebble. It plinked off the glass. No response.

Seidel climbed up out of the hole. Easing a pistol from his pocket, he knocked softly on the front door.

The door flew open, and a squad of Stasi agents aimed machine guns at Seidel. He dropped his pistol. They shoved him outside, kicking him toward the tunnel opening as searchlights flooded the yard.

"Go away!" Seidel shouted toward the hole. "The tunnel is betrayed!"

One of the police officers smacked Seidel on the head with his gun, knocking him out—but his warning saved the other diggers, who raced back to safety in the West.

Harry Seidel was hauled to prison. It turned out the Stasi had known about the tunnel for days. They'd forced the family to give the "all clear" signal, then arrested everyone. The only good news was that Seidel's mother had not yet arrived at the house.

On December 11, the Soviet press officially announced Oleg Penkovsky's arrest and confession. When the news reached Britain, the public was particularly intrigued by the spy's alleged connection with a British citizen named Janet Chisholm. Reporters surrounded Chisholm's home in England, begging for juicy details. She was far too disciplined to offer any. Playing on the public's prejudice that a young mother would never be mixed up in international espionage, she asked, "Do I *look* like a spy?"

In an East German prison, Stasi agents grilled Harry Seidel day after day. He refused to talk. Even when the Stasi threatened him with the death penalty, Seidel would not identify a single fellow tunneler. "I only remember," he said, "that they all had short hair."

In Cuba, crews of Soviet soldiers dismantled the missile sites. They bulldozed the launch pads, drove the missiles to ports, loaded them onto ships, and sailed for home.

Feeling betrayed by his allies, Fidel Castro refused to even meet with the Soviet ambassador in Havana. "Cuba," he roared, "does not want to be a pawn on the world's chessboard!"

The four Soviet submarines limped back to their Arctic base. Promptly ordered to Moscow, the sub commanders were reprimanded for "allowing" themselves to be detected by the Americans. They found no sympathy for the misery and terror they'd endured at sea, no appreciation for the fact that they'd kept their heads under fire and prevented a catastrophic war. "It's a disgrace," charged the deputy minister of defense, shattering his glasses on the table. "You have shamed Russia."

In Washington, John Kennedy watched his approval rating rise to over 70 percent. His early mistakes finally behind him, Kennedy looked forward to winning reelection and taking on big issues at home and around the world. "Wait until 1964," he told friends.

Nikita Khrushchev also claimed victory in the missile crisis. "For the first time in history, the American imperialist beast was forced to swallow a hedgehog, quills and all," he declared. "I'm proud of what we did."

It was a generous interpretation. Most of the world saw Khrushchev's retreat as a sign of weakness. Soviet officials considered the entire episode a national humiliation. This really rankled Khrushchev—one setback was not the end of the world. It literally *could* have been the end of the world, and it wasn't.

It was a bit like a chess match between grandmasters. Such games never end in checkmate. Great players know when their position has become hopeless. They see exactly how they're going to lose, and they resign. It's not the end of the world.

The Soviet Union still had a Cold War to win. They still had an enemy to bury. The only thing to do was reset the pieces and play again.

EPILOGUE
CHOOSE YOUR OWN ENDING

"I PLEAD GUILTY IN ALL respects."

Oleg Penkovsky had to say that. His trial was scripted and judged before it even began.

"Vanity, vainglory, dissatisfaction with my work," he told the court, "and love of an easy life led me to the criminal path."

It was all over in a few hours. The judge found Penkovsky guilty of treason and sentenced him to be shot. On May 16, 1963, the Soviet newspaper *Pravda* noted: "The sentence has been executed."

In total, Penkovsky had passed nearly ten thousand pages of secrets on Soviet strengths and weaknesses to his American and British contacts. A CIA summary would call this "the most productive classic clandestine operation ever conducted by CIA and MI6 against the Soviet target."

Harry Seidel had as much chance of a fair trial in East Germany as Penkovsky did in the Soviet Union. For risking his life over and over to lead dozens of people to freedom, Seidel was charged with "organizing kidnappings, and luring persons to West Berlin." At age twenty-four, he was sentenced to life in prison with hard labor.

In West Berlin, Rotraut Seidel organized protests against her husband's harsh sentence. The pressure paid off. As part of what the press dubbed the "Bodies for Butter" program, East German dictator Walter Ulbricht accepted bribes of food from Western governments in exchange for the release of political prisoners. "For Seidel," the *Boston Globe* reported in 1966, "the Reds got a ransom of $95,000 in fruit."

Harry's mother, meanwhile, had escaped on her own.

Seidel returned to his family and to cycling, winning a national racing title with three teammates in 1973. He passed away in 2020 at age eighty-two.

After his exchange for Rudolf Abel—dramatized in Steven Spielberg's 2015 film *Bridge of Spies*—Francis Gary Powers was taken directly to a CIA safe house in rural Maryland and grilled for days on end. The CIA was particularly concerned that the pilot might have been drugged and brainwashed by the Russians. Between sessions, Powers was permitted to read newspapers. These were more upsetting than the interrogations, with headlines including:

HERO OR BUM?

A HERO OR A MAN WHO FAILED HIS MISSION?

Yes, Powers read in disbelief, they were talking about him.

Ignorant of the facts, articles blamed him for being shot down, for "allowing" himself to be captured by not using his poison pin. The CIA eventually cleared Powers of any suspicion of disloyalty—but did not explain to the public that pilots were never ordered to kill themselves, or even to carry the hollow coin with the poison needle.

Powers resigned from the CIA, split up with Barbara, and began a new life. He remarried, had a son, Francis Gary Powers Jr., and became a helicopter pilot and reporter for a Los Angeles television station. He died in a helicopter crash in 1977, at the age of forty-seven.

Thanks largely to the tireless work of his son, Powers was awarded the Silver Star by the Air Force in 2012.

Rudolf Abel enjoyed a less controversial post-spy life. Reunited with his wife, Elena, and daughter, Evelyn, Abel was greeted as a hero in the Soviet Union, celebrated for living under the Americans' noses for nine years. Abel gave lectures at schools, recounting his experiences in America and encouraging bright young men and women to consider a life of espionage. He was honest, though, about the differences between real-life and movie spies.

"Intelligence work is not a series of rip-roaring adventures, a string of tricks or an entertaining trip abroad," Abel cautioned. "It is, above all, arduous, painstaking work that calls for an intense effort, perseverance, stamina, fortitude, will power, serious knowledge and great mastery." Rudolf Abel died in Moscow in 1971, at the age of sixty-eight.

Lona Cohen, who'd helped the Soviets steal atomic secrets during World War II and was Rudolf Abel's first contact in New York, disappeared behind the iron curtain for several years before reinventing herself as a quirky Canadian named Helen Kroger. She and her husband, Morris, moved to suburban London and continued spying for the Russians. Caught and sentenced to twenty years in prison, she and Morris were eventually exchanged for a British prisoner held in the Soviet Union. Lona lived the rest of her life in a dacha outside Moscow, training younger spies. She died in 1992, at age seventy-nine.

Though he was supposed to be living in hiding in New England, Rudolf Abel's bumbling agent Reino Hayhanen was lured by the promise of $2,000 to appear on *David Brinkley's Journal*, a television news show. His face hidden in shadow, Hayhanen shared his impressions of Abel.

"I didn't like him. He was sneaky."

"But spies are supposed to be sneaky," Brinkley pointed out.

"Yes, but I'm not."

"Would they like to kill you?" Brinkley asked, referring to the KGB. Russian intelligence was—and still is—infamous for hunting down and murdering former agents.

"Hard job to find me," Hayhanen said. "They're trying hard."

They may have succeeded.

James Donovan, Rudolf Abel's lawyer, later wrote that Hayhanen died in what he described as a "mysterious" accident on the Pennsylvania Turnpike in the summer of 1961.

There are no police reports or hospital records of any such accident. The CIA, when questioned, would not comment on the case.

Following their capture at the Bay of Pigs, Pepe San Román, Erneido Oliva, and more than eleven hundred members of the invading brigade were sentenced to thirty years of hard labor. James Donovan, who negotiated the Abel-Powers trade, convinced Fidel Castro in December 1962 to release the prisoners in exchange for a shipment of food and medicine worth $53 million.

Handsome Johnny Rosselli, another of the many people who tried and failed to get rid of Castro, agreed to testify before a Senate committee in 1975. He detailed his role in the CIA's assassination plot, and even named high-level mobsters who helped in the effort. Asked by a friend whether he was worried about angering the mob, the seventy-year-old Rosselli shrugged.

"Who'd want to kill an old man like me?"

The following summer, Miami police fished a fifty-five-gallon oil drum from a city bay. Folded inside, a washcloth taped over the mouth, was the body of Handsome Johnny.

In Cuba, Fidel Castro held on to power long after Kennedy and Khrushchev were gone, even outliving the Cold War. His health failing, he stepped aside in 2006, handing power to his younger brother, Raúl. Castro remained controversial and defiant to the very end, dying in Havana in 2016, at the age of ninety.

Angry about the unfair treatment he and his fellow submariners faced upon their return to port, Vasili Arkhipov spoke little of his mission to Cuba in subsequent years. He died at age seventy-two of kidney cancer, a disease that afflicted many of the sailors who survived the K-19 disaster. In 2012, fifty years after the Cuban missile crisis, Vasili's wife proudly told his story in a documentary titled, fittingly, *The Man Who Saved the World*.

Andrei Sakharov, father of the Soviet Union's hydrogen bomb and designer of the largest explosive ever detonated on earth, did his part to save the world, too. After the Big Ivan test, Sakharov spoke out about the danger of nuclear fallout. Hounded by the government and banned from doing secret military work, he continued to argue against the development of new weapons, and in favor of human rights and greater political freedom for Soviet citizens. "Never trust a government that doesn't trust its own people," he often said. Sakharov was awarded the Nobel Peace

Prize in 1975—though the Soviet government did not permit him to leave the country to receive the prize. Sakharov died in Moscow in 1989, at sixty-eight.

Yuri Gagarin never got back into space. The world-famous cosmonaut was too busy traveling the world, greeting cheering crowds and dining with dignitaries. At a formal breakfast in London's Buckingham Palace, Gagarin stared down at a table setting more perplexing than any cockpit.

"Your Highness," he said, turning to Queen Elizabeth, "you know this is the first time I've had breakfast with the Queen of Great Britain, and it's very difficult to know which cutlery to use."

This was not the proper way to address the monarch. She loved it.

"You know," said the queen, "I was born in this palace, but I still get mixed up."

Returning to the Soviet Union, Gagarin trained five female cosmonaut candidates. In 1963, he proudly watched Valentina Tereshkova become the first woman to fly to space—beating the Americans in this important achievement by twenty years. Gagarin dreamed of getting back in the game himself, but the Soviet government considered him too valuable as a celebrity to risk on space flight. Still, he couldn't shake the dream. When the great rocket designer Sergei Korolev died in 1966, Gagarin said, "I won't feel right until I've taken Korolev's ashes to the moon." Gagarin began training in a MiG fighter jet, relearning the feel of the controls. He was killed in a crash in 1968, less than three weeks after he'd turned thirty-four.

The following year, American astronauts Neil Armstrong and Buzz Aldrin walked on the moon. They left behind, on the dusty gray surface, a medal honoring Yuri Gagarin.

* * *

"As you look back upon your first two years in office, sir, has your experience in the office matched your expectations?"

"Well, I think in the first place the problems are more difficult than I had imagined," John Kennedy told the reporter. "It is much easier to make the speeches than it is to finally make the judgments."

Every president would agree with that.

Kennedy kept his promise to Khrushchev, removing the American missiles from Turkey in April 1963. Asked by the press if this was part of some secret deal with the Soviets, Kennedy dodged the question, claiming it was a matter of routine upgrades—and pointing out that the same targets could easily be hit by American submarines in the Mediterranean Sea.

In June 1963, Kennedy enjoyed his greatest moment on the world stage, speaking to a crowd of nearly half a million in the shadow of the Berlin Wall.

"Freedom has many difficulties," he declared, "and democracy is not perfect, but we have never had to put a wall up to keep our people in." He repeated America's commitment to defend West Berlin and all it stood for. "All free men, wherever they may live, are citizens of Berlin," Kennedy said to a roaring ovation. "And therefore, as a free man, I take pride in the words 'Ich bin ein Berliner!'"

I am a Berliner!

Or, possibly, *I am a jelly doughnut!*

There's a jelly-filled German pastry called a "Berliner."

After some consultation, German grammar experts agreed that Kennedy had spoken correctly.

To deal with each other more effectively in the future, Kennedy and Khrushchev established a "hotline"—a direct phone line from Moscow to Washington. They agreed to the Limited

Test Ban Treaty, the first nuclear arms control agreement, banning nuclear tests everywhere but underground. Kennedy considered the treaty his greatest achievement, a real step away from World War III.

His confidence high, his back feeling better than it had since the tree-planting fiasco over two years before, he traveled to Texas for political events in a state that would be vital to his hopes for reelection. John Kennedy was assassinated in Dallas on November 22, 1963. He was forty-six.

Nearly a year later, at his vacation home on the Black Sea, Nikita Khrushchev picked up the phone and heard the voice of Leonid Brezhnev, the second most powerful man in the Soviet government. Brezhnev told Khrushchev to return immediately to Moscow. The Presidium would be meeting tomorrow.

"Why?" asked Khrushchev. "On what issue?"

"On agriculture and some others."

"Decide things without me!"

"Members have already gathered," Brezhnev said. "We are asking you to come."

Khrushchev knew there was no pressing agriculture issue. His prestige had never fully recovered from the Cuban missile crisis. Younger leaders were impatient for their chance to take over. Clearly, they were ready to make their move.

The next day, his face pink from the sun, Khrushchev walked into the Presidium meeting room and took his chairman's seat at the long table. The scene was a bit like his showdown with Lavrenty Beria eleven years earlier. Only this time, he was the one without the script.

Brezhnev led the attack. Khrushchev made rash decisions, he charged. He didn't listen to advice.

"Why are you doing this?" Khrushchev asked. "Why?"

"Wait a minute. You listen to us for a change."

The other Presidium members took turns taking shots:

"Hasty, erratic, and inclined to intrigues."

"Coarse and rude."

"Infected with conceit."

"You love ovations."

Unlike Beria, Khrushchev was not arrested and executed. He lost his Moscow home and luxurious dachas but was permitted a quiet, comfortable retirement.

He hated it. "He'd repeat bitterly that his life was over," his son Sergei would later recall, "that life made sense as long as people needed him, but now, when nobody needed him, life was meaningless."

Nikita Khrushchev died of a heart attack in 1971. He was seventy-seven.

The drama and danger of the Cold War continued without Kennedy and Khrushchev.

The new Soviet leaders quickly expanded their stockpile of nuclear weapons. They'd been forced to back down in Cuba but did not plan to allow that to happen again. The United States kept pace, and the total number of nuclear weapons in the world rose from around twenty-nine thousand at the time of the Cuban missile crisis to a high of over sixty-nine thousand in the mid-1980s.

This is when I joined the story, as a cynical teenager obsessed with nuclear apocalypse movies—everything from the darkly funny *War Games* to the relentless nightmare of *The Day After*, still the most widely watched TV movie of all time. I was disgusted with supposedly intelligent leaders who talked casually about "mutually assured destruction"—MAD. The idea was that both the United States and the Soviet Union could destroy each other many, many times over—so don't worry! Neither side would be crazy enough to make the first move!

I was pretty sure there'd be a nuclear war before I finished high school.

Then things changed very quickly.

Freedom movements gained ground in Eastern Europe and many parts of the Soviet Union. The Soviets were struggling economically—partly because they were spending so much money trying to keep up in the arms race and partly because their communist system simply didn't work. The tipping point came in Berlin, in November 1989, when the East German government gave in to pressure to ease travel across the Berlin Wall. Crowds on both sides climbed atop the despised divider with pickaxes and literally began knocking it down. Communist governments collapsed all over Eastern Europe, and in 1991, the once mighty Soviet Union broke apart, leaving behind Russia and fourteen newly independent states.

The Cold War was over.

Though, as you've no doubt noticed, the United States and Russia have remained rivals.

Today, arms control agreements have lowered the global nuclear stockpile to about thirteen thousand, mostly in the hands of Russia and the United States. Seven other countries possess nuclear arsenals: China, France, the United Kingdom, Pakistan, India, Israel, and North Korea. Will any of these weapons ever be used?

That story is still unfolding. We don't know how it ends.

Finally, with hindsight, how close did the world really come to World War III in October 1962? How close did humans come to wiping our species off the planet? How does the Cuban missile crisis compare with twenty-first-century threats such as terrorism, climate change, and pandemic disease?

This is open to discussion and debate. But it's interesting to hear from the people who were there.

After the Cold War, former U.S. and Soviet officials began meeting to share their recollections of the crisis, their fears, even their secrets. It was at these meetings that Americans first learned that the four Soviet subs had been armed with nuclear torpedoes. And that the Soviets had dozens of hydrogen bomb warheads in Cuba during the crisis—plus tactical nukes that Soviet commanders were ready and willing to use if attacked.

"This was not only the most dangerous moment of the Cold War," concluded Arthur Schlesinger, a Kennedy aide during the crisis. "It was the most dangerous moment in human history."

Robert McNamara, secretary of defense during the crisis, came to what I consider to be a far more disturbing conclusion. One I believe we'd better keep in mind as we face the dangers of the present and the future.

"At the end, we lucked out," McNamara said of the world's narrow escape in 1962. "It was luck that prevented nuclear war."

My big takeaway is that these guys were smart—and they nearly blew up the planet. We can be smarter. From now on, no matter what type of threat we're facing, let's not depend on luck.

SOURCE NOTES

Each source note includes a key phrase, description, or quote, along with the page number on which the phrase, details, or quote appears. Subsequent quotes from the same conversation are from the same source, unless otherwise noted.

The Paperboy

1 Jimmy Bozart's nickel story: Joseph Donnelly, "Boy's Story of Spy Film in Hollow Nickel," *Daily News* (New York), September 21, 1957; Nathan Ward, "The Hollow Nickel Kid: Real-Life Brooklyn Newsboy Played a Huge Part in 'Bridge of Spies' Case," *Daily News* (New York), November 4, 2015; Associated Press, "RPI Student Helped Nab Soviet Spy," *Troy* (NY) *Record*, September 21, 1957; FBI Rudolf Abel case file 15; Whittell, *Bridge of Spies*, 21–23.

3 "You're Bozart?" and detective's other lines: Jim Dwyer, "Sidelight to a Spy Saga: How a Brooklyn Newsboy's Nickel Would Turn into a Fortune," *New York Times*, November 3, 2015; Whittell, *Bridge of Spies*, 23.

Cold Warrior

10 "It's not suitable for a magic trick": FBI Rudolf Abel case file 15, p. 5.

11 "I would rather perish than betray the secrets": Whittell, *Bridge of Spies*, 15.

11 Rudolf Abel background: Whittell, *Bridge of Spies*, 7–13; J. Donovan, *Strangers*, 18; Andrew and Mitrokhin, *Sword and the Shield*, 146–47.

13 "An iron curtain has descended": The full text of Churchill's famous speech "Sinews of Peace" can be found at the website of the National Churchill Museum at Westminster College, in Fulton, Missouri, where the speech was given on March 5, 1946. nationalchurchillmuseum.org/sinews-of -peace-iron-curtain-speech.html.

13 Abel's journey to New York: Bernikow, *Abel*, 1–3; Whittell, *Bridge of Spies*, 14–15.

Hollow Coin #1

15 Abel's meeting with Cohen: Whittell, *Bridge of Spies*, 17; Albright and Kunstel, *Bombshell*, 197–98; Carr, *Operation Whisper*, 193.

16 Truman's announcement of the hydrogen bomb: Anthony Leviero, "Truman Orders Hydrogen Bomb Built for Security Pending an Atomic Pact," *New York Times*, February 1, 1950.

17 Sokolov's visit to the Cohens' apartment: Albright and Kunstel, *Bombshell*, 3–6.

18 Abel's spy gadgets: Gibney, "Russian Master Spy," 123; Albright and Kunstel, *Bombshell*, 245; FBI Rudolf Abel case file 2, p. 20; Mildred Murphy, "F.B.I. Sifts Abel's Possessions for Possible Clues to Espionage," *New York Times*, August 9, 1957.

The Super

19 "Have you got a problem for me to solve?": Kaplan, *Wizards of Armageddon*, 83.

21 Science behind the idea for the Super: Rhodes, *Dark Sun*, 246–55; DeGroot, *The Bomb: A Life*, 162–63; York, *The Advisors*, 20–21.

22 Oppenheimer opposes Super: Rhodes, *Dark Sun*, 403.

22 Teller's work on Super: Ulam, *Adventures of a Mathematician*, 213–17; Rhodes, *Dark Sun*, 460–62; Hargittai, *Judging Edward Teller*, 207–17.

23 "I found a way to make it work": Françoise Ulam recalls this scene in a postscript to Ulam, *Adventures of a Mathematician*, 311.

23 Teller-Ulam configuration basics: De-Groot, *The Bomb: A Life*, 175; Rhodes, *Dark Sun*, 466–70.

24 "the test program included experiments": Jay Walz, "Experiments for Hydrogen Bomb Held Successfully at Eniwetok," *New York Times*, November 17, 1952.

24 "You would swear": United Press, "Flash Is Described," *New York Times*, November 17, 1952.

24 *Daily News* on test: "U.S. First with H-Bomb," editorial, *Daily News* (New York), November 18, 1952.

The Long Game

27 "Well, go": Khrushchev recalls this scene in N. Khrushchev, *Khrushchev Remembers*, 290.

28 "They think something has happened": N. Khrushchev, *Khrushchev Remembers*, 316.

28 Stalin's stroke and Beria's reaction: Taubman, *Khrushchev*, 237–39; N. Khrushchev, *Khrushchev Remembers*, 317–21.

29 Khrushchev background: Taubman, *Khrushchev*, 21–109; Beschloss, *Mayday*, 164–71; S. Khrushchev, *Nikita Khrushchev*, 6–21; Zubok and Pleshakov, *Inside the Kremlin's Cold War*, 175–80.

30 "Our hand must not tremble": Taubman, *Khrushchev*, 99.

30 "Listen, Comrade Malenkov": N. Khrushchev, *Khrushchev Remembers*, 330.

31 *You scoundrel*: Taubman, *Khrushchev*, 252.

31 Beria arrest scene: N. Khrushchev, *Khrushchev Remembers*, 336–37; Taubman, *Khrushchev*, 254–55.

32 "Today Beria has been arrested": Sergei Khrushchev recalls this scene in *Nikita Khrushchev*, 36.

The Worst Spy

33 Abel's life in New York and his Brooklyn studio: Bernikow, *Abel*, 7–10, 17–20; J. Donovan, *Strangers*, 137–38.

35 Hayhanen arrival in New York: Bernikow, *Abel*, 37; Whittell, *Bridge of Spies*, 20–21; FBI Rudolf Abel case file 7, pp. 10–11.

35 Lamphere's work on coded message: Lamphere and Shachtman, *FBI-KGB War*, 270–72.

35 One-time pad description: Singh, *Code Book*, 120–24; Lamphere and Shachtman, *FBI-KGB War*, 80–81.

37 Abel and Hayhanen meet: J. Donovan, *Strangers*, 23; Bernikow, *Abel*, 46–47.

The Turtle and the Dragon

38 Televised atomic bomb test: The film and photos of this test, March 17, 1953, can easily be found online; search for "Operation Doorstep."

39 "Prepare now against the threat": *Operation Doorstep*, Federal Civil Defense Administration film, 1953.

39 government-made instructional film: *Duck and Cover*, Federal Civil Defense Administration film, 1951.

41 *Lucky Dragon* details: Ropeik, "Unlucky Lucky Dragon"; Lapp, *Voyage of the Lucky Dragon*, 27–33. The Atomic Heritage Foundation website has information on the *Lucky Dragon* and a film of the H-bomb test, which was code-named Castle Bravo, atomicheritage.org/history/castle-bravo.

41 "The sun rises in the west!": Lapp, *Voyage of the Lucky Dragon*, 28.

42 "I don't know exactly what happened": Lapp, *Voyage of the Lucky Dragon*, 57.

42 "Please make sure that I am the last victim": Graff, *Raven Rock*, 49.

42 *Godzilla* origin story: Ropeik, "Unlucky Lucky Dragon."

Early Warning

44 "Attention! The plane is over the target": Sakharov, *Memoirs*, 190–92; Rhodes, *Dark Sun*, 569.

44 Sakharov's H-bomb design: Gorelik, "Riddle of the Third Idea."

45 "It worked!": Sakharov, *Memoirs*, 191.

45 Sakharov describes his mixed emotions: Sakharov, *Memoirs*, 193.

45 "May all our devices explode": Sakharov, *Memoirs*, 194.

45 "We, the inventors, scientists, engineers, and craftsmen": Sakharov, *Memoirs*, 194.

46 Nuclear arsenal figures: Rhodes, *Dark Sun*, 562; Norris and Kristensen, "Global Nuclear Weapons Inventories." Current year totals can be found at "World Nuclear Weapon Stockpile," Ploughshares Fund, ploughshares.org/world -nuclear-stockpile-report.

46 Colonel Shoup's Santa call: International News Service, "More May Follow Santa's Route, Youngster Learns," *Pasadena (CA) Independent*, December 1, 1955; Steve Hendrix, "A Child Calling Santa Reached NORAD Instead. Christmas Eve Was Never the Same," *Washington Post*, December 24, 2018.

47 Lieutenant Powers's recruitment: F. G. Powers, *Operation Overflight*, 7–10; also F. G. Powers Jr., *Spy Pilot*, 41–42.

47 "I was told to ask for a Mr. William Collins": F. G. Powers, *Operation Overflight*, 8.

Secret World

48 Barbara Moore background: B. Powers, *Spy Wife*, 15.

48 "Golly, I'd sure like to meet": B. Powers, *Spy Wife*, 14.

49 Frank and Barbara talk over the offer: F. G.

Powers, *Operation Overflight*, 9; B. Powers, *Spy Wife*, 22.

49 "How do you feel about it now?": F. G. Powers, *Operation Overflight*, 11.

50 "What do you call it?": F. G. Powers, *Operation Overflight*, 26.

51 Area 51 and U-2 pilots: F. G. Powers, *Operation Overflight*, 31–32; Whittell, *Bridge of Spies*, 56–58; Reel, *Brotherhood of Spies*, 66–67.

51 U-2 details and challenges: Whittell, *Bridge of Spies*, 59; F. G. Powers, *Operation Overflight*, 33–35; Reel, *Brotherhood of Spies*, 95–96.

52 "Why do you have to go": F. G. Powers Jr., *Spy Pilot*, 49.

53 Eisenhower's mixed feelings on U-2: Beschloss, *Mayday*, 6; Reel, *Brotherhood of Spies*, 102.

53 Soviet reaction to first overflight: Reel, *Brotherhood of Spies*, 118; S. Khrushchev, "Day We Shot Down the U-2."

53 Khrushchev's love of proverbs: Sergei Khrushchev describes this and refers to many of his father's favorites throughout his book *Nikita Khrushchev*; every Khrushchev biography covers this, including Taubman, *Khrushchev*.

We Will Bury You

55 "Most of these are still in progress:" Bernikov, *Abel*, 11; Silverman, "Spy Who Duped My Dad."

57 "Whether you like it or not": "Ambassadors Walk Out: Protest at Speech by Mr. Khrushchev," *Times* (London), November 19, 1956, in Whittell, *Bridge of Spies*, 44; Reeves, *President Kennedy*, 37.

57 Abel's frustrations with Hayhanen: Gibney, "Russian Master Spy," 126; Whittell, *Bridge of Spies*, 29–30.

58 "I'm an officer in the Soviet intelligence service": FBI Rudolf Abel case file 15, p. 5.

58 Abel arrest scene: FBI Rudolf Abel case file 6, pp. 38–46; Whittell, *Bridge of Spies*, 93–94.

59 "WE CONGRATULATE YOU": Lamphere, *FBI-KGB War*, 274.

59 Headlines: "Brooklyn Artist Arrested as Red Spy," *Santa Cruz (CA) Sentinel*, August 7, 1957; "Top Russian Spy Caught," *Corpus Christi (TX) Times*, August 7, 1957; "U.S. Unmasks Master Spy," *Vancouver (BC) Sun*, August 7, 1957.

59 "Ladies and gentlemen": Reel, *Brotherhood of Spies*, 145.

60 "America sleeps under a Soviet moon": "Yuri Gagarin: The Man Who Fell to Earth," *Independent* (London), April 3, 2011.

60 Abel's trial and conviction: See J. Donovan, *Strangers*, 115–265, for full coverage of trial, including testimony; Whittell, *Bridge of Spies*, 101–3.

60 "This is an offense directed at our very existence": Whittell, *Bridge of Spies*, 108.

61 Barbara Powers was lonely: B. Powers, *Spy Wife*, 26.

Man or Monster?

62 "I might as well tell you": B. Powers, *Spy Wife*, 27–28.

63 "There she is, the U-2!": B. Powers, *Spy Wife*, 60.

63 L-pill described: Reel, *Brotherhood of Spies*, 106; Whittell, *Bridge of Spies*, 69.

64 "Khrushchev: Man or Monster?": This series of articles ran in the New York *Daily News*, September 8–12, 1959.

64 Khrushchev in America: The *American Experience* film *Cold War Roadshow*, first aired in 2014, covers this story, with extensive footage of the visit; also Carlson, "Nikita Khrushchev Goes to Hollywood"; Taubman, *Khrushchev*, 424–35.

65 "Just now, I was told that I could not go": Carlson, "Nikita Khrushchev Goes to Hollywood."

65 Khrushchev and Eisenhower at Camp David: Taubman, *Khrushchev*, 435–38; N. Khrushchev, *Khrushchev Remembers*, 519; Reel, *Brotherhood of Spies*, 160.

67 Eisenhower continues overflights: Beschloss, *Mayday*, 9.

Hollow Coin #2

68 Powers gets the hollow silver dollar: F. G. Powers, *Operation Overflight*, 70–71.

68 "What if something happens": F. G. Powers, 72.

69 Powers describes his May 1 flight: F. G. Powers, 74–84.

70 Khrushchev gets news of overflight: S. Khrushchev, *Nikita Khrushchev*, 369; Taubman, *Khrushchev*, 442.

70 "They've flown over us, again": S. Khrushchev, "Day We Shot Down the U-2"; S. Khrushchev, *Nikita Khrushchev*, 369; Taubman, *Khrushchev*, 443.

71 "My God!" and shoot-down details: F. G. Powers, *Operation Overflight*, 84–90.

72 May Day parade: Taubman, *Khrushchev*, 446; F. G. Powers Jr., *Spy Pilot*, 71; Associated Press, "Millions Attend May Day Fetes," *Los Angeles Times*, May 2, 1960.

Zugzwang

75 Eisenhower at Camp David on May 1: Beschloss, *Mayday*, 33; Reel, *Brotherhood of Spies*, 186.

75 "One of our reconnaissance planes": Beschloss, *Mayday*, 34.

76 "It would be impossible, if things should go wrong": Reel, *Brotherhood of Spies*, 107.

76 Khrushchev's family home: Dobbs, *One Minute to Midnight*, 33; Sergei Khrushchev also described this home to me in a phone interview, May 7, 2020.

77 "Mr. President, I have received word": Beschloss, *Mayday*, 37.

77 "The most powerful weapon in chess": Chernev, *200 Brilliant Endgames*, 59.

77 Khrushchev lays his trap: Zubok and Pleshakov, *Inside the Kremlin's Cold War*, 203.

77 Khrushchev visits trade fair: Associated Press, "Khrushchev Rings the Bell with

a Rifle Shot," *Los Angeles Times*, May 4, 1960; "Khrushchev Fires a Rifle and Barbs," *New York Times*, May 4, 1960.

78   Operation Alert, New York City details: Garrison, *Bracing for Armageddon*, 26; Reel, *Brotherhood of Spies*, 3–6; Peter Kihss, "Nation Takes Cover in Air-Raid Alert," *New York Times*, May 4, 1960; Peter Kihss, "Governor Thanks Workers in Alert," *New York Times*, May 5, 1960; "Civil Defense Drill Briefly Halts Business and Baseball," *Wall Street Journal*, May 4, 1960.

78   President Eisenhower's phony cover story: United Press International, "AF Searching for Lost Plane," *Miami News*, May 4, 1960.

Alive and Kicking

80   "Comrade Deputies, I must report to you": Beschloss, *Mayday*, 43.

81   "Correct! Correct!" and other responses from officials: Beschloss, *Mayday*, 44; Union of Soviet Journalists, *Aggressors Must Be Sent to the Pillory: The Truth About the Provocative Intrusion of the American Plane in the Air Space of the USSR* (Moscow, 1960), 2, in "Soviet Version of the U-2 Incident," CIA, June 9, 1960, cia.gov/library/readingroom/docs /CIA-RDP80T00246A074400420001-9 .pd.CIA report.

81   "Where's my husband?": B. Powers, *Spy Wife*, 67.

82   Operation Alert 1960, White House details: Reel, *Brotherhood of Spies*, 7; Graff, *Raven Rock*, 90.

82   "I am not sure whether I would really want to be living": Graff, *Raven Rock*, 86.

82   Mount Weather details: Reel, *Brotherhood of Spies*, 7–8; Graff, *Raven Rock*, 86; George, *Awaiting Armageddon*, 45; Gup, "Civil Defense Doomsday Hideaway."

83   "It is entirely possible": Reel, *Brotherhood of Spies*, 191.

83   "Comrades, I must let you in on a secret": Beschloss, *Mayday*, 58.

Center Stage

85   "Unbelievable": Beschloss, *Mayday*, 65.

86   "Why should I bother answering": F. G. Powers, *Operation Overflight*, 134.

87   "But they're in Russian": F. G. Powers, 128.

87   Khrushchev meets the student: "Strolling Russian Greets Parisians," *New York Times*, May 17, 1960.

87   "We are gathered here for the Summit": Taubman, *Khrushchev*, 462.

87   "President de Gaulle, Prime Minister Macmillan": "Texts of Khrushchev and Eisenhower Statements on Summit and the Plane Case," *New York Times*, May 17, 1960.

88   "I'm just fed up!": Beschloss, *Mayday*, 290.

88   "If you boo us and attack us": Flanner, *Letter from Paris*, 150; Beschloss, *Mayday*, 299; *Pravda*, May 19, 1960, in Taubman, *Khrushchev*, 466.

89   "Tonight I want to talk with you": Dwight D. Eisenhower, "Radio and Television Report to the American People on the Events in Paris," May 25, 1960, Dwight D. Eisenhower Presidential Library, audio, 28:02 mins., eisenhowerlibrary.gov /eisenhowers/speeches.

89   Powers Moscow trial: F. G. Powers, *Operation Overflight*, 163–96; B. Powers, *Spy Wife*, 99–106.

Little Boy Blue

91   "Drop dead, you scum!": Beschloss, *Mayday*, 338.

91   "Roses are red": Taubman, *Khrushchev*, 474.

92   Castro-Khrushchev meeting: Szulc, *Fidel*, 526–27; Fursenko and Naftali, *"One Hell of a Gamble,"* 60; S. Khrushchev, *Nikita Khrushchev*, 411.

92   Castro at the U.N.: Anita Ehrman, "U.S. Plans Attack, Castro Charges," *San Francisco Examiner*, September 27, 1960; Peter Wallenberg, "Castro Heaps Abuse on Nixon, Kennedy," *Daily News* (New

York), September 27, 1960; "What Is the Longest Speech Given at the United Nations?," Dag Hammarskjöld Library, United Nations, Oct. 15, 2019, ask.un .org/friendly.php?slug=faq/37127.

93 The CIA and Johnny Rosselli: Details of the assassination plot can be found in the agency's "Family Jewels" file— seriously, that's what the agency called it. In 1973, the CIA director ordered employees to tell him about all agency activities, current or past, that might be illegal. The full seven-hundred-page collection of agency misdeeds was declassified and released in 2007. The document can be downloaded from the CIA Library, cia.gov/library /readingroom/collection/family-jewels. Searchable files can be found at the National Security Archive, nsarchive2 .gwu.edu/NSAEBB/NSAEBB222/.

94 "The Soviets have made a spectacle": Beschloss, *Mayday*, 339.

94 "kind of man Mr. Khrushchev": Associated Press, "Economic Proposals Attacked: Republican Talks in Pennsylvania," *Charlotte* (NC) *Observer*, October 25, 1960.

94 "As we Russians say": Kempe, *Berlin*, 37.

95 "the deciding ballot": Beschloss, *Mayday*, 341.

95 "that young whippersnapper" and "Little Boy Blue": Reeves, *President Kennedy*, 22.

95 "It's a high-stakes poker game": Reeves, *President Kennedy*, 32.

95 Nuclear football details: Rasenberger, *Brilliant Disaster*, 108; Kempe, *Berlin*, 49; Dobbs, "Real Story of the 'Football.'"

96 "Watch this": Reeves, *President Kennedy*, 30; "Kennedy Given Example of Fast Helicopter Service," *Washington Post*, January 20, 1961.

96 Francis Gary Powers's life in prison: F. G. Powers, *Operation Overflight*, 208–28.

97 Barbara Powers's life in Georgia: B. Powers, *Spy Wife*, 117–18.

97 Rudolf Abel's life in prison: Bernikov, *Abel*, 248.

97 Reino Hayhanen's life in hiding: Bernikov, *Abel*, 246.

97 Jimmy Bozart details: Jim Dwyer, "Sidelight to a Spy Saga: How a Brooklyn Newsboy's Nickel Would Turn into a Fortune," *New York Times*, November 3, 2015.

97 Rosselli's team: Server, *Handsome Johnny*, 319–86, covers the plot in great detail.

98 "No easy matters will ever come to you": Reeves, *President Kennedy*, 23.

Origin Story

103 "This is how it feels to be killed": Hersey, "Survival."

103 "Everybody into the water!": R. Donovan, *PT 109*, 110.

104 "I'll take McMahon with me": Doyle, *PT 109*, 116.

104 PT-109 details: Doyle, Donovan, and Hersey cover this story in great detail; Paul Vitello, "Eroni Kumana, Who Saved Kennedy and His Shipwrecked Crew, Dies at 96," *New York Times*, August 16, 2014; Brown, "Solomon Islanders." The John F. Kennedy Presidential Library has extensive records of the story, most of which are available at jfklibrary.org/.

105 Kumana and Gasa find PT-109 survivors: Doyle, *PT 109*, 143–48.

106 "Navy! Navy!": R. Donovan, *PT 109*, 48.

106 "And so, my fellow Americans": A film and full transcript of Kennedy's inaugural address are available at the JFK Library website, jfklibrary.org/learn/about-jfk /historic-speeches/inaugural-address; detail of him practicing in tub and at breakfast: Reeves, *President Kennedy*, 34.

107 "It was easy—they sank my boat": Sorensen, *Kennedy*, 18.

107 Kennedy inauguration details: Rasenberger, *Brilliant Disaster*, 114–16; Lincoln, *My Twelve Years*, 227; Reeves, *President Kennedy*, 35–36; Edward T.

Folliard, "Kennedy Takes Oath as President," *Washington Post*, January 21, 1961.

108 "Let every nation know": John F. Kennedy, Inaugural Address, January 20, 1961, transcript, JFK Library.

First Pitch

110 Evelyn Lincoln arrives at the White House and interior details: Lincoln, *My Twelve Years*, 227–30; O'Donnell and Powers, *"Johnny,"* 288; Salinger, *With Kennedy*, 107, 130.

111 "This desk is too big": Lincoln, *My Twelve Years*, 229.

111 Jacqueline Kennedy remodels: Lincoln, *My Twelve Years*, 240; O'Donnell and Powers, *"Johnny,"* 288.

111 North Carolina H-bomb accident: Schlosser, *Command and Control*, 245–47; Lacey-Bordeaux, "Declassified Report"; Ed Pilkington, "U.S. Nearly Detonated Atomic Bomb over North Carolina: Secret Document," *Guardian* (Manchester, UK), September 20, 2013.

112 "By the slightest margin of chance": Bureau of Politico-Military Affairs, "State-Defense Meeting on Group I, II and IV Papers," memorandum of conversation, January 26, 1963, National Archives Record Group 59, available at "Documents on Predelegation of Authority for Nuclear Weapons Use," National Security Archive, nsarchive2.gwu.edu/news/predelegation/pd15_01.htm; "You Won't Believe How Close North Carolina Came to Total Nuclear Annihilation," *Time*, June 12, 2014, video, 2:02 mins., time.com/2866020/north-carolina-nuclear-bombs/.

112 Rosselli plot details: Rasenberger, *Brilliant Disaster*, 142–43; U.S. Senate, *Alleged Assassination Plots Involving Foreign Leaders*, interim report of the Select Committee to Study Governmental Operations with Respect to Intelligence Activities (November 20, 1975), 74–82.

113 "It sounds like D-Day": Reeves, *President Kennedy*, 70.

114 "Did you see the paper?": Senate, *Alleged Assassination Plots*, 82.

115 Kennedy throws out first pitch: Edward T. Folliard, "Kennedy Throws Out First Ball, Eats Hot Dog as Senators Lose," *Washington Post*, April 11, 1961; Arthur Edson, "Baseball Frontier," *Democrat and Chronicle* (Rochester, NY), April 11, 1961.

115 San Román leads men toward invasion: Johnson, *Bay of Pigs*, 77.

The Countdown

116 R-7 taken to launch pad: Cadbury, *Space Race*, 231.

116 Korolev and R-7 details: Harford, *Korolev*, 92; Cadbury, *Space Race*, 139.

117 Ivan Ivanovich story details: Doran and Bizony, *Starman*, 75; Teitel, "Ivan Ivanovich"; Garber, "The Doll." Ivan now lives in the National Air and Space Museum in Washington, DC.

117 "The West will think the cosmonaut has lost his mind": Doran and Bizony, *Starman*, 76.

118 Gagarin training: Doran and Bizony, *Starman*, 29–38; Burchett and Purdy, *Cosmonaut Yuri Gagarin*, 105–6; Golovanov, *Our Gagarin*, 54–60.

119 Gagarin and Titov before launch: Golovanov, *Our Gagarin*, 104; Doran and Bizony, *Starman*, 88–89.

120 "It's been ages since I've had anything so tasty": Golovanov, *Our Gagarin*, 123.

120 Prelaunch details: Doran and Bizony, *Starman*, 91–102.

121 "Yura," he whispered: Doran and Bizony, *Starman*, 94.

121 "Complete silence in the control room": Golovanov, *Our Gagarin*, 133.

121 Control room radio conversation: Golovanov, *Our Gagarin*, 133–34; Cadbury, *Space Race*, 234–37.

122 "Poyekhali": Doran and Bizony, *Starman*, 102.

Over America

124 "T-plus seventy" and other lines between Gagarin and Korolev: Doran and Bizony, *Starman*, 102; Golovanov, *Our Gagarin*, 138.

124 Gagarin's flight details: Cadbury, *Space Race*, 238–40; Golovanov, *Our Gagarin*, 135–140; Doran and Bizony, *Starman*, 104–6.

125 Science of weightlessness: There are lots of explanations and diagrams online; one good explanation is provided in S. May, "What Is Microgravity?"

125 "How far?": Doran and Bizony, *Starman*, 106.

126 "Why is the radio off?": Golovanov, *Our Gagarin*, 143.

126 "The world's first satellite ship": Cadbury, *Space Race*, 239.

126 Gagarin's reentry details: Harford, *Korolev*, 173–74; Cadbury, *Space Race*, 240; Doran and Bizony, *Starman*, 112–13.

127 "I'm a friend, comrades!": Doran and Bizony, *Starman*, 119.

128 "It's 3 in the morning": United Press International, "Puts Snooze Before News," *Daily News* (New York), April 13, 1961.

128 Headlines: "Spokesman Says U.S. Asleep": Shepard and Slayton, *Moon Shot*, 97, in Doran and Bizony, *Starman*, 114; "Puts Snooze Before News": *Daily News* (New York), April 13, 1961.

128 "Tell me, how did you feel": Doran and Bizony, *Starman*, 124.

128 "What can we do? How can we catch up": Doran and Bizony, *Starman*, 142.

129 "Well," Kennedy began: John F. Kennedy, press conference, Washington, DC, April 12, 1963, in Reeves, *President Kennedy*, 86.

129 Castro watches Kennedy: Rasenberger, *Brilliant Disaster*, 185.

The Bay of Pigs

130 "Have no fear" and Castro revolution details: Perrottet, "How Cuba Remembers"; Szulc, *Fidel*, 376–459; Triay, *Bay of Pigs*, 3–5; "Fidel Castro, Cuban Revolutionary Who Defied U.S., Dies at 90," *New York Times*, November 26, 2016.

132 Bay of Pigs landing details: Triay, *Bay of Pigs: An Oral History*, includes many accounts from San Román's brigade; Johnson, *Bay of Pigs*, 103–11; Rasenberger, *Brilliant Disaster*, 231–37; Dille, "We Who Tried," 21–33, 69–83.

132 "Chico," Castro said: Rasenberger, *Brilliant Disaster*, 239.

133 General Cabell meets with Rusk: Rasenberger, *Brilliant Disaster*, 240–41.

134 "Sea Fury!": Rasenberger, *Brilliant Disaster*, 248.

134 "I don't think it's going as well": Reeves, *President Kennedy*, 92.

135 "I don't understand Kennedy": Kempe, *Berlin*, 177.

135 "We really blew this one": Salinger, *With Kennedy*, 196.

136 "Let me take two jets": Rasenberger, *Brilliant Disaster*, 282.

136 "He must be the loneliest man": O'Donnell and Powers, *"Johnny,"* 314; Salinger, *With Kennedy*, 196.

137 "Have you quit?": Rasenberger, *Brilliant Disaster*, 295.

137 "I have nothing": Johnson, *Bay of Pigs*, 167.

137 "We look like fools": C. L. Sulzberger, "And Nothing Fails Like Failure," *Foreign Affairs*, *New York Times*, April 22, 1961.

137 "How could I have been so far off base?": Sorensen, *Kennedy*, 309.

137 "No one knows how tough this job is": Ambrose, *Eisenhower*, 638.

The Headless Spy

140 Powers describes his food fantasies: F. G. Powers, *Operation Overflight*, 237.

140 "Hey, listen" and trade idea: Whittell, *Bridge of Spies*, 202; J. Donovan, *Strangers*, 352.

141 "I beg you to help me": Schecter and Deriabin, *Spy*, 5–6.

142 Embassy officials meet in the "bubble": Schecter and Deriabin, *Spy*, 11.

142 "It is your good friend": Oleg Penkovsky, "Letter to Be Passed to Appropriate Authorities of the United States of America," CIA, cia.gov/library/readingroom/document/0000012268. The CIA has declassified many of its Penkovsky-related files and placed them in the CIA online library under "Lt. Col. Oleg Penkovsky: Western Spy in Soviet GRU," cia.gov/library/readingroom/collection/lt-col-oleg-penkovsky-western-spy-soviet-gru.

142 Penkovsky's suggested dead-drop site: A sketch is printed in Duns, *Dead Drop*, 328.

143 Bulik's detective work: Schecter and Deriabin, *Spy*, 11–15.

144 CIA's early attempts to contact Penkovsky: Schecter and Deriabin, *Spy*, 19–38; Ashley, *CIA SpyMaster*, 150.

145 "I can't believe it, Greville": Wynne, *Contact on Gorky Street*, 76.

145 "What do we speak, what language?": Ashley, *CIA SpyMaster*, 27.

146 Penkovsky background: Ashley, *CIA SpyMaster*, 154–58; Schecter and Deriabin, *Spy*, 53–59; "Meeting No. 1 (London) at Mount Royal Hotel," April 20, 1961, transcript, CIA, cia.gov/library/readingroom/docs/DOC_0000012392.pdf.

Light the Candle

147 Shepard launch details: Thompson, *Light This Candle*, 293–94; Cadbury, *Space Race*, 244–45; Wolfe, *The Right Stuff*, 238–50; Alan B. Shepard oral history transcript, available on NASA website: historycollection.jsc.nasa.gov/JSCHistoryPortal/history/oral_histories/ShepardAB/ABS_2-20-98.pdf.

147 "Gordo!" and subsequent lines: Shepard and Slayton, *Moon Shot*, 293; Thompson, *Light This Candle*, 293–94.

149 Kennedy watches launch from White House: Reeves, *President Kennedy*, 117–18.

150 "The people are afraid to do anything": Schecter and Deriabin, *Spy*, 82.

150 "You could throw me on a U.S. airplane": Ashley, *CIA SpyMaster*, 195.

150 Penkovsky returns to Moscow: Schecter and Deriabin, *Spy*, 175; Duns, *Dead Drop*, 96.

151 Kennedy's back injury: Schlesinger, *A Thousand Days*, 342.

152 Berlin crisis background: Fursenko and Naftali, "One Hell of a Gamble," 104–5; Schlesinger, *A Thousand Days*, 344–47; Taubman, *Khrushchev*, 482–83; Zubok and Pleshakov, *Inside the Kremlin's Cold War*, 194–99.

153 Kennedy prepares for Vienna: Kempe, *Berlin*, 6–7; Reeves, *President Kennedy*, 157–58; Fursenko and Naftali, "One Hell of a Gamble," 129.

154 "Berlin is the testicles of the West": Dean Rusk, *As I Saw It*, as told to Richard Rusk (New York: Norton, 1990), 227, in Gaddis, *Cold War*, 71.

Vienna

155 "Khrushchev will be here any minute": Reeves, *President Kennedy*, 158; Beschloss, *Crisis Years*, 193.

155 Kennedy and Khrushchev meet, banter: Kempe, *Berlin*, 221; O'Donnell and Powers, "Johnny," 340.

156 Details of the Khrushchev-Kennedy discussions: Reeves, *President Kennedy*, 160–63; Schlesinger, *A Thousand Days*, 358–65; Zubok and Pleshakov, *Inside the Kremlin's Cold War*, 243–48. The Vienna talks are also covered in exhaustive detail in the U.S. State Department records of the meeting: *Foreign Relations of the United States, 1961–1963*, vol. 5, *Soviet Union* eds. Charles S. Sampson and John Michael Joyce (Washington, DC: U.S. Government Printing Office, 1998), 206–30.

157 "You're an old country": Hugh Sidey, "What the Ks Really Told Each Other," *Life*, June 16, 1961.

157 "How did it go?": Lincoln, *My Twelve Years*, 270.

157 "He treated me like a little boy": Reeves, *President Kennedy*, 166.

157 "This man is very inexperienced": Kempe, *Berlin*, 234.

158 "Mr. Khrushchev, won't you shake hands" and Khrushchev's reply: Eddy Gilmore, "Jacqueline Charms All Vienna, Especially K.," *Washington Post*, June 4, 1961; Associated Press, "First Lady Wins Khrushchev, Too," *New York Times*, June 4, 1961.

158 "I see one of your space dogs": J. Kennedy, *Historic Conversations*, 210.

158 "He got halfway": Associated Press, "Kennedy Barely Avoids Mme. Khrushchev's Lap," *New York Times*, June 4, 1961.

159 "the bone in my throat": Reeves, *President Kennedy*, 168.

159 "If the U.S. wants to start a war": *Foreign Relations of the United States*, 5:223.

159 "We can destroy each other" exchange: Reeves, *President Kennedy*, 171; Kempe, *Berlin*, 253.

160 "How was it": John F. Stacks, *Scotty: James B. Reston and the Rise and Fall of American Journalism* (Boston: Little, Brown, 2003), 4, 198, 200, in Kempe, *Berlin*, 257.

160 Khrushchev partying: United Press International, "Khrushchev Lives It Up at Party for Sukarno," *Orlando Sentinel*, June 7, 1961; Stanley Johnson, "Nikita Life of Party for Sukarno," *Democrat and Chronicle* (Rochester, NY), June 7, 1961.

Time to Start

161 Pushinka arrives: J. Kennedy, *Historic Conversations*, 210; O'Donnell and Powers, "*Johnny*," 348; Beschloss, *Crisis Years*, 238.

162 Penkovsky meets Janet Chisholm: Schecter and Deriabin, *Spy*, 184; Duns, *Dead Drop*, 113–18.

163 "You know, they have an atom bomb": Sidey, "Were the Russians Hiding a Nuke?" 31.

164 "Ever since the longbow": Hugh Sidey, introduction, *Prelude to Leadership: The European Diary of John F. Kennedy* (Washington, DC: Regnery, 1995), *xxviii*, in Stern, *Averting 'the Final Failure*,' 35.

164 Sakharov and Oval Hall scene: Sakharov, *Memoirs*, 215–17. Khrushchev recalls his disagreement with Sakharov over the H-bomb in *Khrushchev Remembers: The Last Testament*, 68–71.

165 Kennedy's televised address details: Kempe, *Berlin*, 310–14. A film and the full text of Kennedy's "Radio and Television Report to the American People on the Berlin Crisis," July 25, 1961, is available at the JFK Library, jfklibrary.org/asset-viewer /archives/TNC/TNC-258/TNC-258.

166 "If war never comes": "A Spare Room Fallout Shelter," *Life*, January 25, 1960, in Rose, *One Nation Underground*, 191.

166 "When I get my shelter finished": *Time*, "Gun Thy Neighbor?," 58.

166 The head of civil defense in Las Vegas: Associated Press, "Nevada Militia Proposed to Give Protection," *Reno Gazette-Journal*, July 29, 1961.

167 "The United States is openly preparing": CIA, "Foreign Radio and Press Reaction to President Kennedy's Speech on Berlin Crisis," Daily Report, supplement, World Reaction Series, no. 4, July 27, 1961, in Reeves, *President Kennedy*, 203–4.

167 "When would it be best for you": Kempe, *Berlin*, 317.

The Berlin Wall

169 "Mother, go away": Galante, *Berlin Wall*, 48.

170 Harry Seidel background: Galante, *Berlin Wall*, 1–4; Mitchell, *Tunnels*, 1–2.

170 "Please do something. It's my son": Galante, *Berlin Wall*, 49.

170 "It's not a very nice solution": O'Donnell and Powers, "*Johnny*," 350.

171 taunting them with insults: Kempe, *Berlin*, 354; Harry Gilroy, "Mood of Berlin: Controlled Fury," *New York Times*,

August 14, 1961; Associated Press, "Red Forces Stoned, Retaliate with Tear Gas," *Baltimore Evening Sun*, August 14, 1961.

171 Ida Siekmann's death: Galante, *Berlin Wall*, 79.

171 Günter Litfin's death: Kempe, *Berlin*, 365–66.

172 "To use the language of chess": N. Khrushchev, *Last Testament*, 504–5.

172 Seidel's escape: Mitchell, *Tunnels*, 3–4.

173 "Hello, comrade" and Seidel rescues his family: Galante, *Berlin Wall*, 100–102.

174 "with a heavy heart": "Excerpts from the Soviet Union's Statement on Resumption of Nuclear Testing," *New York Times*, August 31, 1961; Chalmers M. Roberts, "Reds Warn Their Scientists Have Created Superbombs," *Washington Post*, August 31, 1961.

175 "F***ed again" conversation: Halberstam, *Best and the Brightest*, 84; Reeves, *President Kennedy*, 223.

175 Big Ivan design: Adamsky and Smirnov, "Moscow's Biggest Bomb"; Atomic Heritage Foundation, "Tsar Bomba," August 8, 2014, atomicheritage.org/history/tsar-bomba.

Human Race

176 Lemnitzer briefing scene: Dallek, *Unfinished Life*, 346.

177 "Under any circumstances": Reeves, *President Kennedy*, 230.

177 "And we call ourselves the human race": Thomas J. Schoenbaum, *Waging Peace and War: Dean Rusk in the Truman, Kennedy, and Johnson Years* (New York: Simon & Schuster, 1988), 330, in Reeves, *President Kennedy*, 230.

177 "Their Achilles' heels": Galante, *Berlin Wall*, 114.

177 Berlin Wall details and escapes: Mitchell, *Tunnels*, 46–50; Galante, *Berlin Wall*, 130; Associated Press, "Hijacks East German Train, Races Past Guards to West Berlin," *St. Louis Post-Dispatch*, December 6, 1961; Associated Press, "They Highballed Through Iron Curtain to Freedom," *Kansas City Star*, December 31, 1961.

178 "We were going to be married": Galante, *Berlin Wall*, 112, 116.

179 Chisholm and Penkovsky's meetings: Schecter and Deriabin, *Spy*, 282–83; Duns, *Dead Drop*, 150–53; CIA Penkovsky files in the CIA online library.

180 Kennedy gets Penkovsky product: Schecter and Deriabin, *Spy*, 190, 318.

180 Big Ivan test details: *Time*, "Russia: A Bang in Asia"; Sakharov, *Memoirs*, 219–21; Atomic Heritage Foundation, "Tsar Bomba," August 8, 2014, atomicheritage.org/history/tsar-bomba.

181 "There is no escaping the fact": U.S. Department of Defense, *Fallout Protection*, 6–37.

181 "I urge you to read and consider seriously": John F. Kennedy, "A Message to You from the President," September 7, 1961, in *Life*, "Fallout Shelters," 96.

182 "It comes down in rain": O'Donnell and Powers, "*Johnny*," 328.

Out of the East

184 Seidel's tunnel: Galante, *Berlin Wall*, 141–46; Mitchell, *Tunnels*, 13–16.

186 "How would you like to go to Moscow": F. G. Powers, *Operation Overflight*, 281–83.

187 "Of course not": J. Donovan, *Strangers*, 420.

188 "However, if anything goes wrong": F. G. Powers, *Operation Overflight*, 285.

188 Powers-Abel exchange details: F. G. Powers, *Operation Overflight*, 286–88; J. Donovan, *Strangers*, 421–23; Whittell, *Bridge of Spies*, 249–51; Carl Hartman, "Powers and Abel Cross Same Freedom Bridge," *Washington Post*, February 11, 1962; Jerry Greene, "Powers on His Way Home," *Daily News* (New York), February 11, 1962.

189 Salinger calls reporters: Salinger, *With Kennedy*, 165.

The Decision

190 Penkovsky spots car watching him: Schecter and Deriabin, *Spy*, 296–300.

192 "Be careful. They are watching you": Ashley, *CIA SpyMaster*, 216.

192 Heinz Jercha killed: Mitchell, *Tunnels*, 17; Galante, *Berlin Wall*, 151–52; Hertle and Nooke, *Victims*, 74–75.

193 "I am sick and tired of all this": Schecter and Deriabin, *Spy*, 308.

194 Watching nuclear tests from Hawaii: *Life*, "First a Light Man Had Never Seen," July 20, 1962, in Beschloss, *Crisis Years*, 369.

194 CIA's Castro plots: Lebow and Stein, *We All Lost*, 25.

194 "The book says one of those men": Reeves, *President Kennedy*, 306.

195 "I see U.S. missiles": Dobbs, *One Minute to Midnight*, 37.

195 "Rodion, what if we throw a hedgehog": Fursenko and Naftali, *"One Hell of a Gamble,"* 171; Taubman, *Khrushchev*, 541.

Grave Issues

201 Yucatán asteroid: Riley Black, "What Happened the Day a Giant, Dinosaur-Killing Asteroid Hit the Earth," *Smithsonian*, September 9, 2019, smithsonianmag.com/science-nature/dinosaur-killing-asteroid-impact-chicxulub-crater-timeline-destruction-180973075/; Michelle Z. Donahue, "Dino-Killing Asteroid Hit Just the Right Spot to Trigger Extinction," *National Geographic*, November 9, 2017, nationalgeographic.com/news/2017/11/dinosaurs-extinction-asteroid-chicxulub-soot-earth-science/.

201 Mount Tambora: Erik Klemetti, "Tambora 1815: Just How Big Was the Eruption?" *Wired*, April 10, 2015, wired.com/2015/04/tambora-1815-just-big-eruption/; Michael Greshko, "201 Years Ago, This Volcano Caused a Climate Catastrophe," *National Geographic*, April 8, 2016, nationalgeographic.com/news/2016/04/160408-tambora-eruption-volcano-anniversary-indonesia-science/.

202 nuclear winter: Matthew R. Francis, "When Carl Sagan Warned the World About Nuclear Winter," *Smithsonian*, November 15, 2017, smithsonianmag.com/science-nature/when-carl-sagan-warned-world-about-nuclear-winter-180967198/; DeGroot, *The Bomb*, 264.

202 Kennedy's routine: Salinger, *With Kennedy*, 124–25.

202 Kennedy's reaction to *Guns of August*: Dallek, *Unfinished Life*, 505.

203 "It is insane": Richard N. Goodwin, *Remembering America: A Voice from the Sixties* (Boston: Little, Brown, 1988), 218, in Dobbs, *One Minute to Midnight*, 229.

204 "do-nothing president": Reeves, *President Kennedy*, 347.

204 "Were it to be otherwise": John F. Kennedy, "U.S. Reaffirms Policy on Prevention of Aggressive Actions by Cuba," September 4, 1962, *U.S. State Department Bulletin* 47, no. 1213 (September 24, 1962), 450, in R. S. Thompson, *Missiles of October*, 165.

204 Khrushchev's Black Sea villa details: Taubman, *Khrushchev*, 3–4.

204 "War in this day and age": "Memorandum of Conversation Between Secretary of the Interior Udall and Chairman Khrushchev," September 6, 1962, *Foreign Relations of the United States, 1961–1963*, vol. 15, *Berlin Crisis, 1962–1963* (Washington, DC: U.S. Government Printing Office, 1994), 309; Smith, *Stewart L. Udall*, 164; Fursenko and Naftali, *"One Hell of a Gamble,"* 209.

205 "Soon the storm will break loose": Taubman, *Khrushchev*, 557.

Special Weapons

207 "Each of you has been entrusted": Reed, *Red November*, 71; additional meeting details in Huchthausen, *October Fury*, 51–53. The authors of these books based their accounts on extensive interviews with the participants.

208 Shumkov tests nuclear torpedo: Weir and Boyne, *Rising Tide*, 80.

208 "I suggest to you": Savranskaya, "Role of Soviet Submarines," 240.

208 "Once your face has been slapped": Weir and Boyne, *Rising Tide*, 83.

209 Arkhipov and K-19 details: Matt Bivens, "Horror of Soviet Nuclear Sub's '61 Tragedy Told," *Los Angeles Times*, January 3, 1994; Huchthausen, *K-19*, 112–43; *The Man Who Saved the World*, documentary film.

209 Subs depart and read orders: Reed, *Red November*, 73–76; Huchthausen, *October Fury*, 59–65.

Milk Run

212 Wynne-Penkovsky meeting, including "I must go": Wynne, *Contact on Gorky Street*, 195.

213 "They could begin it": CIA, "Foreign Radio Broadcasts," Daily Report, October 11, 1962, HHHH 7, in Fursenko and Naftali, "One Hell of a Gamble," 219.

213 "for the sake of the revolution": Dobbs, *One Minute to Midnight*, 29.

214 Heyser U-2 flight and "milk run" quote: Brugioni, *Eyeball to Eyeball*, 182–86.

215 Identifying the missile sites with Penkovsky's intelligence: Andrew and Mitrokhin, *Sword and the Shield*, 182.

215 "I understand you fellows have found a beauty": Brugioni, *Eyeball to Eyeball*, 201.

215 "Ray, our worst fears": Brugioni, *Eyeball to Eyeball*, 203.

215 "Those things we've been worrying about": Beschloss, *Crisis Years*, 4.

215 Bundy delays telling Kennedy: Bundy, *Danger and Survival*, 395–96; Sorensen, *Kennedy*, 673.

215 Soviet submarine details: Huchthausen, *October Fury*, 80–81; Vladimir Isachenko, "Book Recounts the Real Hunt for Red October," *Moscow Times*, June 24, 2002.

Bullfighter

218 "No walls were built": Tom Wicker, "Eisenhower Calls President Weak on Foreign Policy," *New York Times*, October 16, 1962.

219 Bundy tells Kennedy about photos: Fursenko and Naftali, "One Hell of a Gamble," 222.

219 "He can't do this to me": Dobbs, *One Minute to Midnight*, 6.

219 "We have some big trouble": Reeves, *President Kennedy*, 368.

219 "Oh sh**! Sh**! Sh**!": Brugioni, *Eyeball to Eyeball*, 223.

219 Kennedy meets Schirra: United Press International, "Kennedy, Schirras Chat at White House," *Detroit Free Press*, October 17, 1962.

219 "Caroline, have you been eating candy": Reeves, *President Kennedy*, 371.

220 Kennedy's recording system: Dobbs, *One Minute to Midnight*, 15.

220 The first meeting on the Cuban missiles, October 16, 1962: May and Zelikow, *Kennedy Tapes*, 32–36; Stern, *Averting 'the Final Failure,'* 59–75. The JFK Library has made some White House recordings from the Cuban Missile Crisis available in its online exhibit, "World on the Brink: John F. Kennedy and the Cuban Missile Crisis; Thirteen Days in October 1962," microsites.jfklibrary.org /cmc/.

221 Kennedy recites poem: Frankel, *High Noon*, 83.

221 Greenbrier shelter details: Ted Gup, "The Ultimate Congressional Hideaway," *Washington Post*, May 31, 1992; Garrison, *Bracing for Armageddon*, 72.

Pretty Bad Fix

223 October 18 ExComm meeting: Stern, *Averting 'the Final Failure,'* 95–117.

225 "Assume combat readiness": Reed, *Red November*, 98.

226 "Fry it": Brugioni, *Eyeball to Eyeball*, 265.

227 "Well, maybe if we do this overflight right" and LeMay's outlook: Rhodes, *Dark Sun*, 566; Paul Lashmar, "Stranger Than 'Strangelove': A General's Forays

into the Nuclear Zone," *Washington Post*, July 3, 1994.

227 October 19 ExComm meeting: Stern, *Averting 'the Final Failure,'* 121–27; Dobbs, *One Minute to Midnight*, 22.

228 "You pulled the rug right out from under him": Dobbs, *One Minute to Midnight*, 22.

228 "These brass hats have one great advantage": O'Donnell and Powers, *"Johnny,"* 368.

Your Move

230 Kennedy's campaign trip to Midwest: Schlesinger, *A Thousand Days*, 806.

230 LeMay's position: Meetings of the Joint Chiefs of Staff, October–November 1962, transcript at National Security Archive, nsarchive2.gwu.edu/nsa/cuba_mis _cri/621000%20Notes%20Taken%20 from%20Transcripts.pdf.

230 Press notices lights burning: "Capital Tense; Big Action on Cuba May Be Imminent," *Detroit Free Press*, October 22, 1962.

231 Penkovsky missing and signal system: Duns, *Dead Drop*, 142; Schecter and Deriabin, *Spy*, 262.

231 President's cold in Chicago: Salinger, *With Kennedy*, 316.

232 "We have completed the assignments": Dobbs, *One Minute to Midnight*, 26.

232 "Gentlemen, today we're going to earn our pay": Brugioni, *Eyeball to Eyeball*, 314.

232 "There isn't any good solution": Sorensen, *Kennedy*, 693.

233 The Trumans and the shaky chandelier: West, *Upstairs at the White House*, 96–97.

234 White House renovation details, including bomb shelter: Klara, *Hidden White House*, 155–61; Graff, *Raven Rock*, 28; Associated Press, "White House Piano Puts Hole on Floor," *News-Press* (Fort Myers, FL), November 10, 1948.

234 "We are very, very close to war": Reeves, *President Kennedy*, 390.

234 "We have to wait": S. Khrushchev, *Nikita Khrushchev*, 554.

235 "We have just submitted to the networks": Salinger, *With Kennedy*, 327.

235 "In Washington they've announced": S. Khrushchev, *Nikita Khrushchev*, 554; Taubman, *Khrushchev*, 560–61.

236 "Call the members of the Presidium": S. Khrushchev, *Nikita Khrushchev*, 555.

236 "Khrushchev will *not* take this": Stern, *Averting 'the Final Failure,'* 151.

236 "This is going to go very far": May and Zelikow, *Kennedy Tapes*, 154.

236 Kennedy's meeting with congressional leaders: Stern, *Averting 'the Final Failure,'* 159–74; Fursenko and Naftali, *"One Hell of a Gamble,"* 244–45.

236 "We decided that was not the wisest first move": O'Donnell and Powers, *"Johnny,"* 380.

236 "I gotta go and make this speech": Stern, *Averting 'the Final Failure,'* 173.

The Cuban Missile Crisis

237 Oval Office speech scene: Thompson, *Missiles of October*, 268; O'Donnell and Powers, *"Johnny,"* 380.

237 "Good evening, my fellow citizens": John F. Kennedy, "Radio and Television Address to the American People on the Soviet Arms Build-Up in Cuba," October 22, 1962, audio and transcript, JFK Library, jfklibrary.org/learn/about -jfk/historic-speeches/address-during-the -cuban-missile-crisis.

238 Americans watching speech: Thompson, *Missiles of October*, 269.

239 DEFCON levels: Sagan, "Nuclear Alerts," 100.

239 "If the buzzer blows": Jones, "Full Retaliatory Response."

239 "What have you got?": S. Khrushchev, *Nikita Khrushchev*, 559.

240 "Let's stay here until the morning": S. Khrushchev, *Nikita Khrushchev*, 560.

240 "Well, it looks like war": James G. Blight, Bruce J. Allyn, and David A. Welch,

Cuba on the Brink: Castro, the Missile Crisis, and the Soviet Collapse, with David Lewis (New York: Pantheon, 1993), 213, in Dobbs, *One Minute to Midnight*, 150.

240 "The nation has woken up": Dobbs, *One Minute to Midnight*, 150.

240 Khrushchev with Presidium: Taubman, *Khrushchev*, 563.

241 American public's response to crisis: Graff, *Raven Rock*, 140–41; George, *Awaiting Armageddon*, 67–83.

242 U.S. detects Soviet subs: Stern, *Averting 'the Final Failure,'* 150; Savranskaya, "Role of Soviet Submarines," 249.

If Time Permits

243 Khrushchev's response to Kennedy: S. Khrushchev, *Nikita Khrushchev*, 565; Chang and Kornbluh, *Cuban Missile Crisis*, 173–74.

244 "Okay. Now what do we do tomorrow morning": Stern, *Averting 'the Final Failure,'* 193.

244 John and Bobby Kennedy's conversation: May and Zelikow, *Kennedy Tapes*, 219; Stern, *Averting 'the Final Failure,'* 204.

244 "Will there be war?": S. Khrushchev, *Nikita Khrushchev*, 565.

244 "All of us, men and women": Dobbs, *One Minute to Midnight*, 75.

245 "Here lie the Soviet diplomats": Reeves, *President Kennedy*, 397.

245 "So you've brought us a lot of potatoes": Dobbs, *One Minute to Midnight*, 62.

245 "Low today, 48: high, 4,800": Saul Pett, "What That Lump in the Throat Is Made Of," *Daily News* (New York), October 28, 1962.

246 "survival crackers": Graff, *Raven Rock*, 141.

246 "Iowa is not ready": Pett, "Lump in the Throat."

246 Civil defense in New York and Chicago: George, *Awaiting Armageddon*, 72, 77.

246 "Shelters? There are none": Oberdorfer, "Survival of the Fewest," 17.

246 Strategic Air Command details: Graff, *Raven Rock*, 138–39.

247 "Why do you want us to restrain ourselves": Kaplan, *Wizards of Armageddon*, 246; Dobbs, *One Minute to Midnight*, 94–95.

247 "This is General Power speaking": Dobbs, *One Minute to Midnight*, 95; Graff, *Raven Rock*, 137.

248 "They're trying to intimidate us": S. Khrushchev, *Nikita Khrushchev*, 581.

248 Evacuation details: Salinger, *With Kennedy*, 52; O'Donnell and Powers, "Johnny," 375; Lincoln, *My Twelve Years*, 328.

248 "Is this a joke?": Reeves, *President Kennedy*, 400.

249 "No, they haven't met the Russian ships": Pett, "Lump in the Throat."

Blink

251 Russians' sentiments: Jerry Cooke, "We'll Show the Americans We're Serious," *Saturday Evening Post*, December 8, 1962, 21.

251 White House Cabinet Room meeting: Stern, *Averting 'the Final Failure,'* 224–30.

252 Bobby Kennedy recalls tense moments: R. Kennedy, *Thirteen Days*, 54.

253 "We're eyeball to eyeball": Stewart Alsop and Charles Bartlett, "In Time of Crisis," *Saturday Evening Post*, December 8, 1962, in Beschloss, *Crisis Years*, 498.

253 Korolev's Mars rocket details: Harford, *Korolev*, 151.

254 "It looks like I'm going" and slow messages to Moscow: Dobbs, *One Minute to Midnight*, 117–18; Reeves, *President Kennedy*, 420; Dobrynin, *In Confidence*, 96.

255 "The Americans have chickened out": Dobbs, *One Minute to Midnight*, 112.

255 Khrushchev and Sergei talk about retreat: S. Khrushchev, *Nikita Khrushchev*, 581–82.

256 Duluth intruder: Sagan, *Limits of Safety*, 99–100; Dobbs, *One Minute to Midnight*, 132–34.

257 "Nadezhda Petrovna": S. Khrushchev, *Nikita Khrushchev*, 584.

Knot of War

259 "I'm getting more concerned": Stern, *Averting 'the Final Failure,'* 284.

260 "It's very evil stuff": Dobbs, *One Minute to Midnight*, 146.

260 B-130 scene: Savranskaya, "Role of Soviet Submarines," 243–44.

261 "They're asking us, 'Do you need assistance'": Huchthausen, *October Fury*, 217.

261 "This reads as if he wrote it himself": Reeves, *President Kennedy*, 409.

261 "If indeed war should break out": Nikita Khrushchev to President Kennedy, October 26, 1962, embassy translation from Russian, in Chang and Kornbluh, *Cuban Missile Crisis*, 195–98.

262 Castro meets with Alekseyev: S. Khrushchev, *Nikita Khrushchev*, 628–29; Chang and Kornbluh, *Cuban Missile Crisis*, 199.

263 Chuck Maultsby's flight details: Sherman and Tougias, *Above & Beyond*, 221–42. Maultsby tells the story in his own words in McIlmoyle and Bromley, *Remembering the Dragon Lady*, 393–402.

Final Offer

265 "He's scared": Reeves, *President Kennedy*, 411.

265 "Premier Khrushchev told President Kennedy": Dobbs, *One Minute to Midnight*, 231.

265 Khrushchev's second letter: Chang and Kornbluh, *Cuban Missile Crisis*, 207–9.

266 "It's very odd, Mr. President": Chang and Kornbluh, *Cuban Missile Crisis*, 211.

266 "We have a problem": Dobbs, *One Minute to Midnight*, 259.

267 Okimoto's directions to Maultsby: Teitel, "Aurora Borealis."

267 Maultsby's recollections of this moment: McIlmoyle and Bromley, *Remembering the Dragon Lady*, 395.

267 McNamara and LeMay in the "tank": Dobbs, *One Minute to Midnight*, 266–67.

268 "This means war" and Kennedy's reaction: Reeves, *President Kennedy*, 416; Sagan, *Limits of Safety*, 118.

269 "My bladder was about to burst": McIlmoyle and Bromley, *Remembering the Dragon Lady*, 399.

269 Rudolf Anderson news: May and Zelikow, *Kennedy Tapes*, 325.

269 "I just think somebody": Stern, *Averting 'the Final Failure,'* 337.

270 The scene aboard B-59: Reed, *Red November*, 150–55; Weir and Boyne, *Rising Tide*, 102–3, 301–2; Savranskaya, "Role of Soviet Submarines," 244–46. Many Soviet submariners from this mission are interviewed in the PBS documentary *The Man Who Saved the World*.

270 "I will *never* surface": Reed, *Red November*, 152.

First Shot

272 "The U-2 was shot down": Stern, *Averting 'the Final Failure,'* 344–45.

273 "We are in an entirely new ball game": R. F. Kennedy, *Thirteen Days*, 98.

274 "No! The conditions for firing have not been met" and Savitsky's response: Reed, *Red November*, 153.

275 "It would seem the appropriate time": Fidel Castro to Comrade Khrushchev, October 27, 1962, in S. Khrushchev, *Nikita Khrushchev*, 629.

275 "What?" Khrushchev gasped: S. Khrushchev, "How My Father."

275 Kennedy meets with close advisers: Dobbs, *One Minute to Midnight*, 307.

275 "assurances against an invasion of Cuba": President Kennedy to Premier Khrushchev, October 27, 1962, in Chang and Kornbluh, *Cuban Missile Crisis*, 233–35.

276 Dobrynin and Bobby Kennedy's meeting: Dobrynin, *In Confidence*, 86–88; Fursenko and Naftali. "One Hell of a Gamble," 281–82; Dobbs, *One Minute to Midnight*, 308–9; Hershberg, "Anatomy of a Controversy," 71–78.

277 "How did it go" and "God, Dave": O'Donnell and Powers, *"Johnny,"* 394.

Moscow Time

278 "What's new?": S. Khrushchev, "How My Father."

278 Novo-Ogaryovo details: S. Khrushchev, *Nikita Khrushchev,* 583.

279 "The continuation of this threat": Kennedy to Khrushchev, October 27, 1962.

279 "We find ourselves face to face": Taubman, *Khrushchev,* 574.

279 Sergei Khrushchev's phone calls: S. Khrushchev, *Nikita Khrushchev,* 633.

280 Dobrynin's telegram arrives: S. Khrushchev, "How My Father."

281 "At five o'clock whose time?": S. Khrushchev, *Nikita Khrushchev,* 625.

281 "Let's begin, Nadezhda Petrovna": S. Khrushchev, "How My Father."

281 Ilychev's trip to Radio Moscow: S. Khrushchev, *Nikita Khrushchev, xiii–xvii;* Lebow and Stein, *We All Lost the Cold War,* 142.

282 "Attention, this is Radio Moscow" and Khrushchev's letter: Chairman Khrushchev to President Kennedy, October 28, 1962, in S. Khrushchev, *Nikita Khrushchev,* 633–34.

282 *Well, that's it:* S. Khrushchev, *Nikita Khrushchev,* 634.

283 "I feel like a new man now": O'Donnell and Powers, *"Johnny,"* 395.

283 "Wasn't it great about the news": Lincoln, *My Twelve Years,* 330.

284 "This is the greatest defeat": Stern, *Averting 'the Final Failure,'* 385.

284 "Fidel, what should we do about this news": Franqui, *Family Portrait with Fidel,* 194; Beschloss, *Crisis Years,* 543.

284 "I welcome Chairman Khrushchev's statesmanlike decision": Reeves, *President Kennedy,* 424.

285 "Why don't we go to the theater?": S. Khrushchev, *Nikita Khrushchev,* 636.

286 "This is the night I should go to the theater": Beschloss, *Crisis Years,* 542.

286 The call with Penkovsky's signal: Schecter and Deriabin, *Spy,* 337.

Rematch

287 Richard Jacob's arrest at dead-drop: Schecter and Deriabin, *Spy,* 339–42.

289 "This source will be of no further value": Schecter and Deriabin, *Spy,* 347.

289 Seidel's final tunnel: Galante, *Berlin Wall,* 193–200; Mitchell, *Tunnels,* 282–88.

289 "Be a good boy": Galante, *Berlin Wall,* 196.

289 "Go away! The tunnel is betrayed": Mitchell, *Tunnels,* 287.

290 "Do I *look* like a spy": "Obituary: Janet Chisholm," BBC News, August 12, 2004, news.bbc.co.uk/2/hi/uk_news/3559020.stm.

291 "I only remember": Mitchell, *Tunnels,* 311.

291 "Cuba does not want to be a pawn": Beschloss, *Crisis Years,* 550.

291 "It's a disgrace": Dobbs, *One Minute to Midnight,* 328.

291 "Wait until 1964": Beschloss, *Crisis Years,* 557.

291 "For the first time in history": Beschloss, *Crisis Years,* 562.

Epilogue: Choose Your Own Ending

293 "I plead guilty in all respects": Schecter and Deriabin, *Spy,* 355; Mark Frankland, "Penkovsky to Be Shot: Wynne Sentenced to Eight Years," *Observer* (London), May 12, 1963.

293 "the most productive classic clandestine operation": Schecter and Deriabin, *Spy,* 353.

294 "organizing kidnappings, and luring persons to West Berlin": United Press International, "Berlin Refugee Gets Life for Helping Others Flee," *Boston Globe,* December 29, 1962.

294 "For Seidel, the Reds got a ransom": Nino Lo Bello, "Bodies for Butter," *Boston Globe,* August 21, 1966.

294 "Hero or Bum?" and other headlines: F. G. Powers, *Operation Overflight*, 298, 306.

295 Powers's post-CIA life: Francis Gary Powers Jr. covers this extensively in his book, *Spy Pilot*. He gave me additional details in an interview April 29, 2020.

295 "Intelligence work is not a series": "Abel, Red Spy, Dies," *New York Times*, November 17, 1971.

295 Lona Cohen's life in Britain as Helen Kroger: "Obituary: Helen Kroger," *Times* (London), January 13, 1993. Entire books and TV series have covered this, including Carr, *Operation Whisper*.

296 Hayhanen TV appearance, details and dialogue: Berkinow, *Abel*, 249; Fred Danzig, "David Brinkley Talks of Spies and Toys," *Tampa Times*, November 9, 1961.

296 Donovan writes of Hayhanen's "mysterious" death: J. Donovan, *Strangers*, 179–80; "Death of Witness in Abel Case Cited," *New York Times*, March 31, 1964.

296 Bay of Pigs prisoner release: Rasenberger, *Brilliant Disaster*, 371–76; Juanita Greene, "A Wave of Hope Sweeps Exiles in Orange Bowl," *Miami Herald*, December 30, 1962.

297 "Who'd want to kill an old man": Nicholas Gage, "Mafia Said to Have Slain Rosselli Because of His Senate Testimony," *New York Times*, February 25, 1977.

297 Castro wrap-up: Anthony DePalma, "Fidel Castro, Cuban Revolutionary Who Defied U.S., Dies at 90," *New York Times*, November 26, 2016.

297 "Never trust a government" and Sakharov as activist: Gorelik, "Riddle of the Third Idea"; Francis X. Clines, "Andrei Sakharov, 68, Soviet 'Conscience,' Dies," *New York Times*, December 15, 1989; "Andrei D. Sakharov," Atomic Heritage Foundation, atomicheritage.org/profile /andrei-d-sakharov. Sakharov devotes the second half of his *Memoirs* to his activism.

298 "Your Highness": Doran and Bizony, *Starman*, 137.

298 "I won't feel right until I've taken": Doran and Bizony, *Starman*, 187.

299 "As you look back": "After Two Years—a Conversation with the President," December 17, 1962, television and radio interview with William H. Lawrence, *Public Papers of the Presidents: John F. Kennedy, January 1 to December 31, 1962*, p. 889, in Reeves, *President Kennedy*, 437.

299 "Freedom has many difficulties": John F. Kennedy, "Remarks at the Rudolph Wilde Platz," Berlin, June 26, 1963, film and transcript, JFK Library, jfklibrary .org/learn/about-jfk/historic-speeches /remarks-at-the-rudolph-wilde-platz -berlin; Putnam, "*Ich Bin ein Berliner.*"

299 Postcrisis details, including hotline and Limited Test Ban Treaty: Dobrynin, *In Confidence*, 97–98; R. F. Kennedy, *Thirteen Days*, 14; Salinger, *With Kennedy*, 320.

300 "Why? On what issue": Taubman, *Khrushchev*, 5.

301 "Why are you doing this": Taubman, *Khrushchev*, 11–12.

301 "He'd repeat bitterly that his life was over": S. Khrushchev, *Nikita Khrushchev*, 623.

301 Nuclear stockpiles: Current totals by country can be found at "World Nuclear Weapon Stockpile," Ploughshares Fund, ploughshares.org/world-nuclear-stockpile -report.

303 "This was not only the most dangerous": Marion Lloyd, "Soviets Close to Using A-Bomb in 1962 Crisis, Forum Is Told," *Boston Globe*, October 13, 2002.

303 "At the end, we lucked out": Robert McNamara, quoted in the 2003 documentary *Fog of War*.

BIBLIOGRAPHY

Books, Magazines, Journals

Abel, Elie. *The Missile Crisis*. New York: Bantam Books, 1966.

Adamsky, Viktor, and Yuri Smirnov. "Moscow's Biggest Bomb: The 50-Megaton Test of October 1961." *Cold War International History Project Bulletin* 4 (Fall 1994): 3, 19–20.

Albright, Joseph, and Marcia Kunstel. *Bombshell: The Secret Story of America's Unknown Atomic Spy Conspiracy*. New York: Times Books, 1997.

Allain, Rhett. "Why Do Astronauts Float Around in Space?" *Wired*, July 9, 2011. wired .com/2011/07/why-do-astronauts-float-around-in-space/.

Ambrose, Stephen E. *Eisenhower*. Vol. 2, *The President*. New York: Simon & Schuster, 1984.

Andrew, Christopher, and Vasili Mitrokhin. *The Sword and the Shield: The Mitrokhin Archive and the Secret History of the KGB*. New York: Basic Books, 1999.

Appelbaum, Yoni. "Yes, Virginia, There Is a NORAD." *Atlantic*, December 24, 2015.

Applebaum, Anne. *Iron Curtain: The Crushing of Eastern Europe, 1944–1956*. New York: Doubleday, 2012.

Ashley, Clarence. *CIA SpyMaster*. Gretna, LA: Pelican, 2004.

Bernikow, Louise. *Abel*. New York: Trident, 1970.

Beschloss, Michael R. *Mayday: The Crisis Years: Kennedy and Khrushchev, 1960–1963*. New York: HarperCollins, 1991.

———. *Eisenhower, Khrushchev and the U-2 Affair*. New York: Harper & Row, 1986.

Bird, Kai, and Martin Sherwin. *American Prometheus: The Triumph and Tragedy of J. Robert Oppenheimer*. New York: Vintage Books, 2006.

Boot, Max. "Operation Mongoose: The Story of America's Efforts to Overthrow Castro." *Atlantic*, January 5, 2018.

Brown, Rob. "The Solomon Islanders Who Saved JFK." *BBC News Magazine*, August 6, 2014. bbc.com/news/magazine-28644830.

Brugioni, Dino A. *Eyeball to Eyeball: The Inside Story of the Cuban Missile Crisis.* New York: Random House, 1990.

Bundy, McGeorge. *Danger and Survival: Choices About the Bomb in the First Fifty Years.* New York: Random House, 1988.

Burchett, Wilfred, and Anthony Purdy. *Cosmonaut Yuri Gagarin: First Man in Space.* London: Panther Books, 1961.

Cadbury, Deborah. *Space Race: The Epic Battle Between America and the Soviet Union for Dominion of Space.* New York: HarperCollins, 2006.

Carlson, Peter. "Nikita Khrushchev Goes to Hollywood." *Smithsonian,* July 2009. smithsonianmag.com/history/nikita-khrushchev-goes-to-hollywood-30668979/.

Carr, Barnes. *Operation Whisper: The Capture of Soviet Spies Morris and Lona Cohen.* Lebanon, NH: University Press of New England, 2016.

Castro, Fidel, and José Ramón Fernández. *Playa Girón: Bay of Pigs; Washington's First Military Defeat in the Americas.* New York: Pathfinder, 2001.

Chang, Laurence, and Peter Kornbluh, eds. *The Cuban Missile Crisis, 1962: A National Security Archive Documents Reader.* New York: New Press, 1999.

Chernev, Irving. *200 Brilliant Endgames.* New York: Simon & Schuster, 1989.

Dallek, Robert. *An Unfinished Life: John F. Kennedy, 1917–1963.* New York: Little, Brown, 2003.

———. "JFK vs. the Military." In "JFK: In His Time and Ours," special issue. *Atlantic* (Fall 2013).

———. "The Medical Ordeals of JFK." *Atlantic,* December 2002.

DeGroot, Gerard J. *The Bomb: A Life.* Cambridge, MA: Harvard University Press, 2005.

Detzer, David. *The Brink: Cuban Missile Crisis, 1962.* New York: Thomas Y. Crowell, 1979.

Dille, John. "We Who Tried: The Untold Battle Story of the Men on the Beach at the Bay of Pigs." *Life,* May 10, 1963.

Dobbs, Michael. "Gary Powers Kept a Secret Diary with Him After He Was Captured by the Soviets." *Smithsonian,* October 15, 2015. smithsonianmag.com/smithsonian -institution/-180956939/.

———. *One Minute to Midnight: Kennedy, Khrushchev, and Castro on the Brink of Nuclear War.* New York: Alfred A. Knopf, 2008.

———. "The Real Story of the 'Football' That Follows the President Everywhere." *Smithsonian,* October 2014. smithsonianmag.com/history/real-story-football-follows -president-everywhere-180952779/.

Dobrynin, Anatoly. *In Confidence: Moscow's Ambassador to America's Six Cold War Presidents.* New York: Times Books, 1995.

Donovan, James B. *Strangers on a Bridge: The Case of Colonel Abel and Francis Gary Powers.* New York: Scribner, 2015. First published 1964 by Atheneum (New York).

Donovan, Robert J. *PT 109: John F. Kennedy in World War II*. New York: McGraw-Hill, 1961.

Doran, Jamie, and Piers Bizony. *Starman: The Truth Behind the Legend of Yuri Gagarin*. New York: Walker, 1998.

Doyle, William. *PT 109: An American Epic of War, Survival, and the Destiny of John F. Kennedy*. New York: William Morrow, 2015.

Duns, Jeremy. *Dead Drop: The True Story of Oleg Penkovsky and the Cold War's Most Dangerous Operation*. London: Simon & Schuster UK, 2013.

——. "The Spy Who Saved the World—Then Tried to Destroy It." *Daily Beast*, November 11, 2013. thedailybeast.com/the-spy-who-saved-the-worldthen-tried-to -destroy-it.

Ellsberg, Daniel. *The Doomsday Machine: Confessions of a Nuclear War Planner*. New York: Bloomsbury, 2017.

Flanner, Janet. "Letter from Paris." *New Yorker*, June 4, 1960.

Frankel, Max. *High Noon in the Cold War: Kennedy, Khrushchev, and the Cuban Missile Crisis*. New York: Ballantine Books, 2004.

Franqui, Carlos. *Family Portrait with Fidel*. Translated by Alfred MacAdam. New York: Random House, 1984.

Fursenko, Aleksandr, and Timothy Naftali. *Khrushchev's Cold War: The Inside Story of an American Adversary*. New York: W. W. Norton, 2006.

——. *"One Hell of a Gamble": Khrushchev, Castro, and Kennedy, 1958–1964*. New York: W. W. Norton, 1997.

Gaddis, John Lewis. *The Cold War: A New History*. New York: Penguin, 2005.

Galante, Pierre. *The Berlin Wall*. With Jack Miller. New York: Doubleday, 1965.

Garber, Megan. "The Doll That Helped the Soviets Beat the U.S. to Space." *Atlantic*, March 28, 2013.

Garrison, Dee. *Bracing for Armageddon: Why Civil Defense Never Worked*. New York: Oxford University Press, 2006.

Gee, Alison. "Pushinka: A Cold War Puppy the Kennedys Loved." BBC News Magazine, January 6, 2014. bbc.com/news/magazine-24837199.

George, Alice L. *Awaiting Armageddon: How Americans Faced the Cuban Missile Crisis*. Chapel Hill: University of North Carolina Press, 2003.

Gibney, Frank. "A Russian Master Spy." *Life*, November 11, 1957, 123–30.

Golovanov, Yaroslav. *Our Gagarin*. Translated by David Sinclair-Loutit. Moscow: Progress, 1978.

Gorelik, Gennady. "The Riddle of the Third Idea: How Did the Soviets Build a Thermonuclear Bomb So Suspiciously Fast?" guest blog, *Scientific American*, August 21, 2011. blogs.scientificamerican.com/guest-blog/the-riddle-of-the-third-idea-how-did -the-soviets-build-a-thermonuclear-bomb-so-suspiciously-fast/.

———. *The World of Andrei Sakharov: A Russian Physicist's Path to Freedom.* With Antonina W. Bouis. New York: Oxford University Press, 2005.

Gouré, Leon. "Soviet Civil Defense." Santa Monica, CA: RAND Corporation, 1960. rand.org/pubs/papers/P1887.html.

Graff, Garrett M. *Raven Rock: The Story of the U.S. Government's Secret Plan to Save Itself—While the Rest of Us Die.* New York: Simon & Schuster, 2017.

Gup, Ted. "Civil Defense Doomsday Hideaway." *Time,* December 9, 1991. content .time.com/time/magazine/article/0,9171,156041,00.html.

———. "The Doomsday Blueprints." *Time,* August 10, 1992.

Halberstam, David. *The Best and the Brightest.* New York: Penguin, 1983.

Harford, James. *Korolev: How One Man Masterminded the Soviet Drive to Beat America to the Moon.* New York: John Wiley & Sons, 1997.

Hargittai, Istvan. *Judging Edward Teller: A Closer Look at One of the Most Influential Scientists of the Twentieth Century.* Amherst, NY: Prometheus Books, 2010.

Hersey, John. "Survival." Reporter at Large. *New Yorker,* June 17, 1944. newyorker.com /magazine/1944/06/17/survival.

Hershberg, Jim. "Anatomy of a Controversy: Anatoly F. Dobrynin's Meeting with Robert F. Kennedy, Saturday, 27 October 1962." *Cold War International History Project Bulletin* 5 (Spring 1995).

Hertle, Hans-Hermann, and Maria Nooke, eds. *The Victims at the Berlin Wall, 1961– 1989: A Biographical Handbook.* Berlin: Ch. Links, 2011.

Hirsh, Seymour M. *The Dark Side of Camelot.* Boston: Little, Brown, 1997.

Holloway, David. "Research Note: Soviet Thermonuclear Development." *International Security* 20, no. 4 (Winter 1979–80): 192–97.

———. *Stalin and the Bomb: The Soviet Union and Atomic Energy 1939–1956.* New Haven, CT: Yale University Press, 1996.

Huchthausen, Peter A. *K-19: The Widowmaker; The Secret Story of the Soviet Nuclear Submarine.* Washington, DC: National Geographic, 2002.

———. *October Fury.* Hoboken, NJ: John Wiley & Sons, 2002.

Jacobsen, Annie. *Area 51: An Uncensored History of America's Top Secret Military Base.* New York: Little, Brown, 2011.

Jogalekar, Ashutosh. "The Many Tragedies of Edward Teller." *Scientific American,* January 15, 2014. blogs.scientificamerican.com/the-curious-wavefunction/the-many -tragedies-of-edward-teller/.

Johnson, Haynes. *The Bay of Pigs: The Leaders' Story of Brigade 2506.* With Manuel Artime, José Peréz San Román, Erneido Oliva, and Enrique Ruiz-Williams. New York: W. W. Norton, 1964.

Jones, Thomas. "A Full Retaliatory Response." *Air & Space,* November 2005. airspace- mag.com/history-of-flight/a-full-retaliatory-response-6909238/.

Jungk, Robert. *Brighter Than a Thousand Suns: A Personal History of the Atomic Scientists.* Translated by James Cleugh. New York: Harcourt Brace, 1956.

Kaplan, Fred. "JFK's First-Strike Plan." *Atlantic,* October 2001.

———. *The Wizards of Armageddon.* Stanford, CA: Stanford University Press, 1991. First published in 1983 by Simon & Schuster (New York).

Keeney, L. Douglas. *15 Minutes: General Curtis LeMay and the Countdown to Nuclear Annihilation.* New York: St. Martin's, 2011.

Kempe, Frederick. *Berlin, 1961: Kennedy, Khrushchev, and the Most Dangerous Place on Earth.* New York: G. P. Putnam's Sons, 2011.

Kennedy, Jacqueline. *Historic Conversations on Life with John F. Kennedy: Interviews with Arthur M. Schlesinger, Jr., 1964.* New York: Hyperion, 2011.

Kennedy, Robert F. *Thirteen Days: A Memoir of the Cuban Missile Crisis.* New York: W. W. Norton, 1969.

Khrushchev, Nikita. *Khrushchev Remembers.* Edited and translated by Strobe Talbott. New York: Little, Brown, 1970.

———. *Khrushchev Remembers: The Last Testament.* Edited and translated by Strobe Talbott. New York: Little, Brown, 1974.

Khrushchev, Sergei N. "The Day We Shot Down the U-2." *American Heritage* 51, no. 5 (September 2000). americanheritage.com/day-we-shot-down-u-2.

———. "How My Father and President Kennedy Saved the World." *American Heritage* 53, no. 5 (October 2002). americanheritage.com/how-my-father-and-president -kennedy-saved-world.

———. *Nikita Khrushchev and the Creation of a Superpower.* Translated by Shirley Benson. University Park: Pennsylvania State University Press, 2000.

Klara, Robert. *The Hidden White House: Harry Truman and the Reconstruction of America's Most Famous Residence.* New York: St. Martin's, 2013.

Kozak, Warren. *Curtis LeMay: Strategist and Tactician.* Washington, DC: Regency History, 2009.

Krugler, David F. *This Is Only a Test: How Washington D.C. Prepared for Nuclear War.* New York: Palgrave Macmillan, 2006.

Krulwich, Robert. "You (and Almost Everyone You Know) Owe Your Life to This Man." *National Geographic,* March 2016.

Lacey-Bordeaux, Emma. "Declassified Report: Two Nuclear Bombs Nearly Detonated in North Carolina." CNN, June 12, 2014. cnn.com/2014/06/12/us/north-carolina -nuclear-bomb-drop/index.html.

Lamphere, Robert J., and Tom Shachtman. *The FBI-KGB War: A Special Agent's Story.* New York: Random House, 1986.

Lapp, Ralph E. *The Voyage of the Lucky Dragon.* New York: Harper & Brothers, 1957.

Lebow, Richard Ned, and Janice Gross Stein. *We All Lost the Cold War.* Princeton, NJ: Princeton University Press, 1994.

Life. "Fallout Shelters: A New Urgency, Big Things to Do—and What You Must Learn." September 15, 1961.

Lincoln, Evelyn. *My Twelve Years with John F. Kennedy.* New York: David McKay, 1965.

Lindsay, James M. "TWE Remembers: Maj. Richard Heyser Flies a U-2 Over Cuba." *The Water's Edge* (blog), Council on Foreign Relations, October 14, 2012. cfr.org /blog/twe-remembers-maj-richard-heyser-flies-u-2-over-cuba.

May, Ernest R., and Philip D. Zelikow, eds. *The Kennedy Tapes: Inside the White House During the Cuban Missile Crisis.* Cambridge, MA: Harvard University Press, 1997.

May, Sandra, ed. "What Is Microgravity?" NASA, February 15, 2012. nasa.gov/audience /forstudents/5-8/features/nasa-knows/what-is-microgravity-58.html.

McIlmoyle, Gerald E., and Linda Rios Bromley. *Remembering the Dragon Lady: Memoirs of the Men Who Experienced the Legend of the U-2 Spy Plane.* Solihull, England: Helion, 2011.

Mitchell, Greg. *The Tunnels: Escapes Under the Berlin Wall and the Historic Films the JFK White House Tried to Kill.* New York: Crown, 2016.

Mydans, Carl. "A Red Show Tries the U.S. By Proxy." *Life,* August 29, 1960, 14–18.

Newsweek. "Survival: Are Shelters the Answer?" November 6, 1961, 19–20.

Norris, Robert S., and Hans M. Kristensen. "Global Nuclear Weapons Inventories, 1945–2010." *Bulletin of the Atomic Scientists* 66, no. 4 (July/August 2010). tandfon line.com/doi/pdf/10.2968/066004008.

NPR. "The Secret Bunker Congress Never Used." *All Things Considered,* March 26, 2011. npr.org/2011/03/26/134379296/.

Oberdorfer, Don. "Survival of the Fewest." *Saturday Evening Post,* March 23, 1963.

O'Donnell, Kenneth P., and David F. Powers. *"Johnny, We Hardly Knew Ye": Memories of John Fitzgerald Kennedy.* With Joe McCarthy. Boston: Little, Brown, 1972.

Pastore, Rose. "7 of the Creepiest Cold War Fallout Shelters." *Popular Science,* February 21, 2013. popsci.com/science/article/2013-02/7-creepiest-cold-war-fallout -shelters/.

Perrottet, Tony. "How Cuba Remembers Its Revolutionary Past and Present." *Smithsonian,* October 2016. smithsonianmag.com/history/cuba-remembers-revolutionary -past-present-180960447/.

Powers, Barbara. *Spy Wife.* With W. W. Diehl. New York: Pyramid Books, 1965.

Powers, Francis Gary. *Operation Overflight.* With Curt Gentry. New York: Tower, 1970.

Powers, Francis Gary, Jr., and Keith Dunnavant. *Spy Pilot: Francis Gary Powers, the U-2 Incident, and a Controversial Cold War Legacy.* Amherst, NY: Prometheus Books, 2019.

Putnam, Thomas. "The Real Meaning of *Ich Bin ein Berliner*." In "JFK: In His Time and Ours," special issue, *Atlantic* (Fall 2013). theatlantic.com/magazine/archive /2013/08/the-real-meaning-of-ich-bin-ein-berliner/309500/.

Rasenberger, Jim. *The Brilliant Disaster: JFK, Castro, and America's Doomed Invasion of Cuba's Bay of Pigs*. New York: Scribner, 2011.

Reed, W. Craig. *Red November: Inside the Secret U.S.-Soviet Submarine War*. New York: HarperCollins, 2010.

Reel, Monte. *A Brotherhood of Spies: The U-2 and the CIA's Secret War*. New York: Doubleday, 2018.

Reeves, Richard. *President Kennedy: Profile of Power*. New York: Simon & Schuster, 1993.

Reid-Henry, Simon. *Fidel and Che: A Revolutionary Friendship*. New York: Walker, 2009.

Reston, James. *Deadline: A Memoir*. New York: Times Books, 1992.

Rhodes, Richard. *Dark Sun: The Making of the Hydrogen Bomb*. New York: Simon & Schuster, 1995.

Ropeik, David. "How the Unlucky Lucky Dragon Birthed an Era of Nuclear Fear." *Bulletin of the Atomic Scientists*, February 28, 2018. thebulletin.org/2018/02/how -the-unlucky-lucky-dragon-birthed-an-era-of-nuclear-fear/.

Rose, Kenneth D. *One Nation Underground: The Fallout Shelter in American Culture*. New York: New York University Press, 2001.

Rowberry, Ariana. "Castle Bravo: The Largest U.S. Nuclear Explosion." Brookings, February 27, 2014. brookings.edu/blog/up-front/2014/02/27/castle-bravo-the-largest-u-s -nuclear-explosion/.

Sagan, Scott D. *The Limits of Safety: Organizations, Accidents, and Nuclear Weapons*. Princeton, NJ: Princeton University Press, 1993.

——. "Nuclear Alerts and Crisis Management." *International Security* 9, no. 4 (Spring 1985): 99–119. jstor.org/stable/2538543.

Sakharov, Andrei. *Memoirs*. Translated by Richard Lourie. New York: Alfred A. Knopf, 1990.

Salinger, Pierre: *With Kennedy*. New York: Avon Books, 1967.

Savranskaya, Svetlana. "New Sources on the Role of Soviet Submarines in the Cuban Missile Crisis." *Journal of Strategic Studies* 28, no. 2 (April 2005): 233–59.

Schecter, Jerrold L., and Peter S. Deriabin. *The Spy Who Saved the World: How a Soviet Colonel Changed the Course of the Cold War*. New York: Charles Scribner's Sons, 1992.

Schlesinger, Arthur M., Jr. *A Thousand Days: John F. Kennedy in the White House*. Boston: Houghton Mifflin, 1965.

Schlosser, Eric. *Command and Control: Nuclear Weapons, the Damascus Accident, and the Illusion of Safety*. New York: Penguin Books, 2014.

Server, Lee. *Handsome Johnny: The Life and Death of Johnny Rosselli, Gentleman Gangster, Hollywood Producer, CIA Assassin.* New York: St. Martin's, 2018.

Shepard, Alan, and Deke Slayton. *Moon Shot: The Inside Story of America's Apollo Moon Landings.* Rev. ed. With Jay Barbree. Open Road Media, 2014.

Sherman, Casey, and Michael J. Tougias. *Above & Beyond: John F. Kennedy and America's Most Dangerous Cold War Spy Mission.* New York: Public Affairs, 2018.

Sidey, Hugh. "Were the Russians Hiding a Nuke in D.C.?" *Time,* November 12, 2001.

Silverman, Robert. "The Russian Spy Who Duped My Dad." Salon, February 8, 2014. salon.com/2014/02/09/the_russian_spy_who_duped_my_dad_partner/.

Singh, Simon. *The Code Book: The Science of Secrecy from Ancient Egypt to Quantum Cryptography.* New York: Anchor Books, 2000.

Smith, Thomas G. *Stewart L. Udall: Steward of the Land.* Albuquerque: University of New Mexico Press, 2017.

Sorensen, Theodore C. *Kennedy.* New York: Harper & Row, 1965.

Stern, Sheldon M. *Averting 'the Final Failure': John F. Kennedy and the Secret Cuban Missile Crisis Meetings.* Stanford, CA: Stanford University Press, 2003.

Szulc, Tad. *Fidel: A Critical Portrait.* New York: William Morrow, 1986.

Taubman, William. *Khrushchev, The Man and His Era.* New York: W. W. Norton, 2003.

Taylor, Frederick. *The Berlin Wall: A World Divided, 1961–1989.* New York: Harper-Collins, 2006.

Teitel, Amy Shira. "How the Aurora Borealis Nearly Started World War III." *Discover,* March 12, 2013. discovermagazine.com/the-sciences/how-the-aurora-borealis-nearly-started-world-war-iii.

———. "Ivan Ivanovich Cleared the Way for Yuri Gagarin's Spaceflight." *Discover,* September 21, 2017. discovermagazine.com/the-sciences/ivan-ivanovich-cleared-the-way-for-yuri-gagarins-spaceflight.

Thompson, Neal. *Light This Candle: The Life and Times of Alan Shepard.* New York: Random House, 2004.

Thompson, Robert Smith. *The Missiles of October: The Declassified Story of John F. Kennedy and the Cuban Missile Crisis.* New York: Simon & Schuster, 1992.

Time. "The Cruise of the Vostok." April 21, 1961, 46–52.

———. "Gun Thy Neighbor?" August 18, 1961, 58.

———. "The Presidency: Measuring Mission." June 9, 1961, 9–13.

———. "Russia: A Bang in Asia." September 8, 1961, 26–30.

Tregaskis, Richard. *John F. Kennedy and PT-109.* New York: Landmark Books, 1962.

Triay, Victor Andres. *Bay of Pigs: An Oral History of Brigade 2506.* Gainesville: University Press of Florida, 2001.

Ulam, S. M. *Adventures of a Mathematician*. Berkeley: University of California Press, 1991.

U.S. Department of Defense. *Fallout Protection: What to Know and Do about Nuclear Attack*. Washington, DC: U.S. Government Printing Office, 1961.

Weir, Gary E., and Walter J. Boyne. *Rising Tide: The Untold Story of the Russian Submarines That Fought the Cold War*. New York: Basic Books, 2003.

West, J. B. *Upstairs at the White House: My Life with the First Ladies*. With Mary Lynn Kotz. New York: Warner, 1974.

Whittell, Giles. *Bridge of Spies: A True Story of the Cold War*. New York: Broadway Books, 2010.

Wills, Garry. "Did Kennedy Cause the Crisis?" In "JFK: In His Time and Ours," special issue, *Atlantic* (Fall 2013).

Wolfe, Tom. *The Right Stuff*. New York: Picador, 2008. First published in 1979 by Farrar, Straus & Giroux (New York).

Wynne, Greville. *Contact on Gorky Street*. New York: Atheneum, 1968.

———. *The Man from Odessa*. London: Robert Hale, 1981.

York, Herbert F. *The Advisors: Oppenheimer, Teller, and the Superbomb*. Stanford, CA: Stanford University Press, 1976.

Zaloga, Steven J. *Target America: The Soviet Union and the Strategic Arms Race, 1945–1964*. Novato, CA: Presidio, 1993.

Zubok, Vladislav, and Constantine Pleshakov. *Inside the Kremlin's Cold War: From Stalin to Khrushchev*. Cambridge, MA: Harvard University Press, 1996.

Documentaries and Films

Cold War Roadshow. Directed and edited by Robert Stone and Tim B. Toidze. Episode 7, Season 26, *American Experience*, PBS, November 18, 2014.

Command and Control. Directed by Robert Kenner. Episode 3, Season 29, *American Experience*, PBS, April 15, 2017.

Duck and Cover. Directed by Anthony Rizzo. Federal Civil Defense Administration, 1951. youtube.com/watch?v=IKqXu-5jw60.

The Fog of War: Eleven Lessons from the Life of Robert S. McNamara. Produced and directed by Errol Morris. Sony Pictures Classics, 2003.

JFK, pt. 2. Produced and directed by Susan Bellows. Episode 8, Season 25, *American Experience*, PBS, November 12, 2013.

The Man Who Saved the World. Written and produced by Nick Green. Episode 6, Season 12, *Secrets of the Dead*, PBS, October 23, 2012.

Operation Doorstep. Produced by Byron Inc. Federal Civil Defense Administration, 1953. youtube.com/watch?v=uIWAs_avpbY.

Race for the Superbomb. Directed by Thomas Ott. Episode 2, Season 11. *American Experience*, PBS, January 11, 1999.

Newspapers

Baltimore Evening Sun

Boston Globe

Charlotte (NC) Observer

Corpus Christi (TX) Times

Daily News (New York)

Democrat and Chronicle (Rochester, NY)

Detroit Free Press

Guardian (Manchester, UK)

Los Angeles Times

Miami Herald

Miami News

Moscow Times

News-Press (Fort Myers, FL)

New York Times

Observer (London)

Orlando Sentinel

Reno (NV) Gazette-Journal

San Francisco Examiner

Santa Cruz (CA) Sentinel

St. Louis Post-Dispatch

Tampa Times

Times (London)

Troy (NY) Record

Vancouver (BC) Sun

Wall Street Journal

Washington Post

Government Sources & Online Archives

Atomic Heritage Foundation, atomicheritage.org

Central Intelligence Agency Library, cia.gov/library

Dwight D. Eisenhower Presidential Library, eisenhowerlibrary.gov

Federal Bureau of Investigation, Rudolf Abel case files

John F. Kennedy Presidential Library, jfklibrary.org

Miller Center, University of Virginia, millercenter.org

NASA, "Missions A-Z," nasa.gov/missions

National Air and Space Museum, "Space Race," airandspace.si.edu/exhibitions/space
-race

National Security Archive, George Washington University, nsarchive.gwu.edu

The Public Papers of the Presidents of the United States, University of Michigan Digital
Library, quod.lib.umich.edu/p/ppotpus

U.S. Department of State, Office of the Historian, history.state.gov

U.S. Senate, "Hearings & Meetings," senate.gov/committees/hearings_meetings.htm

ACKNOWLEDGMENTS

Research for this book was proceeding normally—and then 2020 happened. With all my nerdy detective travel canceled, I was even more reliant than usual on the generosity of libraries and archives. These invaluable sources are listed in the bibliography. Special thanks to Francis Gary Powers Jr., founder of the Cold War Museum in Virginia, who shared stories about his father's experiences and even sent me a replica hollow silver dollar. I'll show it to you sometime. Thanks to Jane Chisholm, daughter of Janet Chisholm, for sharing a few little-known details about her mother's life as a spy in Moscow.

I'm especially grateful to Dr. Sergei Khrushchev, who generously agreed to answer my questions about those private talks he had with his father during the missile crisis. Dr. Khrushchev, who became a U.S. citizen in 1999, died in June 2020. Through his writing and lectures, he has given us insight into key moments of Cold War history that literally could not have come from anywhere else.

My single biggest thank-you is to Connie Hsu for her expert editing and overall guidance. I've never written so much I didn't end up using—my file of deleted scenes is 338 pages. Seriously, I just checked. Connie knew exactly what I was going for, and helped me craft the mass of material into a story.

For their continued support, I'm very grateful to the entire team at Macmillan, including Jon Yaged, Jen Besser, and Allison Verost. Thanks to Mekisha Telfer for her edits and suggestions, and to Aurora Parlagreco and John Nora for making the book look so cool. For getting the book out in the world, thank you to Morgan Kane, Katie Quinn, Mary Van Akin, Elysse Villalobos, and Jennifer Edwards. And for their incredibly demanding (in a good way) commitment to accuracy, a huge thanks to Jen Healey and the "nonfiction A-team"—Sherri Schmidt, Janet Renard, and Susan Bishansky.

As always, a big thanks to my wonderful agent, Susan Cohen, and the team at Writers House.

And finally, of course, thank you to Rachel, Anna, and David. I've run out of clever ways to say it, but I could not do any of this without you.

IMAGE CREDITS

INDEX

Page references in italic indicate a photograph; those with *f* denote figures, including maps.